KU-419-614

BATH SPA UNIVERSITY
DISCARD
LIBRARY

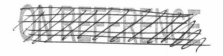
ON REFERENCE

NOT TO BE REMOVED FROM LIBRARY

B.C.H.E. - LIBRARY
DISCARD
00089073

THE CONTEMPORARY ISLAMIC REVIVAL

THE CONTEMPORARY ISLAMIC REVIVAL

A Critical Survey and Bibliography

YVONNE YAZBECK HADDAD,
JOHN OBERT VOLL,
and JOHN L. ESPOSITO

with KATHLEEN MOORE
and DAVID SAWAN

Bibliographies and Indexes in Religious Studies, Number 20
Gary E. Gorman, Advisory Editor

Greenwood Press
New York • Westport, Connecticut • London

BATH COLLEGE OF
HIGHER EDUCATION
NEWTON PARK LIBRARY

CLASS NO.
016.297 HAD

SUPPLIER

BNBC

Library of Congress Cataloging-in-Publication Data

Haddad, Yvonne Yazbeck.
  The contemporary Islamic revival : a critical survey and
bibliography / Yvonne Yazbeck Haddad, John Obert Voll, and John L.
Esposito ; with Kathleen Moore and David Sawan.
    p. cm.—(Bibliographies and indexes in religious studies,
ISSN 0742-6836 ; no. 20)
  Includes indexes.
  ISBN 0-313-24719-6 (alk. paper)
  1. Islam—20th century—Bibliography. I. Voll, John Obert, 1936-   .
II. Esposito, John L.   III. Title.   IV. Series.
Z7835.M6H23   1991
[BP60]
016.297 '09 '045—dc20   91-12618

British Library Cataloguing in Publication Data is available.

Copyright © 1991 by Yvonne Yazbeck Haddad, John Obert Voll, and John L. Esposito

All rights reserved. No portion of this book may be
reproduced, by any process or technique, without the
express written consent of the publisher.

Library of Congress Catalog Card Number: 91-12618
ISBN: 0-313-24719-6
ISSN: 0742-6836

First published in 1991

Greenwood Press, 88 Post Road West, Westport, CT 06881
An imprint of Greenwood Publishing Group, Inc.

Printed in the United States of America

The paper used in this book complies with the
Permanent Paper Standard issued by the National
Information Standards Organization (Z39.48-1984).

10 9 8 7 6 5 4 3 2 1

Contents

Foreword

As these words are being written, *The Times* reports that Salman Rushdie has met with Islamic scholars in an attempt to quash the *fatwa*--legal opinion--imposing a death sentence by the late Ayatollah Khomeini for Rushdie's controversial novel, *The Satanic Verses*. This novel portrays the conflict between the material and spiritual worlds through the story of Gibreel and might be read as a parable of how man can be destroyed by the loss of Islamic faith. Apparently the charge against Mr. Rushdie remains, for Iran's present spiritual leader, Ayatollah Ali Khamenei, is reported as stating that the death penalty will not be repealed "even if he [Rushdie] were to repent and become the most pious Muslim of his time." Ironically, this story appeared on Christmas eve, and received at least the same prominence as "traditional" Christmas stories in *The Times*.

In one sense the Rushdie affair embodies many feature characteristics of the Islamic revival that has occurred in recent decades: an overriding concern with the destructive influence of secularism on religion, the power of Islamic religious leaders, the unbending rigor of Islamic law, the transnational impact of Islam even in non-Islamic societies. All of this exemplifies how small the world has grown in the last forty years as Middle Eastern oil and Asian trading power have forever altered the Eurocentric balance of economic and political--not to mention social and religious--power.

Since the 1960s the Islamic world has developed a new sense of unity through recognition of a common heritage that overrides economic, political, social and ethnic differences. Both the Quran and the Sunna Muslim nations and peoples share a common doctrine that stresses social justice and communal solidarity which powerfully transcends mere nationalism. On its own this transnational solidarity is not unique in the semitic religious tradition--both Judaism and Christianity share a similarly supranational identity. Within Islam, however, there is also an unequivocal call to rebel against the existing order when it departs from the salvific norms established by Allah and articulated by the Prophet. When one's salvation is at risk because of an imperfect social order, traditional Islamic teaching maintains that religious ideology and military power must combine to overthrow imperfection and recreate a more ideal religious state.

There is at present an emerging consensus among Muslims and their leaders, both political and spiritual, that the established order is inadequate and that Islam contains a viable alternative to the status quo that has been imposed by the non-

Islamic world. On the one hand Western capitalism has meant domination of local free enterprise by foreign competition, while the Eastern Bloc socialist alternative has involved excessive bureaucracy and the introduction of large-scale trading conglomerates at the expense of traditional small-scale trading patterns. Traditional Islam, on the other hand, presents a moderating influence similar to Catholic social responsibility of the early twentieth century: a free market philosophy shaped by social responsibility in which private ownership carries with it an imperative to behave in a socially beneficial manner. In short Islam contains viable alternatives to the developed world social, political and cultural patterns that sit uneasily on Muslim shoulders.

This is not to suggest that Islam is a seamless fabric, for in fact there is a significant rift between the apparent secularism of the entrepreneurial and professional elite and the generally traditional worldview of the ordinary people in Islamic countries. Also, one suspects, the political elite to some extent have used Islamic rhetoric and traditional Islamic views to mobilize the masses, through modern communication technology, by presenting a somewhat mythic view of a resurgence in Islam when in fact the faith has been a powerful force in Islamic states for decades. It is the pervasive power of this faith--witness events in Iran and Iraq in the last five years--that is being emphasized through communication and the media.

Those of us who are of other faiths tend not to see the subtle, positive attributes of Islam; we are too entranced by the extremes of the Ayatollahs, General Zia, Saddam Hussein, Colonel Qaddafi and a host of other Islamic rulers who seem to emphasize the more unsavory tenets of this religion. At the same time Islam has produced such pragmatic reformers as Ibn Khaldun, who ably offered a moderate interpretation of Islam in tune with the realities of his time. A similar flexibility has been exhibited by Islamic leaders in Saudi Arabia and the Gulf States, Nigeria, Indonesia, and other countries--quiet achievers for whom Islam has been a way of life that does not require flamboyant sabre-rattling.

If the Muslim sabre-rattlers permit us to see in a new century, it is more than likely that Islam will be recognized as an articulate and powerful source in the future development of the world. Accordingly, it is incumbent upon us all to understand the reasons behind the Islamic resurgence, and I believe that Professor Haddad and her colleagues have aided us substantially in this task with their valuable collection of essays and bibliography on Islam in the last two decades.

G.E. Gorman
Advisory Editor

Preface

The need for an annotated bibliography on contemporary Islamic revival became evident in the 1980s as printing presses, academic journals, magazines and newspapers initiated a deluge of information about Islam and the perceived menace of fundamentalism and terrorism. The Islamic revolution in Iran which brought the Ayatullah Khomeini to power and the crisis it precipitated, created a demand for additional materials. Writing on Islamic topics soon developed into a "growth industry" as scholars, journalists and others came out with studies, analyses and opinions on Islam and the role it plays in public life, on Islamic revival and Muslim revolutionary and opposition movements in various parts of the world.

The greatly enhanced opportunities for publishing in these areas turned into a boom for some scholars in the field by providing outlets for their otherwise rather esoteric studies. A professor of art history at a major university, reflecting on this phenomenon, commented: "For years, I thought that my career was going nowhere. And then, boom, I have become a serious scholar with two published books to my credit and requests for articles and lectures. You can say that my career, like that of many others, should be stamped 'MADE BY KHOMEINI.'"

It is estimated that by the early 1980s production had increased to the point where an average of some 200 books per year were published in the English language on topics dealing with the Middle East, Islam and Islamic revival. The periodical literature, keeping pace, has been extensive in its scope. While this material has provided an important corrective to the earlier prevalent scholarly opinion that the religion of Islam is irrelevant to the modern world, a great deal of the literature is repetitious in nature, reiterating or even borrowing from material published elsewhere. This phenomenon has been described by a former editor of the *International Journal of Middle East Studies* as "plagiarism and self-plagiarism."

This bibliography is designed to provide a useful reference of available literature on the subject of contemporary Islamic revival published in English between 1970 and 1988 for students and researchers. It does not include material from the popular press, which can be located through databases. It concentrates on academic studies of, as well as primary sources on, contemporary Islamic revival. A few texts printed prior to 1970 have been included, because they have not been superceded by the more current publications, or because they continue to be the only available, indispensable sources of background information on a given subject.

Some, but not all, of the entries are annotated. In cases in which a title may not be clearly indicative of the range of material contained in the entry, an annotation has been added for purposes of fuller clarification. Given the fact that much of the material contained in this bibliography is not available in such places as *The Reader's Guide to Periodical Literature* or *Index Islamicus*, the editors chose to forego fuller annotation for the purpose of providing as many substantive references as possible. While this inclusiveness allows for some overlap in subject matter, the intent is to provide the reader access to as much written material as possible on any given subject.

Most of the entries are classified according to geographical areas with subdivisions for specific countries where appropriate, determined in large part by the availability of literature relevant to the topic. In a few cases where very little has been reported on Islamic revivalist activities in such areas as China, the Soviet Union, parts of Southeast Asia and Sub-Saharan Africa, studies addressing issues facing Islamic communities in the modern world have been included in order to provide background information for comparative studies on an international scope.

Because the emigration of Muslims to Europe and North America and the development of Islamic institutions in the west have become increasingly important in influencing revivalist Islam, entries on these communities and a selection of their literary output have been included in the bibliographic sections. Material that is not area specific has been placed under the general heading of "Interpretive Studies." These include writings by western scholars on revival, as well as Islamic sources on the subject: translations of revivalist texts and/or commentary by Muslim scholars attempting to explain revivalism to a western audience. Most of these entries deal with political Islam or address comparative or general issues. Studies on women and Islamic economics have been placed under separate headings, since the two topics have been identified by Muslim revivalists as crucial areas in need of Islamization, that is, radical transformation in order to manifest Islamic values.

The three introductory chapters are an overview of the field from somewhat different perspectives. They provide an historical framework for a field of studies dominated by social scientists who, in many cases, have not taken the historical antecedents of their studies into full consideration, as well as a general summary of the revivalist heritage as it has developed over the last century. These chapters also attempt to acquaint the student with the types of literature written by Western scholars on contemporary Islamic revival as well as with some of the themes in the literature written by Muslim revivalists themselves. Specific case studies of revivalist activities in various Muslim countries are offered as illustrative examples.

The compilation and annotation of the bibliography has been done primarily by Yvonne Haddad, Kathleen Moore and David Sawan. John Esposito and John Voll assisted in the selection and annotation of entries. Valuable input was provided on the material on Southeast Asia by Fred R. von der Mehden and on Russia and China by Jonathan Lipman and Drew Gladney. Susan Kolb researched the subject index and Alice Izer, officer manager of the Department of History at the University of Massachusetts/Amherst edited it. For all these contributions we express our appreciation and thanks.

Abbreviations

AA	*Asian Affairs.* Journal of the Royal Society for Asian Affairs. Formerly: The Royal Central Asian Society.
AAA	*American-Arab Affairs.* Washington, DC.
AAAPSS	*Annals of the American Academy of Political and Social Sciences.*
ABS	*The American Behavioral Society.*
AcAs	*Acta Asiatica.* Tokyo.
AES	*Archives Europeenes de Sociologie.*
AFJI	*Armed Forces Journal International.*
AfLS	*African Language Studies.*
AJCL	*American Journal of Comparative Law.*
AJIS	*American Journal of Islamic Studies.*
AJISS	*American Journal of Islamic Social Science.* Herndon, VA.
AnthQ	*Anthropological Quarterly.*
AP	*Asian Profile.*
ArOr	*Archiv Orientalni.*
AS	*Asian Survey.*
ASQ	*Arab Studies Quarterly.*
ATS	*Asian Thought and Society.*
BAS	*Bulletin of Atomic Scientists.*
BCII	*The Bulletin of the Christian Institute of Islamic Studies.* Hyderabad, India.
BICMRA	*Bulletin for Islamic and Christian-Muslim Relations in Africa.*
BJS	*British Journal of Sociology.*
CAS	*Central Asian Survey.*
CH	*Current History.*
CLR	*Cambridge Law Review.*
CSA	*Contemporary Southeast Asia.*
CSSH	*Comparative Studies in Society and History.*
CTT	*Current Turkish Thought.*
DI	*Der Islam.* Hamburg, FRGermany.
EAJ	*East Asia Journal of Theology.* Singapore.
EI	*Echo of Islam.*
FA	*Foreign Affairs.*
FCR	*Free China Review.*
FI	*Feminist Issues.*
HamdIs	*Hamdard Islamicus.* Karachi, Pakistan.
HamdMed	*Hamdard Medicus.* Karachi, Pakistan.
HT	*History Today.*
IC	*Islamic Culture.* Hyderabad, India.
ICF	*Islamic Culture Forum.*
IDR	*Islamic Defense Review.*
IH	*Islamic Horizons.* Plainfield, IN.
IJ	*International Journal.* Toronto, Canada.

IJIAS	*International Journal of Islamic and Arabic Studies*. Bloomington, IN.
IJMES	*International Journal of Middle East Studies*. New York, NY.
IL	*Islamic Literature*.
IMA	*Islam and the Modern Age*. New Delhi, India.
InSt	*International Studies*.
IO	*Islamic Order*.
IP	*Islamic Perspectives*.
IQ	*The Islamic Quarterly*. London.
IR	*Islamic Revolution*.
IRE	*International Review of Education*.
IRM	*International Review of Missions*. World Council of Churches, Geneva.
IrSt	*Iranian Studies*. Hanover, NH.
IS	*Islamic Studies*. Islamabad, Pakistan.
Islamo	*Islamochristiana*. Rome.
IT	*Islam Today*.
Itt	*al-Ittihad*. Plainfield, IN.
JAA	*Journal of Arab Affairs*. Fresno, CA.
JAAR	*Journal of the American Academy of Religion*. Chambersburg, PA.
JAAS	*Journal of Asian and African Studies*.
JAL	*Journal of Arabic Literature*. Leiden, The Netherlands.
JARCE	*Journal of the American Research Center in Egypt*.
JAS	*Journal of Asian Studies*.
JCA	*Journal of Contemporary Asia*.
JCCP	*Journal of Commonwealth and Comparative Politics*.
JHSN	*Journal of the Historical Society of Nigeria*.
JIA	*Journal of International Affairs*.
JIBF	*Journal of Islamic Banking and Finance*.
JIMMA	*Journal Institute of Muslim Minority Affairs*. King Abdulaziz University, Saudi Arabia.
JNES	*Journal of Near Eastern Studies*. Chicago, IL.
JPHS	*Journal Presbyterian Historical Society*.
JPS	*Journal of Palestine Studies*. Washington, DC.
JRA	*Journal of Religion in Africa*. Leiden, The Netherlands.
JRIE	*Journal of Research in Islamic Economics*.
JSAMES	*Journal of South Asian and Middle Eastern Studies*. Los Angeles, CA.
JSSR	*Journal for the Scientific Study of Religion*.
MEJ	*Middle East Journal*. Washington, DC.
MEQ	*Muslim Educational Quarterly*.
MERIP	*Middle East Report*.
MES	*Middle East Studies*.
MonR	*Monthly Review*.
MR	*The Magreb Review*.
MSE	*Muslims of the Soviet East*.
MW	*The Muslim World*.
MWLJ	*Muslim World League Journal*.
NR	*The New Republic*.
OM	*Oriente Moderno*. Rome.
ORITA	*Ibadan Journal of Religious Studies*.
PA	*Pacific Affairs*.
PMVB	*Pro Mundi Vita Bulletin*.
RAL	*Research in African Literature*.
RC	*Race and Class*.
RCL	*Religion in Communist Lands*.
RelSt	*Religious Studies*.
RIMMA	*Review of Indonesian and Malaysian Affairs*. Sydney, Australia.
RIPEH	*Review of Iranian Political Economy and History*.
SAC	*Southeast Asia Chronicle*.
SAIS	*SAIS Review*. Washington, DC.
SC	*Social Compass*.
SCC	*Studies in Comparative Communism*.
SCR	*Studies in Comparative Religion*.
SOS	*Soviet Oriental Studies*. Moscow.
TWQ	*Third World Quarterly*.
UM	*The Universal Method*.
WD	*World Development*.

WMR	*World Marxist Review.*
WP	*World Politics.*
WT	*The World Today.*

THE CONTEMPORARY
ISLAMIC REVIVAL

1

The Revivalist Literature and the Literature on Revival: An Introduction
Yvonne Yazbeck Haddad

Contemporary Islamic revivalist literature is but the latest episode in the ongoing saga of Muslim encounter with the west and corresponding recognition of its own internal circumstances. It is the product of the attempt of a variety of Muslims in different parts of the world to mobilize the energies of their constituencies to continue the process of decolonization and the creation of a viable, modern, independent Islamic society. Unlike the writers of earlier revivalist literature, which was dominant from the nineteenth to the middle of the twentieth century, its authors appear to have given up on what they perceived to be mere social reform and to be committing themselves to social engineering as the most efficient way to bring about the social, political, economic, and cultural change desired.

European conquests of Muslim lands beginning in the sixteenth century demonstrated the superiority of western technology of war while providing the conquerors with economic control over Muslim natural resources. At the same time, these conquests gave rise to a feeling of frustration among the people due to the failure of their governments to remove the yoke of foreign rule. They thus served as an impetus for change. The intensification of western cultural penetration and military domination of Muslim people in the nineteenth century, generally justified in colonial and Christian missionary rhetoric as efforts to elevate Muslims from their decadent conditions, to civilize them, and to make them worthy members of the new world order, hastened the decay and collapse of Muslim empires.[1] It also challenged religious and secular leaders to provide an adequate response to meet the new challenges facing the community.

Revivalist literature written during the second half of the nineteenth century to the present time reflects the history of the encounter with the west. It is based on a perception of reality formed during several centuries of western domination of the Muslim world, including the carving up of Islamic territory by colonial powers into forty four nation states after the Second World War. This division created new boundaries that delineated new national identities on aggregates of people according to areas of residence and based on geographical considerations that were mapped out in Paris and London. It left one third of the Muslim population of the world living in minority status under the domination of other religious and ethnic majority groups.

Revivalist ideas are not generated in a vacuum but are a response to external and internal stimuli, in this case to the realization of general societal decay as well as the perceived challenge and experience of oppression by western powers. Ideas that resonate with the experiences of the people in moments of crisis and times of stress tend to generate their own momentum, driving old myths and doctrines to extinction while creating new complexes of beliefs and values that are affirmed as being at the heart of the faith. Revival is seen by its advocates as a crucial means of infusing life into a community that is bogged down in centuries-old customs and traditions whose concentration on the imitation of the past has led to ossification of Islamic society, restricting its ability to move quickly into the modern world.

Throughout history, the Muslim community has had to grapple with the tension between faithfulness to the prophetic model and relevance for contemporary times. While Muslims agree that Islam is valid for all time and all places and that the prophetic message is appropriate to all conditions the world has faced or could possibly face, there is no consensus on the question of whether it is necessary to strive continually to create and maintain a society that is a replica of prophetic times. In recent history, groups such as the Ahli-Hadis of India and the contemporary Salafis of Kuwait have believed in a perception of history that looks to the past for its model, considered by its detractors to be retrogressive.[2] According to this view the farther the community moves from the perfect time of the Prophet the farther it is from perfection. Ideal time is past time, and the duty of the Muslim is to avoid new ideas, customs or interpretations since they are simply innovations which act as barriers and impediments to the realization of ideal society.

Most revivalist literature of the last century has disagreed with this kind of perspective. The efforts of its authors have been redirected and reinterpreted over the decades to portray an Islam that is forward looking, creative and open to movement and change. Revivalists seek to appropriate the ethos of the original model and to apply it to contemporary circumstances so as to affirm Islam as vibrant and relevant to modernity. Contemporary revivalist literature, while not denying that prophetic time is perfect time, has developed a theology of history which sees Islam as always unfolding.[3] It is up to Muslims to take control of their lives and build a better future. Consequently, the literature focuses on the shape of the future that is sought and the potential for its success.[4] It posits a new role for human beings as responsible agents of God charged with establishing a viable civilization, a righteous order guided by the revelation of the Qur'an.[5]

Efforts at revitalizing the Islamic community to meet the challenge of the modern world and western domination have thus been part of Muslim thinking and writing for the past two centuries. While sharing the sense of urgency that some kind of change is essential, they nonetheless have taken somewhat different forms. At the end of the last century Islamic thinking was invigorated by the responses of individual Islamic thinkers who saw the experience of western involvement as a special challenge. They developed an Islamic rationale for the necessity of change and legitimated the impetus on the part of the Muslim community for adapting to new circumstances. They called for a movement of *islah* (reform), posited in opposition to those who advocated *taqlid* (imitation) of the times and thinking of the past.[6] Leaders such as Sir Sayyid Ahmad Khan of India, Khayr al-Din Basha of Tunisia, Muhammad Abdu of Egypt, and Jamal al-Din al-Afghani of Iran, referred to as "modernists" by western scholars, attempted to harmonize Islamic teaching with European philosophy and science which they perceived as the key to western civilization.[7]

They found scriptural support for their focus on change in Surah 13:12 of the Qur'an, "God will not alter what is in a people until they alter what is in themselves." This verse they interpreted as stressing the accountability of human endeavor while placing the responsibility for development on the Islamic society itself.   Muslims were not to see themselves as predestined to backwardness, subservience, weakness or dependency by the will of God.   To the extent that they were not competitive in the modern world, especially with the west, it was due to the fact that they had failed to take the initiative in developing their societies.   The modernists emphasized the importance of taking the world seriously, insisting that Islamic societies had deviated from the truth of Islam by following Sufi teachings that emphasize the spiritual dimension of life at the expense of the material.   Islam, they affirmed, is both *din wa dunya* (religion and the world).

A second phase of response is that formulated by Muslim socialists in the middle of the twentieth century.   They were responding most directly to the challenge of decolonization and under-development.   They perceived that an ideology fusing socialist ideals with Islamic values would help mobilize the masses for development. The model was the Soviet Union, perceived as having achieved industrialization without the Christianization prescribed as necessary by missionaries and European colonialists.   This enchantment with socialism was in part a reaction to colonialism. Repulsed by capitalist exploitation of wealth and resources, alongside the poverty prevalent in their societies, the revivalists wrote on issues of social and economic justice in Islam.[8]   Some, especially the ideologues of the Ba'th Party in Syria, advocated a secularist socialism.   Still others advocated Islam as socialism and socialism as Islam.   While this literature became very prominent during the Nasser regime in Egypt, parallel developments took place in Pakistan under Zulfiqar Ali Bhutto and in Iran under Mosadegh.   The prescribed ideology focused especially on the concept of *tajdid* (renewal) in its concern for change, referring to the classical Islamic concept which recognized the necessity for a centennial renewal, reform and regeneration of the faith.   This is based on the understanding that every century God will send a *mujaddid*, a renewer of the faith who is to restore the teaching of Islam in ways that are relevant for the age.   Different authors provide different candidates for the title of *mujaddids* past and present, their choice reflecting their own ideological orientation.[9]

The incorporation of socialist ideology as Islam by the Nasser regime introduced a new threshold in the debate over the proposed Islamic future.   Issues of renewal and imitation, authenticity, and borrowing, as well as the reliability of what was advocated as genuine sources of socialist teachings within Islam became central in the struggle between the Egyptian government and its opposition.   Monographs on the socialism of Muhammad and his wife Khadija, as well as the early companions of the Prophet, were published in an effort to justify the ideology of the state.[10]   This literature initiated an intellectual controversy which was hotly pursued on the pages of two Kuwaiti magazines, *al-'Arabi* and *al-Muslim al-Mu'asir*.   It focused on whether the companions of the Prophet Muhammad were leftist or rightist and whether the sources of the formative period of Islam can be subjected to modern re-interpretation to justify claims of Islamic precedent to proponents of "Islamic Left" and "Islamic Right".   Others argued that Islam is unique in its perception of reality and should not be distorted to conform to modern ideologies, constructs or stereotypes.[11]

It is clear that the contemporary revivalist literature developed in the 1970s and 1980s taps into the rhetoric, language, and arguments that have been developed over a century of confrontation with the west.   It is also clear that the arguments reflect the present realities.   Not only is the material different in tone and level of engagement from that which preceded, but it addresses new challenges and confronts new problems.   Contemporary revivalists refer to their efforts as trying to engender *al-sahwa al-Islamiyya*, Islamic awakening or alertness or vigilance.[12]   It is the search for an identity that is truly Islamic, grounded in the best of the Muslim heritage while awake and responsive to the changes demanded by the exigencies of modern living.

Proponents of the Islamic awakening are loosely bound by their commitment to find an Islamic solution to the issues and challenges confronting Muslim society in the modern world. While they all strive for a better future, and agree that prevalent conditions in Muslim countries are unacceptable, there is no consensus on what constitutes the best solution: which Islamic ideology to adopt, what course to take, or what change to implement. Some advocate an ideology that is reminiscent of the liberation theology of Latin America, in that it addresses economic and political issues from a perspective which rejects colonial domination and economic dependency. Egyptian economists 'Adil Husayn, Tariq al-Bishri, and Jalal Amin, who see such a perspective as the necessary means of raising consciousness and mobilizing the public for development, have been dismissed by those who disagree with them as "neo-salafis", "Muslim Marxists" or as "new pretenders" to Islamic identity. Hasan Hanafi of Egypt attempted to organize an international Islamic leftist political movement with the publication of *Al-Yasar al-Islami* (Islamic Left) and was consequently jailed by Anwar al-Sadat.[13] The great support he received from students at Cairo University appears to have waned soon after his release from jail.

Other authors, more moderate and progressive in their interpretations, include Egyptians Kamal Abu al-Majd, 'Abd al-'Aziz Kamil, Kuwaiti Muhammad al-Rumayhi, Jordanian Fahmi Jad'an, Tunisians Ehmeida Enneifer, and Salah al-Din al-Jourchi.[14] While their writings circulate among the intellectuals in various countries, it is the works of authors such as Muhammad al-Ghazali, Anwar al-Jundi, Fathi Yakan, Yusuf al-Qaradawi, Muhammad Qutb, Sa'id Hawwa, and Zainab al-Ghazali, who are considered more right of center, that command a wide readership in the general public.

The literature of the contemporary revivalist movement depicts Islam and the Muslims as surrounded by a variety of hostile forces bent on their destruction.[15] These range from the Judeo-Christian conspiracy against Islam and the communist threat to Muslim nations to a whole array of perpetrators of evil as well as deviant ideologies such as materialism, secularism, atheism, internationalism, Freudianism, and existentialism.[16] At issue is survival itself.[17] The literature of the awakening calls for struggle against the hostile forces that encircle the Muslims; but the language used is very careful not to advocate violence, unless used as a defensive measure. The condemnation of violence and the advocacy of measured struggle by authors in the mainstream of the Islamic movement on one hand is a reaction to the persecution the earlier generation of members of the Muslim Brotherhood suffered under different regimes. On the other hand, it is an attempt to rein in the revolutionary zeal of young members that led to the assassination of Anwar al-Sadat by members of the Jihad movement in Egypt.[18] The trial of the assassins was not restricted to the conspirators; also on trial was the literature of revival, especially the book *Ma'alim fi al-Tariq* by Sayyid Qutb which sanctioned the use of force to eliminate leaders who were impediments to the welfare of the Islamic movement.[19]

Islamic revivalists includes advocates of Islamic revolutionism which they see as the only means left for bringing about change.[20] For them, Islam is not only the alternative to the nation-state systems fashioned after the western or Marxist models. They view revolution as a divine imperative to which Muslims are commissioned to supervise the implementation of God's will throughout the world. As believers, Muslims are perceived not only to have been selected to form a Muslim community where Islamic law dominates, but to be destined to convert the world to this precise vision. Thus while Sunni Islam has traditionally frowned on revolution and advocated compliance and obedience to those in power, adherents of Islamic revolutionism see it as an ongoing process of transformation that molds and shapes all aspects of life preordained by God in primordial times.[21]

One of the most persistent themes of contemporary revivalist literature is that the west, and in particular the United States, has lost its moral hegemony.[22] While it clearly still has military might, it has abandoned (at least in matters of policies pertaining to Israel) its values of democracy, self-determination, and separation of religion and state that were so respected by the Muslim world at an earlier time. At present it is generally perceived as being bankrupt in terms of morality and social values. The west, therefore, is no longer a model to be emulated. Rising crime rates, race riots, substance abuse, AIDS, pornography, unfortunate consequences of the feminist movement such as the breakdown of the family and pregnancy outside of marriage, social and economic inequality and inequity, and many other ills plague the very structure of American life. Muslims are particularly aware of what they see as the technological collapse of the United States. No longer reliant on itself, it has become an importer of materials from all over the world; as one Muslim put it, "the steel belt has been transformed into the rust belt."

Today there is a consensus among a large number of Muslims that given the circumstances of this time in history, and particularly of the relationship of Muslim nations to the west and the necessity of restructuring their societies, change is imperative. The challenging question, still very much in the process of resolve, is, change to what?

The present discourse on change, then, taps into the legacy of revival as a dominant and recurring theme in Islam.[23] In reading the literature of the revivalists one finds several forms of discourse appearing with regularity. First there is the particular justification that any given author offers for the necessity of change. Then there is the attempt to legitimate whatever kind of change is advocated. This generally is accompanied by an emphasis on authenticity, in which individual authors try to clarify that their approach is original and not mere emulation of what has been advocated by defenders of the western model. Finally there is an emphasis on autonomy, insisting that one's ideas are especially suited to the Islamic situation and will not in any way lead to dependency on the west. This revivalist literature, then, is clearly focused on issues of modernity.[24] It seeks parity with those who are the moving forces of the world, at the same time that it stresses what is authentic in the Islamic tradition and what is viable and workable for Muslim communities both technically and theoretically. It is world affirming in ways consonant with the recurring themes and emphases of the tradition of Islam.

While change clearly has been seen as necessary, cooperative efforts and movements for Islamic unity have been crucial for gaining independence and freedom from foreign domination. Consequently, as various authors have responded to conditions in their respective parts of the world, their prescription for revival has not been simply local in scope but has envisioned a reconstituted Islamic world, united and strong, able to withstand outside intervention. The obvious tie by which they have sought to bind the disparate ethnic and linguistic peoples is Islam. Thus, for example, we see Indian Muslims during the last part of the nineteenth and early part of the twentieth centuries advocating pan-Islamism and *jihad* (struggle, holy war) as means for rallying external support from Muslims in other countries to withstand the onslaught of western hegemony. The mandate for unity was grounded in the vision of one Ummah, a nation of Muslims bound together by their common beliefs in the sovereignty of God and the message of the Prophet Muhammad. This same theme became the cornerstone of the teachings of the Muslim Brotherhood in Egypt which came into being in 1928 as a reaction to British colonial domination of that country as well as to the elimination of the last symbol of unity, the office of the caliphate, by the secular government of Kemal Ataturk in Turkey.

Western intervention in Muslim countries served not only to engender the dream of Muslim unity, helping them to break out of the confines of local reality by seeking support for collective action; it also introduced new means of transportation and communication which facilitated the spread of such ideas. Better ships, for example, made travel to Mecca for the *hajj* (pilgrimage) easier, and while there the growing number of *hajjis* who came in contact with other Muslims from all parts of the world became aware of the dynamic hold of Islam worldwide and the potential for mobilizing all Muslims. They also came in contact with new ideas for a revitalized Muslim community. This experience has led to advocacy by a number of thinkers, from 'Abd al-Rahman al-Kawakibi at the turn of the century to Gamal 'Abdul Nasser in the 1950s and Ali Shari'ati in the 1970s, of the use of the *hajj* as an international Islamic forum to discuss issues facing the Muslim Ummah worldwide and to disseminate new ideas for regenerating the whole community of Islam.[25]

Western intervention also brought with it a new system of education, printing presses, and the beginning of the dissemination of ideas through periodical literature. These means of communication with the young literate public, eager to build a better world than the one they inherited from their parents, began to take hold at the turn of the century in India, Iran, and Egypt. The expulsion of Muslim activists to Europe gave them the opportunity to learn more about European ideas and techniques and helped encourage a literature in dialogue with the west, one that stresses the ideals of Islam and proposes Islamic solutions in opposition to those of western societies. It also afforded them the opportunity to meet activists from other parts of the world and realize the discrepancy between European ideals as proclaimed and European policies as actually practiced in colonial countries.

Magazines and tracts published in Europe by these activists have had great influence in generating support for their ideas throughout the Muslim world. The journal *al-'Urwa al-Wuthqa* published by Muhammad Abdu, for example, continues to have an international readership, impacting the religious ideas of people in such distant places as Indonesia. Today the same factors appear to be operative. Some of the most important journals on Islamic topics are published in the west, including *Inquiry*, *The Muslim World Book Review* and *al-Muslimun* which are printed in Britain and disseminated worldwide. Furthermore, Muslim activists living in western countries away from the watchful eyes of their governments have been able to generate and disseminate new ideas about the potential of Islamic unity and revival as well as to forge international connections and relations with Muslim activists elsewhere in the world. The best modern example is the utilization of the tape recorder and the cassette in spreading Ayatullah Khomeini's and Ali Shari'ati's revolutionary ideas in Iran.

Thus the efforts for unity continue, although they have had a checkered history in terms of success. In the latter half of this century Saudi Arabia, in a bid to generate support for the Islamic Pact against Nasser's socialism, created the Muslim World League as a permanent congress for consultation on Islamic issues. More recently, Saudi Arabia helped form an international *fiqh* council of Islamic jurisprudence experts from all over the Muslim world representing the various legal schools to help reach a consensus on Islamic answers to conditions created by modern technology and other realities of the contemporary world. Among the various issues they have addressed are human rights, organ transplants, genetic engineering, and artificial insemination. Since 1969 the Organization of Islamic Conference has attempted to play the important role of enhancing the circumstance of Muslims throughout the world.[26] Supported by 44 governments that identify themselves as Islamic, this organization came into being as a result of the fire in the Aqsa mosque in Jerusalem and has been involved in political as well as cultural and educational matters. It seeks to foster unified action based on a common vision for safeguarding international Islamic interests.

The meetings of these international bodies, as well as those of scores of other conferences sponsored by various organizations, have produced a healthy collection of articles, conference reports and documents. But while they are heavy on Qur'anic injunctions for unity and the urgency, validity and imperative for such unity, in fact they have had little direct influence on state policy. Some of the ideas generated by these international conferences have filtered down to the general public, but for the most part the meetings have become forums for a rhetoric indulged in by a select group of older recognized Muslim religious leaders and a new group of international Islamic professionals who are subsidized by various governments and revivalist institutions in an effort to maintain legitimacy and control.

Modern means of communication, of course, have also made it easier for other ideas to cross boundaries and take hold of the imagination of Muslim leaders in various countries. (The secular thought of Kemal Ataturk, for example, was very influential in the considerations of Bangladeshi leaders seeking an alternate identity to the kind of pan-Islamism fostered by Indian Muslims that brought about the creation of Pakistan as an Islamic state.) As major issues get debated and become part of the political and ideological discussions taking place in Muslim countries, these same means of communication make the general literate public in various Muslim countries aware of the international dimensions of the revivalist struggle against those who oppose them. When secularist Egyptians seek to detract from the influence of the revivalists in their country, for example, they talk about their opponents as advocates of the "Pakistanization" (*Bakstanat*) of Islam. And when a woman in Bangladesh puts on an Islamic headdress, she may well be said to be emulating "Arab" culture. Advocates of the radical transformation of society in many countries are often accused either of being influenced by or being in the pay of the Saudi, Iranian or Libyan governments and in some cases the Central Intelligence Agency of the United States.

Many factors in contemporary Islamic society contribute to the growth of the revivalist movement. Prominent is the strong intrusion of western culture, today present and obvious and overbearing in movies and television, the news media, clothing styles and many other aspects of contemporary Muslim culture. In the early part of this century the challenge was experienced primarily through western military and political power; the dimension of cultural influence was not as overwhelming as it has been from the middle to the latter part of the century. The challenge of conflicting cultures was present, but distant; the west was an area to be visited and admired and selectively emulated, but it had not intruded in the kinds of immediate ways that provide the present challenge to the revivalists to counter western ways as dangerous, corruptive, and essentially un-Islamic. As we will see, much of the contemporary revivalist literature is written in the attempt to come to terms with these more recent western influences, and to establish Islam as the only viable alternative to what is increasingly described as a decadent and morally bankrupt western society.

A very important factor in the rise of Islamic revivalism has been the migration of workers to assist in the economic development of oil rich countries as well as to seek employment in western industrial nations. This movement has had significant effects on individuals and families, on perceptions of self-identity, and on the development of religious consciousness. The Arab nationalist ideology of the brotherhood of all Arabs suffers when workers from Jordan, Egypt and Palestine are treated as alien, transient and inferior in Kuwait and Saudi Arabia. The experience of "migrancy" has in many instances engendered a new superior identity found in the universal bond of Islam, transcending national and regional identities.

The movement of a large number of rural people into urban areas has been of great significance. Bringing with them values clearly opposed to an urbanized, levantine, culture they have enthusiastically endorsed the elements of revivalist ideology that reaffirm the traditional values of Islam over against the so-called middle class westernized pseudo-Europeanized culture. At the same time the very growth in their numbers has forced many urban areas of the Middle East, most notably Cairo, to sustain a population far exceeding that for which they were designed and for which they have anything resembling adequate resources. This has led to the kinds of deep frustrations in the populace that make fertile grounds for the dissemination of revivalist ideology. The revivalists appear to be most effective in reaching the young, educated and recently urbanized members of society. These persons have never experienced direct colonial rule, yet seem to resonate with the fear of the specter of colonial hegemony and the western threat to the righteous Muslim order that is ordained by God.

A phenomenal growth in the publication and dissemination of literature in many Islamic countries has played a key role in the increase in the number of people committed to an Islamist solution to the problems their countries face. Qur'ans and other religious texts, tracts and pamphlets, magazines and books on Islamic law and life are readily available in bookstores and sidewalk stalls. Publishing houses are proliferating, and publication is aided by donations from a variety of sources. Those who espouse a revivalist interpretation of Islam find a ready outlet for their materials, and one can easily know all sides of a religious debate. Access to Islamic literature is aided by the availability of public education; people in rural as well as urban areas are learning to read and the literature of the revivalists is ready for their perusal.

It is clear that literacy and the availability of contemporary commentaries that address current issues have made the Qur'an more accessible to the general Muslim public and has made it an important source not only for devotions and spiritual growth, but for reflection, consciousness raising, and politicization.[27] Unlike the volumes written by earlier generations of Muslim scholars, the contemporary commentaries may not shed any new light on exegetical problems of the Qur'an that Western scholars have been grappling with but they do provide us with an understanding of the function scripture has in forging and maintaining a community of believers, as well as the new ways in which contemporary Muslims find meaning for their lives in the Qur'anic text.[28] (Several new attempts at reinterpreting the Qur'an for modern life, as well as several studies analyzing the contemporary exegetical movement, have also appeared in Urdu, Bengali, Farsi and Bhasa Malaysia.)[29]

Discussion of religious topics is no longer in the hands of the clergy, therefore, but has entered the public realm. And it is clear that the revivalist movement itself is very much that of the lay population. Much of the religious literature is produced outside of government presses. In content and ethos it has a different emphasis from the Islamic materials prepared by government agencies who use religion to buttress their political legitimacy. Often written by professionals such as lawyers, businessmen, doctors, and engineers, this literature is aimed at providing an impetus to progress for those who wish to see a developed and modern Islamic state.[30]

Political realities have contributed to the rise of revivalism. Leaders such as Anwar al-Sadat of Egypt, Ja'far al-Numayri of Sudan, Muhamad Ershad of Bangladesh, Mu'ammar al-Qadhafi of Libya, Muhammad Mahathir of Malaysia, and Zia ul-Haqq of Pakistan have empowered Muslim groups to gain hegemony at the expense of nationalists and socialists. At the same time the decline of the power and influence of Egypt since the Camp David Agreement of 1979 has meant that Saudi Arabia has become a more important regional power, helping to disseminate Islamic ideology. Saudi Arabia sees its role as a leader of Islamic countries, protector of the holy places of Islam. In the past several decades it has used its financial resources (especially since the rise in the price of oil in the 1970s) to fund Islamic causes and to defend against the encroachment of nationalist, socialist, and/or secularist ideologies in a wide range of Muslim countries, including the Islamic resistance against the Soviet Union in Afghanistan. This aid as well as the availability of other funds for Islamic causes has empowered Muslim groups worldwide. Members of the Muslim Brotherhood and other religious organizations have access to considerable wealth, especially those who left Nasser's persecution in Egypt and were able to get in on the ground floor of the new rising Saudi economy.

Revivalist literature itself is characterized by a number of themes. Underlying most of them is the already acknowledged tension in which Muslims perceive their culture and religion to be in conflict with the west.[31] This tension results in a kind of dialogue in which Muslims may, in fact, be the only partners. That is to say, whether or not westerners are aware of the response and counter-response movement that Muslims feel in relation to the west (and they generally are not), it is the case that many Muslims perceive Islam to be in dialogue not only with western ideas and writers but with western culture itself as viewed from the perspective of the media. At times this response takes the form of a kind of contest with Christianity, in which Muslims presently feel that any challenges set by Christianity and the west have been met successfully by Islam.[32] The victory is theirs whether or not their "opponents" are even aware that the contest is underway.

One of the characteristics of the literature of the current revivalist movement in the Islamic world is its direct reaction to the ways in which Muslims feel that Islam has been perceived by western imperialist powers. In that context it is a literature that is the product of disillusionment and the experience of oppression. Muslims see that they have been exploited, their culture despised, and their history ignored. In effect, Muslim societies have been relegated to the margins of history, while Islamic peoples have been seen essentially as non-persons. Contemporary revivalist literature directly challenges this kind of perception, seeking to liberate Muslims from manipulation by outside forces, to bolster self-confidence, to provide a sense of relevance, and to create a vibrant society whose parameters are defined by themselves rather than by outsiders. They seek to address, participate and be taken seriously in world forums in their own right without interpreters or middlemen.

This literature, then, seeks to create an ethos in which Muslims can operate outside the confines of superpower hegemony. It expresses great anger at United States policy which acknowledges Jewish nationalism as a legitimate expression of Jewish identity but rejects Arab or Islamic nationalism as illegitimate and a threat to United States interests. It despises what it perceives as the American hypocrisy of supporting and using Islam when it is a matter of United States interests in combatting communism (as in Afghanistan), and turning readily against Islam when it is perceived as an impediment to these interests (as in the case of Iran). As a consequence, a continuing theme of this revivalist writing is the portrayal of American policy as one of attempting to divide and subjugate Muslim nations who seek a legitimate manifestation of self-expression and an alternative to both east and west. Islam, therefore, is set forth as the viable and workable distinctive locus of identity, freed from association with any of the world's great powers.

Another important theme of the revivalist literature is what has been called the Islamization of knowledge.[33] It is based on the understanding that knowledge is not value free but is always loaded with some of the baggage of the particular socio-cultural situation out of which it developed and in which it is experienced. In the most immediate sense this has meant for contemporary Muslims the recognition that Muslim students in foreign countries seeking technological and other kinds of training are being imbued with western values, whether these be capitalist or marxist. Even technology which seems to be the most objective and value free is in fact grounded in particular historical circumstances, which endows it with special kinds of meaning. It is a primary task of these revivalist writers, then, to try to counter these influences with a carefully crafted Islamic ideology, based on Islamic values, by which to undergird all areas of knowledge. This attempt at the Islamization of knowledge has been the subject of several international conferences in which scholars from different institutions and different fields of discourse have met to discuss and share strategies. Islamization, then, is proposed as a deliberate effort to provide a modern Muslim alternative to westernization, a comprehensive Islamic vision of life that decries the patchwork of western implants as destroying the fabric of Islam and calls for a restructuring of all of society.

A very important focus of revivalist writing is the proper role for women in Islamic society. Persuaded that the women's liberation movement in the Muslim world has been one of the unwelcome influences of western hegemony and in fact part of the increasingly obvious western agenda to undermine and destroy the religion of Islam, contemporary Muslims have made the issue of the role of women one of the major arenas in which the debate between western and Islamic values is taking place. In general they call for a division of Muslim society according to gender. While there are of course differences among the various writers in the degree to which women are allowed to participate in the public realm, in general they are restricted to the home or allowed to work as teachers, social workers and medical personnel taking care of the female population. The task of the woman, however, has been greatly enhanced in that this literature now validates her shared responsibility of inculcating the elements of the Islamic faith in the members of her family. It is for men to determine and direct Islamic society; it is for women to sustain, nurture, and propagate the faith. The future of religion in one sense thus lies in the hands of women.[34]

It is clear, as has been indicated, that Muslim revivalist writing is very much in tension with and in reaction to Islamic experience of the west, both as it has infringed on life in Muslim countries and as it is perceived in its own context through the various forms of the media. Part of that response is determined by the kinds of writing that is taking place in the western world about the very phenomenon of Islamic revivalism. A number of western scholars are very much aware of the transformations that have taken place in Muslim countries and that Muslims are in process of reviewing their religion and its role in the world. This transformation has received increasing attention from scholars writing in English during the last two decades as contemporary Islamic revival and the movements it inspired began to impinge on western consciousness.

The way in which Islam is being depicted by the scholars of the west is of great interest to the Muslim community. The story is told of a scholar from al-Azhar in Cairo who attended a conference on Islam in Washington D.C. in celebration of the 14th Islamic centennial. His real interest, it turns out, was less in the Islamic materials discussed at the conference than in the latest books that were being published on Islam in the United States. Like others in the Muslim community, he was eager to read what westerners are saying about Islam. Those who have the opportunity to see this kind of literature are ready to classify western authors either as *munsif*, or fair in their scholarship about Islam, or as clearly prejudiced and judgmental. This kind of assessment has indeed become a new locus of discussion, refutation and apologetic on the part of Muslims, a kind of new genre of Islamic writing focussed specifically on how to deal with western scholarly writing about Islam.[35]

Muslim scholars to some small extent are increasingly becoming a part of the context in which discussions affecting that literature are taking place. Up to the 1950s there were almost no Muslims on the faculties of western universities, and Islam was taught mainly by professors who were western Christians, Jewish or in certain cases Christian Arabs. Today that situation has changed somewhat, and Muslims are able to participate in the academic discourse of the west about Islam to the degree to which they hold positions in various universities in America and Europe. It is also the case that a number of significant revivalist writers live and write in the United States, France, Germany, and other western countries. Their works are incubated, in a sense, in these contexts and when published in the Islamic press in the United States or Europe are immediately read and digested in Islamic countries.

For over a century English has been an Islamic language, consciously chosen by Muslims in the Indo-Pakistani subcontinent as the most effective medium in which to communicate their ideas and to defend their faith. In recent times English has been drawn into the service of Islam through the production of Islamic books and other materials in North America and Britain, as a growing number of Muslim immigrants, emigres, and expelled activists take residence in these countries.[36] The Islamic Society of North America, an umbrella organization for over half of the mosques in the United States and Canada, is affiliated with the Muslim Brotherhood of the Arab World and the Jamaati Islami of India/Pakistan. It supports several publishing ventures in the United States, as does the Islamic Foundation of London. These organizations have provided translations as well as original texts of major Sunni revivalist authors. More recently, the Mustazafan Foundation (the Islamized former Pahlevi Foundation) as well as several Iranian government agencies have been distributing English translations of major Shi'i texts composed by revivalist Iranian clerics.

Material written in or translated into English has become an important source of revivalist literature. Muslim communities living in the English speaking diaspora have been publishing this material in significant quantity in order to maintain themselves in the faith. More importantly, this literature is addressing the English speaking world by presenting its perspectives and world views, challenging, arguing, and even pleading with its intended audience, and using this medium to affirm the importance of being able to represent a culture, religion, and lifestyle different from that of the dominant culture.

Muslim contributors to the bibliography in this volume include immigrant scholars, social scientists, and humanists from Muslim countries who have emigrated to the States and are engaged in research and teaching on various campuses, emigree scholars, Muslim scholars who have had to leave their home countries because their ideas were (or because their governments found them) too controversial, and ideologues or political activists who continue to work for the deposing of regimes with which they disagree.[37] There is a new international network of professionals whose work is Islam. They function not as clergy, but as agents in the determination of Islamic policy and the directors of Islamization. They figure prominently in such organizations as the Muslim World League and the Organization of Islamic Conference.

THE LITERATURE ON REVIVAL

The available literature in English on contemporary Islamic revival appears to be directly and indirectly influenced by American strategic interests in various parts of the Muslim world, as well as by the availability of research funds from government foundations and other research organizations that encourage and foster research on specific topics they deem important either for national security considerations or for intellectual purposes. This literature also reflects the history of the academic study of Islam in the west. In the nineteenth and early twentieth centuries, most study of Islam as a religion, to the extent to which it existed at all, was done in two seminaries either as part of Christian missionary training or in an effort to enhance the study of Hebrew and the cultural background of the Bible. In the first two decades of this century, a handful of universities began offering courses on Islam in their Near East centers.

It was not until the middle of the 1950s, when the United States government, faced with the prospect of world leadership, found itself lacking in area specialists conversant with the languages and cultures of the world, that funds were made available to establish centers for Middle East (as well as other area) studies. In order to fill the positions opened at the various centers, foreign, mostly European scholars were hired to teach and direct research. When the centers for Middle and Near East studies were established their students had available only a handful of texts in English on contemporary Islam.[38] It was not until the 1960s that several important contributions to the understanding of the role that Islam played in the modern world and the manner in which it was utilized by various reformers and revivalists appeared.[39]

Western writing on the phenomenon of contemporary Islamic revivalism is clearly market driven. Before the end of the 1970s anyone who was engaged in research on revivalists was generally considered to be doing marginal and perhaps insignificant work. By the 1980s interest in Islam had grown to the extent that such scholarly endeavor was responding to public interest. As the fascination of America and the west with those who assassinated Anwar al-Sadat and in the Khomeini phenomenon developed, the market for the kinds of studies represented in this bibliography took off. Because of the interest of the western press in publishing literature on Islamic revival, both articles and monographs, some scholars have been called on to produce more than might be reasonable given the material available. In addition to some of the excellent scholarship produced there have been a few unfortunate results. In some cases there has been a reworking of information in ways that have led to repetitious presentations. Even more regrettably, otherwise responsible scholars on occasion have been tempted to "borrow" from the materials and the theories of others in their eagerness to join the rush of publication.

In assessing the literature available in English on contemporary revival, it appears that historians and historians of religion have been less interested in the material of Islamic revivalism, than have been representatives of other scholarly disciplines. The majority of authors on contemporary revival are graduates of the Middle East and Near East centers established in the 1950s. They are either Middle East, African or South Asian area specialists, or are grounded in social science disciplines such as political science, economics, sociology and anthropology. The relatively slim contribution of historians of religion has added little to the available information. It is hard to avoid the conclusion that for whatever reasons the majority of historians and historians of religion have ruled out most Islamic materials, certainly those of contemporary movements, as *a priori* insignificant to their overall studies.

Some writers, of course, have their own not so hidden agendas for attempting to describe the phenomena of Islamic revival. There are those who find it hard to hide their own lack of respect, and in certain cases antipathy, for anything that has to do with religion. They find it impossible to take seriously the religious dimensions of the movements of modern Islam and convey this in their writing, even though they may have deep affection for Arab society and culture. Some secular scholars write in a derogatory manner about Islam because they find it a threat to their own absolute claims to truth. There are also supporters of the Zionist cause who try to use revivalist material to raise the specter of Islamic extremism, helping to enhance the standing of and therefore support for Israel in the west.

It is clear that during the past several decades scholars writing in English on Islamic revival have made a major contribution to our understanding of Muslim movements, their organizational structures and their function as opposition political groups as well as their basic teachings. They have provided us with a description of the protoype of Muslim "fundamentalists," their class and economic background, their motives, their role as opposition groups to governments, their apparent motives as well as their ideology. It is also clear that much more needs to be done. There is a serious need for more studies on the religion of Islam as it has been interpreted for Muslims facing the twenty first century and its recasting as an ideology capable of mobilizing society for modernization and development. For example, in order to understand the dynamic of revival, we need more analysis of the issues being raised in the current debate over the reinstitution of the Shari'a in countries such as Egypt, Jordan, Tunisia, Algeria, and Indonesia. Given the fact that the public discussion of these issues uses familiar Islamic language and themes, scholars have been tempted to dismiss the revivalists as seeking to return the Muslim community to the seventh century. It is clear that for most revivalist writers, however, this is not the case, and that exegetical and contextual analysis of the language they are using make it clear that they are seeking a better understanding of the problems besetting their societies and of the ways in which traditional Islamic sources can be interpreted so as to help solve them.

The importance of the Qur'an as a source of inspiration and vindication of new ideas has not been studied adequately by western scholars. There have been no significant studies in English on contemporary Islamic exegetical literature of the Qur'an since the middle of the 1970s, nor on its use by authors, ideologues and revolutionaries as well as by government agencies in defining a relevant worldview for the modern, educated Muslim public. And little work has been done on the role of Qur'anic study groups and circles that appear to proliferate throughout the Muslim world, shaping and reshaping youth as the vanguard of the Islamic movement. Two other phenomena that have received scant attention are the sermon as a means of communicating revivalist ideas and the Sheikh panels that provide instruction on the Islamic way of life.[40]

The revivalist vision of the world calls on every Muslim to be a *da'iya*, someone who summons others to Islam.[41] In recent years the universities of Jordan, Kuwait, and Qatar, among others, have established Shari'a schools with a specialization in *da'wa* (lit. call or propagation, used to designate the outreach dimension of Islam). The graduates (both male and female) of these institutions as well as those of al-Azhar school of *da'wa* choose teaching careers through which the dissemination of the worldview of the revivalist movement is taking place. There are currently neither studies of this phenomenon nor of the literature that describes the role of the *da'iya* and the work of *da'wa*.

A study of the means of dissemination of revivalist ideas by use of modern media is an important ingredient in understanding the spread of the movement. Women and children especially are being targeted as a ripe audience. What are the kinds of ideas that are being spread on the popular level by such means as tape cassettes, religious videotapes, Islamic songs, and poems, women's magazines and special literature developed for children (illustrated books, cartoons and comics)? More work needs to be done on religious instruction in the school systems, the content of the religious curriculum, and the types and preparation of those who are doing this kind of classroom instruction.[42]

Attention also needs to be paid to the role of the *fatwa* (Islamic legal opinion) being offered to counter the challenges of the modern world, both those coming out of official government-controlled *fatwa* offices and those issued by non-clerical leaders of the revivalist cause.[43]

Most of the literature on revival deals with international relations, politics, issues of power and authority, and to some extent the social dimensions of the movement. Little attention has been paid to issues of Islamic economics and banking. Islamic banks generally are established to foster the development of the community rather than personal profit, and to provide interest-free loans. Since the failure of several financial institutions in Egypt, however, and the collapse of the pyramid scheme in

Kuwait's Suq al-Manakh, valued at billions of dollars, there has been some reluctance to invest resources on the scale experienced earlier. Furthermore, the decline in the price of oil and the depletion of oil reserves has led to serious reconsideration of funding. Future literature on revivalist directions needs to take this important economic factor into account.

Another matter to which increased attention needs to be paid is that of the role and status of women. While the general subject of Islamic women has received a good deal of attention in the last decade, most of the studies have focused on the evident phenomenon of veiling in public. The participation of women in the contemporary revivalist movement has been particularly conspicuous because of the insistence on adoption of "Islamic dress." This phenomenon is specially puzzling to western and westernized observers who see veiling as repressive and regressive. While titles of studies such as "Beyond the Veil," "A Look Beyond the Veil," "Behind the Veil," "A Return to the Veil," "Through a Veil Darkly," "Tradition and the Veil," "Veiling Infitah," "Veil of Fears," and "Reveal and Conceal," to some extent may be playful, they do capitalize on persistent western fascination with the "mysterious" East.[44] This attitude has been attacked by Muslim scholars in recent years as condescending, seeming to treat Muslim women as objects to be observed, analyzed, criticized and pitied. It also sets up western women, by contrast, as models of progressive civilization. Third world scholars question whether even the best intentioned of western observers can ever really understand women of other cultures whose values and goals differ so significantly from their own.

In the current age of computer technology, desk top publishing, cellular telephones, live television and the Fax machine, the encounter between Muslim countries and the west has become more direct and intense. Events in various parts of the world dictate the need for experience and expertise in how best to relate to those whom some scholars continue to refer to as "terrorists," "zealots," "militants," "fundamentalists," and "extremists."[45] With growing public demand for information interpreting events overseas that impact United States national and security interests, the market is tempting scholars to get immediate recognition by becoming the instant experts. The temptation for quick publication to outdistance the competition is overwhelming. One wonders whether it is time for a moratorium on such instant analysis, as well as on the seemingly constant reworking of already published material. The time seems to have come for more reasoned reflection on the events shaping the contemporary Islamic world and the ideologues who are attempting to change their circumstances by redefining the values that govern their lives.

Notes

1. Rudolph Peters, *Islam and Colonialism: The Doctrine of Jihad in Modern History* (The Hague: Mouton de Gruyter, 1979); Norman Daniel, *Islam, Europe and Empire* (Edinburgh: The University Press, 1966); Norman Daniel, *Islam and the West, The Making of an Image* (Edinburgh: The University Press, 1966); Muhammad al-Bahi, *Al-Fikr al-Islami al-Hadith wa Silatuhu bi al-Isti'mar al-Gharbi* (Cairo, 1975); Anwar al-Jundi, *Sumum al-Istishraq wa al-Mustashriqin* (Cairo, 1984); Harry Gaylord Dorman, *Toward Understanding Islam: Contemporary Apologetic of Islam and Missionary Policy* (New York: Columbia University, 1948); Mukhtar Sharaf, *Haqa'iq al-Tabshir* (Cairo, 1975).

2. The Salafiyya movement in Kuwait is lead by an Egyptian: 'Abd al-Rahman 'Abd al-Khaliq, *Al-Usul al-'Ilmiyya li-al-Da'wa al-Salafiyya* (Kuwait, 1402H). Another Egyptian lead movement in Kuwait prefers the title of *Usuliyyun* fundamentalists: 'Umar Sulayman al-Ashqar, *Thalath Sha'air: al-'Aqiqa, al-Adhiya, al-Liha'* (Kuwait, 1979); 'Umar Sulayman al-Ashqar, *Ma'alim al-Shakhsiyya al-Islamiyya* (Kuwait, 1984). Their ideas have been criticized by other Muslims. See Muhammad Fathi Uthman, *Al-Salafiyya fi al-Mujtma'at al-Mu'asira* ([Cairo, 1982]).

3. Yvonne Yazbeck Haddad, *Contemporary Islam and the Challenge of History* (Albany: State University of New York Press, 1982); Rashid al-Barrawi, *Al-Tafsir al-Qur'ani li al-Tarikh* (Cairo, 1973); 'Abd al-Rahman 'Ali Al-Hajji, *Nazarat fi Dirasat al-Tarikh al-Islami* (Damascus, 1975); Anwar al-Jundi, *Al-Islam wa Harakat al-Tarikh* (Cairo, 1968); 'Imad al-Din Khalil, *Al-Tafsir al-Islami li al-Tarikh* (Beirut, 1975); Sayyid Qutb, *Fi al-Tarikh: Fikra wa Minhaj* (Beirut, 1974); Mahmud al-Sharqawi, *Al-Tafsir al-Dini li al-Tarikh* (Cairo, 1975).

4. Abd al-Aziz Kamil, *Al-Islam wa al-Mustaqbal* (Cairo, 1975); Fu'ad Muhammad Fakhr al-Din, *Mustaqbal al-Muslimin* (Cairo, [1976]; Ahmad Kamal Abu al-Majd, "Al-Muslimun Da'wa li-Iqtiham al-Mustaqbal," *al-Arabi* 292 (March 1983).

5. Muhammad al-Sayyid al-Jalaynad, *Qadiyyat al-Khayr wa al-Shar fi al-Fikr al-Islami* ([Cairo], 1981); 'Abd al-Karim al-Khatib, *Al-Insan fi al-Qur'an* (Cairo, 1979); Faruq Disuqi, *Hurriyat al-Insan fi al-Fikr al-Islami* (Alexandria, 1982); Bint al-Shati', *Maqal fi al-Islam* (Cairo, n.d.); Hasan Sa'b, *Al-Islam wa al-Insan* (Beirut, 1981).

6. Taha Jabir Fayyad al-Alwani, *Al-Ijtihad wa al-Taqlid fi al-Islam* (Cairo, 1979); Muhammad Qutb, *Ma'rakat al-Taqalid* (Cairo, n.d.).

7. Sayyid Ahmad Khan, *Tafsir al-Qur'an* (Lahore, 1880-95); *Al-Tahrir fi Usul al-Tafsir* (Agra, 1892); *Tahzib al-Akhlaq* (Lahore, n.d.); J.M.S. Baljon, *The Reforms and Religious Ideas of Sir Seyyed Ahmad Khan* (Leiden: Brill, 1949); B.A. Dar, *Religious Thought of Sayyid Ahmad Khan* (Lahore, 1957); Khayr al-Din Basha, *Aqwam al-Masalik fi Ma'rifat Ahwal al-Mamalik* (Tunis, 1284-5H); Muhammad 'Abdu, *Al-A'mal al-Kamila li-al-Imam Muhammad 'Abdu*, 6 vols., Ed. Muhammad 'Amara (Beirut, 1972); Sayyid Jamal al-Din al-Afghani, *Ara' va Mu'taqadat-i Sayyid Jamal ad-Din Afghani*, Ed. Murtaza Mudarrisi Chahardihi (Tehran, 1958-9); Nikki R. Keddie, *Sayyid Jamal ad-Din "al-Afghani": A Political Biography* (Berkeley, University of California Press, 1972).

8. 'Imad al-Din Khalil, *Maqal fi al-'Adl al-Ijtima'i* (Beirut, n.d.); Sayed Kotb, *Social Justice in Islam*, trans. John H. Hardie (Washington,D.C.: American Council of Learned Societies, 1953); John J. Donahue and John Esposito, *Islam in Transition* (New York: Oxford University Press, 1982), pp. 98-168; Kemal Karpat, *Political and Social Thought in the Contemporary Middle East* (New York: Frederick A. Praeger, 1968)

9. Amin al-Khuli, *Al-Mujaddidun fi al-Islam* (Cairo, 1384H); Ahmad 'Abd al-Rahim Mustafa, *Harakat al-Tajdid al-Islami fi al-'Alam al-'Arabi al-Hadith* (Cairo, 1971); Muhammad 'Amara, *Tajdid al-Fikr al-Islami* (Cairo: 1977).

10. Ahmad Sharabasi, *Al-Din wa al-Mithaq* (Cairo, 1962); Mahmud Shalabi, *Ishtirakiyyat Muhammad* ([Cairo, 1962]); Mahmud Shalabi, *Ishtirakiyyat 'Umar* ([Cairo, 1964-5]); Mahmud Shalabi, *Ishtirakiyyat Abi Bakr* ([Cairo, 1963]); Mahammad Shalabi, *Ishtirakiyyat 'Uthman* ([Cairo, 1968]); Mahmud 'Ali Maher, *Muslim Yaqra' al-Mithaq fi Daw' al-Qur'an* (Cairo, 1968); Sa'id al-Sharabasi, *Mabadi' al-Ishtirakiyya fi al-Islam* (Cairo, n.d.); Ahmad Shalabi, *Al-Hayat al-Ijtima'iyya fi al-Tafkir al-Islami* (Cairo, [1968]).

11. Ahmad 'Abbas Salih, *Al-Yamin wa al-Yasar fi al-Islam* (Beirut, 1972); 'Imad al-Din Khalil, *Lu'bat al-Yamin wa al-Yasar* (Beirut, n.d.); Mustafa Mahmud, *Ukdhubat al-Yasar al-Islami* (Cairo, 1978).

12. Ahmad al-Najjar, *Manhaj al-Sahwa al-Islamiyya* (n.p., [1977]); Yusuf al-Qaradawi, *Al-Sahwa al-Islamiyya* (Cairo, 1984); Anwar al-Jundi, *Al-Sahwa al-Islamiyya* (Cairo, n.d.) See also Anwar al-Jundi, *Al-Yaqza al-Islamiyya* (Cairo, 1978); 'Abd al-Hadi Bu Talib, *ISESCO wa al-Sahwa al-Islamiyya* (Casablanca, 1985).

13. Hasan Hanafi, *Al-Turath wa al-Tajdid* (Beirut, 1972).

14. Abu al-Majd is formerly a member of the Egyptian cabinet and later an advisor to the Kuwaiti prime minister. Kamil is a former member of the Egyptian cabinet and advisor to the ruler of Kuwait. Al-Rumayhi is editor of *Al-'Arabi*, an internationally circulating Kuwaiti monthly. Jad'an is professor of Islamic history at the Jordanian University in Amman. Enneifer is a former member of the Islamic Tendency Movement in Tunisia and co-founder of the Progressive Muslims of Tunisia. Al-Jourchi is editor of a weekly magazine, co-founder of the Progressive Muslims of Tunisia and president of the Tunisian Human Rights Campaig14.22n.

15. Muhammad al-Ghazali, *Ma'rakat al-Mushaf fi al-'Alam al-Islami* (Cairo, 1964); Muhammad al-Ghazali, *Kifah Din* (Cairo, n.d.); Muhammad Faraj, *Al-Islam fi Mu'tarak al-Sira' al-Fikri al-Hadith* (Cairo, 1962); Muhammad al-Hasani, *Al-Islam al-Mumtahan* (Cairo, n.d.); Muhammad Jalal Kishk, *al-Ghazu al-Fikri* (Cairo, 1975); 'abd al-Sattar Fathallah Sa'id, *Al-Ghazu al-Fikri wa al-Tayyarat al-Mu'adiya li al-Islam* (Cairo, 1977).

16. 'Imad al-Din Khalil, *Tahafut al-'Almaniyya* (Beirut, n.d.); Anwar al-Jundi, *Suqut al-'Almaniyya* (Beirut, [1973]); Muhammad Mahdi Shams al-Din, *Al-'Almaniyya* (Beirut, 1980).

17. 'Abd al-Halim 'Uways, *Al-Muslimun fi Ma'rakat al-Baqa'* (Cairo, 1979).

18. Johannes J. G. Jansen, *The Neglected Duty: The Creed of Sadat's Assassins and Islamic Resurgence in the Middle East* (New York: Macmillan, 1986).

19. Sayyid Qutb, *Milestones* (Kuwait, 1978); see also his *Islam: the Religion of the Future* (Chicago: Kazi Publications, 1977); and *Islam and Universal Peace* (Indiannapolis, IN: American Trust Publications, 1977). Yvonne Y. Haddad, "Sayyid Qutb: Ideologue of Islamic Revival," in *Voices of Resurgent Islam*, ed. John Esposito (New York: Oxford University Press, 1983), pp. 67-98.

20. Muhammad Mahmud al-Zubayri, *Al-Islam Din wa Thawra* (Beirut, 1982); 'Awn al-Sharif, *Al-Islam wa al-Thawra wa al-Hadara* (Beirut, 1980).

21. Muhammad Mahmud al-Zubayri, *Al-Islam Din wa Thawra* (Beirut, 1982); 'Awn al-Sharif Qasim, *Al-Islam wa al-Thawra wa al-Hadara* (Beirut, 1980).

22. Fayiz Fahd Jabir, *Mawqif al-'Alam al-Islami min Qadiyyat Filastin* (Amman, 1981); Hilmi Muhammad al-Qa'ud, *Al-Harb al-Salibiyya al-'Ashira* (Cairo, 1981).

23. 'Abd al-Salam Yasin, *Al-Islam Bayn al-Da'wa wa al-Dawla: al-Minhaj al-Nabawi li-Taghyir al-Insan* (Casblanca, 1392H); Sabir 'Abd al-Rahman Tu'ayma, *Iradat al-Taghyir fi al-Islam* (Cairo, 1968).

24. Hasan Sa'b, *Al-Islam Tijah Tahadiyyat al-Hayat al-'Asriyya* (Beirut, 1965); Ibrahim al-Fayyumi, *Al-Islam wa Ittijahat al-Fikr al-Mu'asir* (Cairo, 1977); Munir Shafiq, *Al-Islam fi Ma'rakat al-Hadara* (Beirut, 1981); Faruq Hamadih, *Waratha Saliha li al-Hadara al-Mu'asira* (Casablanca, 1979); 'Awn al-Sharif Qasim, *Al-Islam wa al-Thawra al-Hadariyya* (Beirut, 1980); Ahmad Musa Salim, *Al-Islam wa Qadayana al-Mu'asira* (Cairo, n.d.).

25. 'Abd al-Rahman al-Kawakibi, *Sijill Mudhakkirat Jam'iyyat Umm al-Qura aw Mu'tamar al-Nahda al-Islamiyya al-Mun'aqid fi Makka al-Mukarrama 1316H* (Cairo, 1320).

26. 'Abdullah al-Hasan, *The Organization of the Islamic Conference: An Introduction to an Islamic Political Institution* (Herndon, VA: The International Institute of Islamic thought, 1988); Harry F. Kern, "The Organization of the Islamic Conference," *Arab-American Affairs* 20 (Spring 1987), 96-106.

27. For studies on contemporary Qur'an commentary, see 'Abd al-Majid 'Abd al-Salam al-Muhtasib, *Ittijahat al-Tafsir fi al-'Asr al-Rahin* (Amman, 1982); Muhammad Ibrahim Sharif, *Ittijahat al-Tajdid fi Tafsir al-Qur'an al-Karim fi Misr* (Cairo, 1982); 'Iffat Muhammad al-Sharqawi, *Ittijahat al-Tafsir fi Misr fi al-'Asr al-Hadith* (Cairo, 1972); Mustafa Muhammad al-Hadidi al-Tayr, *Ittijah al-Tafsir fi al-'Asr al-Hadith* (Cairo, 1975); 'Abdullah Khurshid al-Birri, *Al-Qur'an wa 'Ulumuhu fi Misr* (Cairo, 1970). Among the Qur'anic commentaries published in Arabic during this century are: Muhammad Farid Wajdi, *al-Mushaf al-Mufassar* (Cairo, n.d.); Mahmud Shaltut, *Tafsir al-Qur'an al-Karim* (Cairo, 1974); Muhammad 'Abd Allah Draz, *Madkhal ila al-Qur'an al-Karim* (Kuwait, 1971); Ahmad Mustafa al-Maraghi, *Tafsir al-Maraghi* (Cairo, 1969); Ibrahim al-Qattan, *Taysir al-Tafsir* (Amman, 1983); Bint al-Shati', *al-Qur'an wa al-Tafsir al-'Asri* (Cairo, 1969); Tantawi Jawhari, *al-Jawahir fi Tafsir al-Qur'an al-Karim* (Cairo, 1350H); Muhammad Mahmud al-Hijazi, *al-Tafsir al-Wadih* (Cairo, 1972); 'Abd al-Karim al-Khatib, *al-Tafsir al-Qur'ani li al-Qur'an* (Cairo, 1967); Ali Merad, *Ibn Badis Commenteur du Coran* (Paris: Paul Geuthner, 1971); Malik Ben Nabi, *The Quranic Phenomenon*, trans. Abu Bilal Kirkary (Indianapolis: American Trust Publication, 1983); 'Imad al-Din Khalil, *Afaq Qur'aniyya* (Beirut, 1979); 'Imad al-Din Khalil, *Ma'a al-Qur'an fi 'Alamihi al-Rahib* (Beirut, n.d.); Muhammad 'Ali al-Hasan, *Al-'Alaqat al-Duwaliyya fi al-Qur'an wa al-Sunna* (Amman, 1982); 'Abd al-Wadud Yusuf, *Tafsir al-Mu'minin* (Damascus, 1975); 'Allal al-Fasi, *Sira' al-Madhab*

wa al-'Aqida fi al-Qur'an (Tunis, 1979); Muhsin 'Abd al-Hamid, *Dirasat fi Usul Tafsir al-Qur'an* (Casablanca, 1984).

28. Commentaries on the Qur'an have been written by authors who are neither grounded in traditional education nor versed in the classical sciences of exegesis. Sayyid Qutb, *Fi Zilal al-Qur'an* (Beirut, 1973-74); 'Izzat Darwaza, *al-Tafsir al-Hadith* (Cairo, 1962).

29. See for example, Mawlana Abu-l-Karim Azad, *The Tarjuman-l-Qur'an*, ed. and trans. by Sayyid Abdu-l-Latif (London: Asian Publishing House, 1962); Sayyid Ahmad Khan, *Tafsiru-l-Qur'an* (Lahore, 1891); Ghulam Ahmad Parwez, *Mafhum-l-Qur'an* (Lahore, 1961); Abu al-'A'la al-Mawdudi, *Tafhim-l-Qur'an* (Lahore, 1967).

30. See, for example, the writings of the lawyer Kamal Abu al-Majd in the widely distributed Kuwaiti monthly *al-'Arabi*: "Al-Shura wa al-Dimuqratiyya wa Ru'yat al-Islam al-Siyasiyya," *al-'Arabi* 257 (April 1980); "Bal al-Islam wa al-'Uruba Ma'an," *al-'Arabi* 263 (October 1980); "Basha'ir Nahda Islamiyya Jadida," *al-'Arabi* 295 (June 1980); "Al-Turath wa al-Ijtihad wa Nazariyyat al-Islam wa al-Siyasa," *al-'Arabi* 308 (July 1984); Muhammad Kamal 'Atiyya, *Muhasabat al-Sharikat wa al-Masarif fi al-Nizam al-Islami* (Cairo, 1984). The medical doctor, Mustafa Mahmud, has become a popular television evangelist and has established a mosque which attempts to recreate the original role of the mosque by providing social, economic as well as spiritual services. See his controversial book, *al-Qur'an Muhawala li-Fahm 'Asri* (Beirut, n.d.); also his *Bahth fi al-Wujud wa al-'Adam* (Cairo, 1977). Two controversial books written from opposing Muslim perspectives were authored by engineers. Wa'il 'Uthman, *Hizb Allah fi Muwajahat Hizb al-Shaytan* (Cairo, 1975); Faraj Fuda, *Qabl al-Suqut* (Cairo, 1985).

31. 'Abd al-Mun'im al-Nimr, *al-Islam wa al-Gharb Wajhan li-Wajh* (Beirut, 1982); Abu al-'A'la al-Mawdudi, *Nahnu wa al-Hadara al-Gharbiyya* (Damascus, n.d.); Abu al-Hasan 'Ali al-Nadawi, *Al-Sira' Bayn al-Fikra al-Islamiyya wa al-Fikra al-Gharbiyya fi al-Aqtar al-Islamiyya* (Kuwait, 1965); Seyyed Hossein Nasr, The Western World and its Challenges to Islam," *The Islamic Quarterly* 17 (June 1973), 3-25; Muhammad Mahmud Husayn, *Al-Islam wa al-Hadara al-Gharbiyya* (Beirut, 1969).

32. For example, hundreds of thousands of copies of the taped television debate between evangelist Jimmy Swaggart and Ahmad Deedat, the Indian Muslim from South Africa on whether the Bible is the word of God are distributed throughout the Muslim world and to Muslim students attending western universities. Muslims believe that the debate proved without a shadow of a doubt the superiority of the Qur'an as the revealed word of God, while exposing the Bible as an inferior document, tampered with by humans.

33. Abdul Hamid Abu Sulayman, "Islamization of Knowledge With Special Reference to Political Science," *American Journal of Islamic Social Sciences*, 2 (1985), 263-89; Isma'il Al Faruqi and Abdullah Omar Nasseef, eds, *Social and Natural Sciences: The Islamic Perspective* (Sevenoaks, Kent: Hodder and Stoughton, 1981); Zaydan 'Abd al-Baqi, *'Ilm al-Ijtima' al-Islami* (Cairo, 1984).

34. Yvonne Haddad, "Islam, Women and Revolution in Twentieth-Century Arab Thought," *MW* 74 (July-October 1984): 137-60; Valerie Hoffman-Ladd, "Religious Life of Muslim Women in Contemporary Egypt," Ph.D. Diss., University of Chicago, 1986. See also 'Abd al-Baqi Ramdun, *Khatar al-Tabarruj wa al-Ikhtilat* (Beirut, 1974); 'Abd al-Ghani 'Abbud, *Al-Usra al-Muslima wa al-Usra al-Mu'asira* [Cairo], 1977; Muhammad 'Abd al-Karim and Mahmud Muhammad al-Jawhari, *Al-Akhawat al-*

Muslimat wa Bina' al-Usra al-Qur'aniyya (Alexandria, 1980); Anwar al-Jundi, *Al-Tarbiya wa Bina' al-Ajyal* (Beirut, 1975).

35. For example, *The Muslim World Review of Books* devotes all its pages to review of books published in the west on Islam and the Muslim world.

36. Three Muslim emigres in the United States whose teaching and research has had an important influence on Muslim students from overseas include: Isma'il al-Faruqi, *Tawhid: Its Relevance for Thought and Life* (Kuala Lampur: The International Institute of Islamic Thought, 1982); Seyyed Hossein Nasr, *Islam and the Plight of Modern Man* (London: Longman, 1975); Fazlur Rahman, *Islam and Modernity: Transformation of an Intellectual Tradition* (Chicago: University of Chicago Press, 1982).

37. The Association of Muslim Social Scientists publishes the *American Journal of Islamic Social Sciences. (Herndon, Virginia).*

38. Among them were two books by Wilfred Cantwell Smith, *Modern Islam in India* (London: Gollancz, 1946) and *Islam in Modern History* (Princeton: Princeton University Press, 1957); C. C. Adams, *Islam and Modernism in Egypt* (London: Oxford University Press, 1933); H.A.R. Gibb, *Modern Trends in Islam* (Chicago: University of Chicago Press, 1947); J.N.D. Anderson, *Islamic Law in the Modern World* (New York: New York University Press, 1959).

39. These include Montgomery Watt, *Islamic Revelation in the Modern World* (Edinburgh: Edinburgh University Press, 1969); Elie Kedourie, *Afghani and 'Abduh* (London: Cass, 1966); Malcolm Kerr, *Islamic Reform* (Berkeley: University of California Press, 1966); Martin Lings, *A Moslem Saint of the Twentieth Century: Shaykh Ahmad al-'Alawi* (London: Allen and Unwin, 1961); J.M.S. Baljon, *Modern Muslim Koran Interpretation, 1880-1960* (Leiden: Brill, 1961); Clifford Geertz, *The Religion of Java* (Glencoe: Free Press, 1960) and *Islam Observed: Religious Developments in Morocco and Indonesia* (New Haven: Yale University Press, 1968); G. Von Grunebaum, *Modern Islam: The Search for Cultural Identity* (Berkeley: University of California Press, 1962); R.P. Mitchell, *The Society of Muslim Brothers* (London: Oxford University Press, 1969).

40. Ibrahim Muhammad al-Jamal, *Al-Khutba al-'Asriyya* (Cairo, 1983); Abu al-A'la al-Mawdudi, *Khutab al-Jum'a* (Cairo, n.d.); Ahmad al-Shahawi Sa'id Sharaf al-Din, *Sarakhat 'Ala al-Minbar,* 2 vols. (Cairo, 1975); Qarni Abu 'Amira, *Bughyat al-Khatib fi al-Khutab al-Minbariyya* (Cairo, 1982).

41. Sabir Tu'ayma, *Al-Islam wa 'Alamuna al-Mu'asir: Dirasa fi al-Da'wa wa al-Du'at* (Riyad, 1981); Sabir Tu'ayma, *Al-Ma'rifa fi Manhaj al-Qur'an: Dirasa fi al-Da'wa wa al-Du'at* (Beirut, n.d.); Yusuf al-Qaradawi, *Thaqafat al-Da'iya* (Beirut, 1980); Fathi Yakan, *Mushkilat al-Da'wa wa al-Da'iya* (Beirut, 1980).

42. Ahmad al-latif al-Jad'an wa Husni Adham Jarrar, *Shu'ara' al-Da'wa al-Islamiyya fi al-'Asr al-Hadith,* 7 vols. (Beirut, 1983); The texts used in the school systems in Jordan, Tunisia, Morocco, Egypt, and Syria are written by government officials. It would be valuable to have a comparative study of what is taught as Islamic ideology on issues of political, economic, social and cultural significance.

43. Dar al-Ifta' al-Islamiyya, *Al-Fatawa al-Islamiyya* (Cairo, 1982); Yusuf al-Qaradawi, *Fatawa Mu'asira* (Cairo, 1981); 'Abd al-Halim Mahmud, *Fatawa* (Cairo, [1981]); al-Mutawalli al-Sha'rawi, *Fatawa* (Cairo, 1982).

44. Fatima Mernissi, *Beyond the Veil: Male-Female Dynamics in Modern Muslim Society*. 2d ed. (Bloomington, IN: Indiana University Press, 1987); Elizabeth W. Fernea and Robert A. Fernea, "A Look Behind the Veil," *Human Nature* 2(1979): 68-77; Nesta Ramazani, "Behind the Veil: Status of Women in Revolutionary Iran," *RIPEH*, 3 (Spring, 1979): 53-64; John A. Williams, "A Return to the Veil in Egypt," *Middle East Review* 11 (1979): 49-65; David Waines, "Through a Veil Darkly: The Study of Women in Muslim Societies," *Comparative Studies in Society and History* 24, 4 (October 1982): 642-659; Susan E. Marshall and Randall G. Stokes, "Tradition and the Veil: Female Status in Tunisia and Algeria," *Journal of Modern African Studies* 19, 4 (1981): 625-646; Fadwa El Guindi, "Veiling Infitah with Muslim Ethic: Egypt's Contemporary Islamic Movement," *Social Problems* 28 (1981): 465-483; Haleh E. Bakhash, "Veil of Fears: Iran's Retreat from Women's Rights," *NRep*, 3693 (28 October 1985): 15-16; Andrea B. Rugh, *Reveal and Conceal: Dress in Contemporary Egypt* (New York: Syracuse University Press, 1986).

45. Lucien S. Vandenbroucke, "Why Allah's Zealots? A Study of the Causes of Islamic Fundamentalism in Egypt and Saudi Arabia," *Middle East Review* 16, 1 (Fall 1983); Hamied al-Ansari, "The Islamic Militants in the Politics of Egypt," *International Journal of Middle East Studies* 16 (1984): 123-144; Saad Eddin Ibrahim, "Egypt's Islamic Militants," *MERIP Report*, 12, 103 (February, 1983); Nesta Ramazani, "Islamic Fundamentalism and the Women of Kuwait," *Middle East Insight* 5, 5 (January-February, 1988); G. Keppel, *The Prophet and Pharoah: Muslim Extremism in Egypt* (London: al-Saqi, 1985).

2

The Revivalist Heritage
John Obert Voll

The contemporary Islamic revival is a special response to the particular conditions of the late twentieth century and must be seen in the context of the conflicts and challenges of the modern world. At the same time it is also part of the historical experience of renewal within Muslim societies over the centuries. The current experiences of Muslim revivalists cannot be separated from the heritage which they reaffirm. Both are important to the contemporary revivalist experience and neither can be ignored if that experience is to be understood.

The intellectual content of the contemporary Islamic revival reflects its dual character as both a special, new experience and part of a broader historical tradition. Muslim intellectuals and activists have identified a variety of issues and concepts which involve redefinition of old ideas as well as necessitating new symbols and concepts. The very process itself is a part both of the experience of movements and individuals as they deal with modern situations and of the continuity of concepts and ideas reflected in their heritage.

The conscious combination of these elements in the process of redefinition is an important component of contemporary revival. It represents a new stage in the modern intellectual history of Islam with a significant redirection away from the focus of much activity in the previous century and a half.

For much of the nineteenth and twentieth centuries, a significant proportion of the intellectual and ideological efforts of Muslims was aimed at creating a "modernized" Islam, or even what was in effect an alternative to Islam. Concepts which had little relationship to the Islamic heritage became vital parts of mainstream political and cultural discourses. Nationalism, secular reformism, democratic capitalism, and social radicalism of a Marxist style provided important bases for new ideological perspectives for many in the Islamic world. While many people worked to show how Islam was actually socialist or capitalist or in accord with some other modern perspective, this effort was primarily to adjust Islamic concepts to modern western perceptions rather than to reaffirm the Islamic heritage itself.

The Islamic revival reverses this effort by affirming the Islamic discourse in a way that does not attempt to start with western forms of modern ideas. This new phase shows the disillusion with the foreign ideologies and forms and the willingness to create an Islamic rather than a western worldview for the contemporary era: western ideological formulations, whether liberal or radical, capitalist or communist, are seen by many Muslims as having failed. The emphasis therefore has shifted from "modernizing" Islam to the Islamization of the modern experience.

The intellectual content in the messages presented by the major individuals and movements in the contemporary Islamic revival reflects this changing context. While the local conditions vary, there are certain broad themes that have emerged in the late twentieth century that are frequently shared by Muslim revivalists throughout the Islamic world. These themes show the different ways in which the Islamic heritage influences contemporary revivalist thought.

Three different types of conceptual development can be identified as the revivalist mode of Islamic experience has evolved in recent years. One involves major concepts that have been central to pre-modern revivalism and have continued to have relevance in the contemporary reaffirmation of Islam. A second type of development is the transformation of older concepts into terms and symbols of special significance in the modern context, while a third involves the development of new concepts arising out of specific modern and contemporary conditions.

THE CONTINUING REVIVALIST TRADITION

Throughout Islamic history there have been dynamic responses to the conditions created by historic change. As adaptations have been made to changing conditions, voices have been raised to call for a return to the pure fundamentals of Islam. It is possible through this interaction to identify a tradition of revivalism and renewal in the history of Muslim societies.[1] In this tradition there have been certain concepts which have had continuing meaning and force and play a role in the discourses of renewal both in the pre-modern and contemporary eras.

One such concept is the idea of renewal itself, embodied in the terms *tajdid*, meaning "regeneration" or "renewal," and the related term, *mujaddid*, which means "the person who leads renewal." In the early centuries of Islamic history it became clear that Muslims had not succeeded in creating and maintaining a truly Islamic society following the death of the Prophet Muhammad. As a result, there were periodic calls for a renewal *tajdid* of the commitment to the fundamental principles of Islam and the related reconstruction of society in accord with the Qur'an and the Traditions of the Prophet.

These efforts were often seen in the perspective of a well-known Tradition of the Prophet that "God will send to His community at the head of each century those who will renew its faith for it." Over the centuries Muslims have looked back at important reforming leaders of the faith and identified them as *mujaddids* or "renewers." While there is disagreement over who might be identified as "the mujaddid" of a particular century, there is little disagreement over the existence of *mujaddids* as an important force in the history of Islamic societies. "Renewal" is a vital aspect of the efforts of Muslims to follow the imperatives of their faith.

In the twentieth century, the concept of *tajdid* has been an important part of contemporary revival, and a significant concept in the intellectual formulations of many of the key revivalist thinkers. Mawlana Abul 'A'la Mawdudi (1903-1979), the South Asian activist, wrote a major study of the history of *tajdid* movements and *mujaddids*.[2] The idea of renewal is an important part of his general analysis of the requirements of the modern age. Maryam Jameelah, another influential writer in the contemporary revival, noted that upon *mujaddids* "depend not only Islam's renaissance but its very survival."[3]

In the final quarter of the twentieth century, the concept of renewal has become an important legitimizing concept in the struggle against existing conditions.

Mawdudi had carefully distinguished between *tajdid*, which was opposition to existing conditions while reaffirming Islam, and innovation, which involved adopting new non-Islamic elements. His successors in many parts of the Islamic world continue this conceptualization. Hasan Turabi, the leader of the Muslim Brotherhood in the Sudan, for example, called his revivalist analysis of the foundations of Islamic law in the contemporary world *tajdid*. In Nigeria intellectuals involved in Islamic revivalism see *tajdid* as the critical aspect of the Islamization process. In a discussion of the nineteenth century West African revivalist Uthman dan Fodio, Ibrahim Sulayman, a prominent Islamist writer, says that the "tajdid process... was essentially a struggle between believers and unbelievers; and in a political context, a struggle between tyrants and the advocates of justice -- in short,... a repetition of the ever-recurrent drama involving the conflict between David and Goliath."[4]

The concept of "renewal" is thus a part of the Islamic heritage which continues in the contemporary revival. There is a sense of the continuing need to "purge Islam of... evils, and to present it once again in its original pure forms," resulting in a feeling that, as Mawdudi stated, "Islam needed in every age and still needs such strong men, groups of men and institutions which could change the course of the times and bring the world round to bow before the authority of the One, Almighty."[5] This special sense of a mission to restore purity is part of the conceptual continuity between past and present movements of Islamic revival.

A second great theme of revival is the call to judge existing societies. The mission of renewal involves an act of judgement which identifies existing practices and faith of Muslims as not being in accord with "the original pure form" of Islam. Essentially, this involves the act of identifying a person, group, or institution as being "unbelieving" or *kafir*. This action is called *takfir*; the concept of *takfir*, like *tajdid*, has deep roots in Islamic history.

All Muslims accept the general obligation to encourage what is good and to condemn what is bad, but many Muslims do not believe that it is appropriate to make the charge of "unbelief" against another professing Muslim. This is seen as attempting to usurp the authority of God as Judge. As a result, from the very early days of the Islamic community, *takfir* has been controversial and has distinguished more militant revivalists from other Muslims. Among the first people to engage in the act of *takfir* were the Kharijites, uncompromising militants who revolted against the majority leadership of the community in the first century of Islam. Since that time activists who have called their opponents "unbelievers" have frequently been called Kharijites by their political and ideological enemies.

The debate over whether or not a Muslim has the responsibility and the right to judge another person as an "unbeliever" has continued in revivalist discourses over the centuries. In the modern era, although the specific conditions and issues may have changed, the basic concepts and principles involved show significant continuity. Contemporary arguments reflect old issues and often utilize the medieval scholars as authorities for positions.

Recent debates in Egypt illustrate the basic arguments of the past three decades. The leading revivalist thinker of the 1960s, Sayyid Qutb, set the tone for those who accepted the obligation to condemn the existing society as "infidel." His ideas became an important foundation for the movements of Islamic militants during the 1970s. However, even among those involved in the Islamic resurgence, some felt that *takfir* was improper. Qutb was accused of being a Kharijite by a major scholar from al-Azhar and even the leader of the Muslim Brotherhood at the time, Hasan al-Hudaybi, argued that Muslims must be "preachers, not judges."[6]

Late in the 1970s, the Jihad group argued that the "Rulers of this age are in apostasy from Islam" and killed the Egyptian president, Anwar al-Sadat. In the trial of the killers and in the subsequent debates, comparisons again were made with the Kharijites and *takfir* was seen as the action of extremists.[7] This was not just the position of the religious establishment, as reflected in the ruling of the Mufti of Egypt, but was also the stance of such an important intellectual of the resurgence as Yusuf al-Qaradawi.[8]

The concept of *takfir* and the debate about it remain part of the continuing tradition of renewal in the Islamic community. The deep roots of the arguments are recognized by all participants and in this area, at least, the issues and experiences of the present resurgence reflect a profound continuity with past Muslim life.

A third continuing theme of revival is *jihad*. This is a complex concept which is often understood simply as meaning a military "holy war." It is much broader than this, encompassing the whole range of special efforts to adhere to, affirm, and support the message of God. It includes, of course, military efforts to defend Islam, but it also is used to apply to other activities as well. From the early days of Islam to the present, activists have spoken of the need for "jihad" in the path of God, and *jihad* has become an important concept in the message of renewal. Medieval mystics spoke of the inner *jihad* of spiritual renewal while militants called people to arms. It is this complex heritage that modern renewalists utilize in their efforts to reaffirm the Islamic message in the contemporary world.

During the past two centuries, *jihad* has been applied in many different contexts, but its basic meaning has not been altered. It provided an important mobilizing concept for the early resistance to European imperial forces. Algerian resistance to French conquest and control in the nineteenth century, for example, was usually conceived of as *jihad*, as was the anti-imperial movement of Muhammad ibn Abdallah in Somalia at the beginning of the twentieth. Even more secularly oriented nationalist movements in the twentieth century often used the term to describe their efforts.

In the recent Islamic resurgence, *jihad* has become a programmatic issue in the minds of activists. The call for active *jihad* is a natural consequence of the declaration that the ruler or the society is infidel. Contemporary revivalists have, however, differed with regard to how one implements the obligation of "striving (jihad) in the path of God." In Egypt, even among the more radical Islamist groups of the 1970s, for example, there was disagreement. One group (known as "Takfir wa al-Hijrah") argued that the appropriate strategy was withdrawal from society during the phase when their movement was small and weak, while another opted for a more open conflict with the state. The latter led to the organization of the Jihad group which killed Sadat.

The nature of *jihad* is an issue in the better known works of the contemporary resurgence. Sayyid Qutb reflects the more militant position. He criticizes "defeatist-type people" who "want to confine *jihad* to what today is called 'defensive war'" and says that the movement of true religion "does not confine itself to mere preaching to confront physical power" of infidel oppression.[9] In this activist position, Qutb continues the approach of the south Asian revivalist, Abu al-'A'la Mawdudi, who stated that "the real objective of Islam is to remove the lordship of man over man and to establish the kingdom of God on earth. To stake one's life and everything else to achieve this purpose is called *jihad*."[10] Mawdudi explicitly emphasized the military aspect when he noted, "A man who exerts himself physically or mentally or spends his wealth *in the way of Allah* is indeed engaged in *jihad*. But in the language of the *Shari'ah* this word is used particularly for a war that is waged solely in the name of Allah against those who practice oppression as enemies of Islam."[11]

In the modern era as in the past, the narrow, more military focus is countered by revivalists who have a broader definition that also utilizes long-standing interpretations. This position is well represented by Suzanne Haneef. She notes that "Unfortunately the word *jihad* has been represented so often in the western media (and by some well-meaning but ignorant Muslims as well) as meaning 'holy war' that this is now accepted as its real meaning. This is totally incorrect, for *jihad* simply means 'striving'.... The first and most essential *jihad* which the Muslim must carry on is within himself in a never-ceasing effort at self-improvement and self-purification."[12] In this, Haneef follows the long-standing Islamic mystic idea of the "greater *jihad*" of the soul.

The context of the discussion about *jihad* has changed, but the basic themes and issues reflect significant continuities over the centuries. Mawdudi, Qutb, and Haneef express opinions within the traditions of Sunni Islam, but these differences can be seen among contemporary Shi'i groups as well. The Ayatollah Khomeini and other leaders of the Islamic revolution in Iran stressed the more militant definition of *jihad*. Other Shi'i thinkers emphasize the need for *jihad* to be defensive and that unjust rulers can not undertake *jihad*. The just community "may engage in *jihad* to defend itself and strive to establish justice," but rulers must prove that "the *jihad* was not undertaken primarily for territorial expansion."[13]

The great concepts of renewal *tajdid*, condemnation *takfir*, and striving *jihad*, represent aspects of long-term continuity in the contemporary Islamic resurgence. These concepts are widely used in the discourse of the resurgence and their underlying meaning remains similar to what it has been in the past. This is reflected also in the continuity of disagreements as well. The contexts are new but the debates are significantly similar to those of the past. This continuity is an important dimension of the current revival.

TRANSFORMATION OF CONCEPTS

The current resurgence is not simply a repetition of the past experiences of Islamic renewal. In addition to the continuities, there are some significant reformulations of older concepts which give the current movements a distinctive intellectual and action framework. Each of the major figures in the contemporary Islamic world has his own special approach but there are some key conceptualizations that are shared by many of them. These reinterpretations of older concepts provide the special tone for the contemporary revivalist approach.

One of the most important new conceptualizations involves the term *jahiliyyah*. The Arabic term basically means "ignorance." In traditional Islamic usage, "the *Jahiliyyah*" referred to the age of ignorance before the revelation of the Qur'an to Muhammad. However Mawdudi, the early pioneer in contemporary revivalist thought, began to use the term to refer to forces which corrupted historic Muslim societies, seeing *jahiliyyah* as a type of counter-revolution which came to dominate Muslim societies. It was, in his view, the mission of the renewer (*mujaddid*) to combat and ultimately defeat *jahiliyyah*.[14]

This theme has been elaborated by thinkers in the current Islamic resurgence. Sayyid Qutb developed the concept further and identified the enemies of true Muslims as "*Jahiliyyah*." For those who viewed opponents as "unbelievers," that is, persons who engaged in *takfir*, the unbelieving enemy were defined as the *jahiliyyah*. Qutb defined this concept clearly in modern terms: "If we look at the sources and foundations of modern ways of living, it becomes clear that the whole world is steeped in *Jahiliyyah*, and all the marvelous material comforts and high-level inventions do not diminish this ignorance. This *Jahiliyyah* is based on rebellion against God's sovereignty on earth... It is now not in that simple and primitive form of the ancient *Jahiliyyah*, but takes the form of claiming that the right to create values, to legislate rules of collective behavior, and to choose any way of life rests with men, without regard to what God has prescribed."[15] This was the heart of Qutb's attack on the nationalist and socialist state of Nasser in Egypt and it provided the idiom for subsequent Islamist attacks on states throughout the Islamic world.

The identification of the forces opposed to Islam as a new *jahiliyyah* became an important part of activist Muslim rhetoric, particularly in Egypt in the 1970s and

1980s. This conceptualization was also significant in other areas of the Islamic world, especially as the works of Sayyid Qutb became a part of the literature of Islamic revival everywhere. While the terminology is less important among Shi'i Islamic revolutionaries, they certainly understand and utilize the concept. By the 1990s, the re-oriented meaning of *jahiliyyah* has become an accepted and widely-used part of the discourse of Islamic revivalism, understood and used even by those who would not be considered militants.

Another powerful concept which has been reoriented in some ways in the contemporary resurgence is *tawhid*. This is one of the central concepts in the Islamic experience and refers to the oneness of God. In discussions of Islam before the recent resurgence, the meaning of the concept tended to be simple. An introduction to Islam published by Abd al-Rahman Azzam in the early 1960s, for example, states that *tawhid* "means the act of belief in the oneness of God."[16] The usual form for this act of belief is saying the basic statement of faith: "There is no divinity but God."

The concept of *tawhid* has long been one of the starting points for discussions of faith in Islam and is a key concept in Islamic theology. Muhammad Abdu, the Egyptian intellectual who provided the foundation for Islamic modernism, discussed *tawhid* at some length. Although Abdu's conclusions were modernist, his definition of the key term shows fundamental continuity with the longstanding traditions of Islamic theological thought. Abdu stated that the "theology of unity (*tawhid*) is the science that studies the being and attributes of God, the essential and the possible affirmations about Him, as well as the negations that are necessary.... The original meaning of *tawhid* is the belief that God is one in inalienable divinity. Thus the whole science of theology is named from the most important of its parts, namely the demonstration of the unity of God in Himself and in the act of creation."[17]

This relatively static definition has been transformed in the final quarter of the twentieth century. In the older usage, *tawhid* was seen as a "concept" or "belief." However, in recent years, it has increasingly come to be understood as an active, dynamic process as well. Muhammad N. Siddiqi reflects this change when he notes that in addition to being "the key concept in Islam," which presents the "essence of the Islamic civilization," it "is also the one term which describes the *process* of the Islamic transformation of an individual or a society."[18]

An important figure in this developing understanding was Mawdudi, who emphasized that the affirmation that "There is no divinity but God" does not merely proclaim "the unity of God as the Creator or even as the sole object of worship. It also proclaims the uniqueness of God as the Master, Sovereign, Lord and Law-Giver." In his view, it is a "summons that man respond to Him with his whole being in exclusive service and obedience and devotion and worship."[19] Mawdudi argued that the "belief in the Unity and the Sovereignty of Allah is the foundation of the social and moral system propounded by the prophets," and then outlined what were the basic implications of *tawhid* for political, social, and economic life.[20]

Through analyses like Mawdudi's, *tawhid* provides the conceptual foundation for the affirmation that the Islamic message is comprehensive. In this view, Islam does not allow for the separation of religion and politics and does not accept the distinction between sacred and profane. In both principle and practice Islam is to be thoroughly holistic in its approach, with the oneness of God providing the unification of all aspects of life and cosmos. *Tawhid* is not simply a concept or a belief, it is an active transforming process. This perspective is characteristic of the major individuals and movements involved in the Islamic resurgence of the final quarter of the twentieth century.

The transformation of *tawhid* from a faith-concept to an activist process can be seen in most areas of the Islamic world. In the years before the resurgence, Hasan al-Banna, the founder of the Muslim Brotherhood in Egypt, paralleled the work of Mawdudi in defining a *tawhid*-based holistic approach to the transformation of society. This was continued by later Brotherhood writers and was a vital part of the structure of Qutb's thought. Qutb, for example, affirmed that "Islam constructs its foundation of belief and action on the principle of total submission to God alone. Its beliefs, forms of worship and rules of life are uniformly an expression of this submission and are a practical interpretation of the declaration that there is no deity except Allah."[21]

Similar affirmations can be found throughout the Islamic world in the 1970s and 1980s by major Muslim intellectuals. Increasingly, this style of awareness of *tawhid* is not simply associated with militant revivalists but has become the normal usage. One of the most comprehensive discussions in this mode is provided by Isma'il R. al-Faruqi, who was an internationally influential intellectual in the Muslim world. He was a major force in the international effort to accomplish the "Islamization of knowledge," which was to be a part of the active process of *tawhid* in the contemporary world. He felt that "*tawhid* is a general view of reality, of truth, of the world, of space and time, of human history and destiny."[22] On this basis, he showed the importance of the Islamically holistic approach to ethics, social order, politics, economics, and all other aspects of human life. The key is the emphasis on the comprehensive and universal nature of Islam.

Various thinkers in the Iranian Islamic revolution also have approximated the concept of *tawhid* as an active process. Major ideologically-oriented Ayatollahs have based their significant works on *tawhid*, understood as a comprehensive perspective on all of life. The Ayatollah Mahmud Taleghani, for example, saw *tawhid* as the foundation of a just economic and social order.[23] The most significant Iranian contributor to the transformation of the conceptualization of *tawhid* is Ali Shariati, often called the ideological parent of the Iranian revolution. Shariati "is the first Iranian writer on religion to have turned this hitherto theological doctrine into a 'world-view' *jahan-bini*, a term coined originally by Iranian Marxists in the early forties as an equivalent for a secular, political system of beliefs."[24] For Shariati, *tawhid* is "the foundation of the individual and social life of a Muslim. All human activities and relationships, whether political, economic, literary, or artistic, ought to be firmly grounded in *tawhid*."[25]

This transformation of the conceptualization of *tawhid* is an important part of the discourse of the contemporary Islamic resurgent. Along with the reorientation of other key concepts, such as *jahiliyyah*, this provides an important dimension of the contemporary expression of Islamic revivalism. The current resurgence is not simply a continuation of old traditions of renewal *tajdid*. It represents a special response to the new conditions of the contemporary world, reflected in the efforts to reorient concepts central to the Islamic faith.

ISLAMIZATION OF NEW CONCEPTS

The dynamic response of Muslims to the conditions of the contemporary world is also indicated by the fact that new concepts have been adapted and included within the discourse of Islamic revivalism. This reflects the conceptual and programmatic complexity and sophistication of the revival, which thus includes adaptations of new concepts as well as some aspects of direct continuity with past renewals and transformations of old conceptualizations. In this way, revivalism involves both the heritage from the modern experience and the heritage from pre-modern Islamic civilization. The process of incorporating the "non-traditional" legacy into the current Muslim revivalist discourse is in many ways as important as the process of continuing or transforming the older heritage.

The modern experience of interaction between Islamic societies and the west has brought many new terms and concepts to the Islamic world. In the context of imperial conquest and general western domination during the nineteenth and twentieth centuries, some Muslims tended to accept western ideas and methods uncritically. There was an assumption that institutions and forms that worked in western Europe could be transplanted unchanged to Islamic societies and that westernization and modernization were identical. In this way, many terms of western European origin, such as nationalism and secularism, were introduced into political, social, and religious discourses in Islamic societies. These terms became important parts of the debates regarding the nature and future of the Islamic world.

Since western concepts usually have been introduced to the Islamic world as a part of westernizing reform programs, their usage at first simply reflected the broader context of societal change. Western educated Muslims and westernizing reformers used the terms, while others opposed both the concepts and the terminology. However, as concepts such as nationalism came to dominate the political discourse, the broader masses of the population tended to give their own meaning to the policies and pronouncements of the westernized elite. An informed observer in the 1940s noted that as "the nationalist idea penetrated into the popular mind, it was transformed, and could not avoid being transformed, by the pressure of the age-long instincts and impulses of the Muslim masses."[26] In this way there was, for a period of time, a double level of usage, with the elite and the general population saying the same words but meaning quite different things.

Expanding educational systems and the growing integration of even more isolated areas into national economies, social institutions, and political participation meant that some of the double level of meanings began to disappear. By the 1960s there were important challenges to the old westernizing elites, criticizing them for blind borrowing from the west. One of the most influential of these critiques was formulated by the Iranian intellectual, Jalal Al-i Ahmad, who described the uncritical acceptance of western ideas, *gharbzadegi*, as a disease which destroyed the cultural soul.[27] Some Muslims began to reject western terms and to work to develop terminology from within the Muslim cultural traditions. It is in this context that terms like *tawhid* and *jahiliyyah* came to replace more western expressions of revolutionary criticism of the *status quo*.

Some terms from the west, however, have been retained in the discourse in varying forms. "Secularism," for example, continues as a representation of what is being opposed. In other cases there has been an effort to transform the meaning of terms inherited from the interaction with the west along lines needed for contemporary revivalist understandings. As was true in the period before the Islamic resurgence, these are integrated in different ways. Some represent adaptive translations of western terms (like *ishtirakiyya*h for "socialism"), while others are simply direct transliterations of western terms, like *dimuqratiyyah* for "democracy."

Two terms, "democracy" and "fundamentalism," illustrate the way the modern heritage has been used in the conceptualization of the Islamic resurgence. Although the concrete words used are of western origin, they have become integrated to varying degrees in the vocabulary of contemporary Islamic discourse. This integration is a different process from what was seen before the resurgence. In the earlier era the integration effort was a simple one of showing how Islam contained the western concept. Islamic modernists essentially were modernizing (and in the perspective of the time this usually meant westernizing) Islam, shaping Islamic concepts and perceptions to conform to modern western ideas. In the 1970s, a reorientation of effort began which reversed the process. The thinkers of the Islamic resurgence work to Islamize the modern western concepts rather than modernizing Islamic concepts.

The western understanding of democracy was very important in shaping the vision of Muslims who organized nationalist opposition to western imperial control. Westminster-style elected parliaments were the frequently stated goal of constitutional development and there was much talk about the sovereign will of the people in the great revolutionary movements. Mustafa Kemal Ataturk identified the people as the sovereign of the new Turkish state which was created by the Turkish War for Independence following World War I, and the political system was a parliamentary republic. In the period of more radical revolutionary ideologies in the 1960s, Jamal Abd al-Nasir ("Nasser") created a form of Arab Socialism which also spoke of representing the people's will. The result of the Egyptian revolution which began in 1952 was to be true democracy, and that was defined in the National Charter of 1962 as meaning "the assertion of the sovereignty of the people, placing all authority in their hands and the consecration of power to serve their ends."[28] This basically western definition of democracy dominated political discourse until the recent Islamic resurgence.

Democracy is a powerful and appealing concept which has not been rejected by the thinkers of the Islamic resurgence. They have, however, worked to reshape it into something more clearly Islamic. As in many other areas, the south Asian thinker Mawdudi set the tone quite early for the Islamic conceptualization of democracy. He noted that the "philosophical foundation of western democracy is the sovereignty of the people... This is not the case with Islam... [Islam] altogether repudiates the philosophy of popular sovereignty and rears its polity on the foundations of God and the vicegerency (*Khilafat*) of man."[29] He explained that Islam has its own democratic form of organization in which the entire people rule in accord with the Qur'an and the Traditions of the Prophet. He stated, "If I were permitted to coin a new term, I would describe this system of government as a 'theodemocracy,' that is to say divine democratic government, because under it the Muslims have been given a limited popular sovereignty under the suzerainty of God."[30] This brings the concept of Islamic democracy into accord with the developing emphasis on *tawhid* as a comprehensive process.

The limitations on the definition of democracy in Mawdudi's analysis are emphasized by some in the new revivalist tradition. Qutb, for example, writing in the early 1960s at the time of the peak of the popularity of Nasser and his revolutionary ideology, condemned Nasser's definition of the desirable political system. He discussed the way that Islam addressed non-Muslims in the early and, for Qutb, more authentically Islamic community saying that Islam "did not propose similarities with their system or manners to please them, as some do today when they present Islam to the people under the names of 'Islamic Democracy' or 'Islamic Socialism'."[31]

By the 1970s, however, the positive dimensions of democracy as a part of the Islamic message began to receive more attention. The Muslim Brotherhood organizations in a number of countries affirmed the importance of democracy in Islamic institutions and the term was widely used. An active supporter of the Brotherhood in Syria, for example, stated that "endorsement of direct participatory democracy is a traditional position of the Syrian Muslim Brotherhood."[32] This commitment is reflected in the 1980 Manifesto of the Syrian Islamic Revolution which states that "Our most effective weapons in our fight against the enemy and in our struggle to save our country and to put our nation back on its feet are: first, our reliance on Allah and, second, the participation of our people." The meaning of this is spelled out in advocating the "system of mutual consultation (democracy)," the freedom to form political parties, and direct elections "at all levels of representation."[33]

The full meaning of Islamic democracy was discussed by the leader of the Muslim Brotherhood in the Sudan, Hasan Turabi. He stated, while he was attorney-general of the Sudan, that "an Islamic order of government is essentially a form of representative democracy," but he noted that "an Islamic republic is not strictly speaking a direct government of and by the people; it is a government of the *shariah*. But, in a substantive sense, it is popular government since the *shariah* represents the convictions of the people and, therefore, their direct will."[34]

These positions reflect the earlier discussion of Mawdudi and represent an effective Islamization of the concept of democracy. There is an emphasis on participation, consensus, and consultation, all of which are traditional Islamic concepts, and the ever-present reservation based on affirmation of *tawhid* that it is God and not the people who are sovereign. By the 1980s this was a common position and came to be accepted by many as the basis for Islamic political discourse. It was shown in the papers and discussions at an international seminar on "Islamic Political Thought and Institutions" sponsored by the Association of Muslim Social Sciences in 1982. Published papers from this conference were written by both Sunni and Shi'i scholars, and in a summary of these the editor of the volume noted that there "is general agreement among the contributing authors that democracy is the spirit of the Islamic governmental system, even though they reject its philosophical assumptions about the people's sovereignty."[35]

Democracy, despite its western origins, is a term which has been incorporated into Islamic discourse by contemporary Islamic revivalist thinkers. Through the imposition of Islamic definitional limitations, especially on the concept of sovereignty, and the combination with Qur'anic concepts like consultation *shura*, it has become an important concept in contemporary discussions of the nature of the authentically Islamic political system. As a concept, it is now understood in a very different way than it was in the period when western assumptions and definitions were simply accepted by Muslim thinkers and leaders.

Another western term that is being incorporated into the discourse of the Islamic revival is "fundamentalism." This term originally referred to a specific type of American Protestantism. In the 1970s it began to be used by journalists and some analysts in discussions of Islamic revivalism, although many people had reservations. Many Muslims found the term offensive or at least inappropriate, while western scholars saw it as imprecise and possibly misleading.[36] In addition, both Muslims and non-Muslims noted that there is no equivalent in Arabic (or in other languages of major Muslim groups) for the word "fundamentalism."[37] However, by the end of the 1980s this situation was changing, and Muslims (both revivalist and non-revivalist) began to make use of the term and to transform it into a term usable in the discourse of the Islamic resurgence.

In contrast to the use of the term "democracy," "fundamentalism" has sometimes been translated into a parallel Arabic term and appears as *'usuliyyah*. Initially this was seen as simply an artificially constructed term, but by the late 1980s both it and "fundamentalism" have begun to be used as legitimate vocabulary of Islamic revivalist discourse. In 1982, two American Muslims published a book called *Islamic Fundamentalism*, which noted the positive dimensions of the Islamic resurgence and accepted the designation of "Islamic fundamentalism" for the revival.[38] Prominent Muslim scholars writing in English also used the term to apply to the movements of the resurgence, frequently as a part of a critique of the movements. Shi'i scholars such as Hamid Enayat and Seyyed Hossein Nasr used the term in analyzing the broad spectrum of Islamic revivalist movements from the Muslim Brotherhood and the Jama'at-i-Islami to the Iranian Islamic revolutionaries.[39] Similarly, Sunni scholars of varying perspectives, for example Fazlur Rahman and Bassam Tibi, also used "fundamentalism" as a term in their analyses of the Islamic resurgence.[40]

By the end of the 1980s, major Muslim intellectuals and activists were beginning to use *'usuliyyah* as a term in their discourse. Rashid al-Ghanushi, the leader of the Islamist movement in Tunisia, for example, called "realistic fundamentalism" *'usuliyyah waqi'iyyah* the "one path for the liberation and preservation of the Muslim intellect and the Islamic mission from senile and impotent inclinations."[41] A presentation of the platform of the Tunisian organization follows this usage and speaks of its "fundamentalist program" *al-manhaj al-'usuli*.[42] Similarly, the Egyptian philosopher Hasan Hanafi adopted the term *al-'usuliyyah al-islamiyyah* as a useful literal translation of the western "Islamic Fundamentalism" in his major study of Islamic activists and the resurgence in Egypt.[43]

In the discourse of the contemporary resurgence "fundamentalism" becomes a special form of revivalism (*tajdid*). It is, in this usage, a way of distinguishing the response of Islam to modernity from earlier affirmations of the faith. It carries with it an implication of similarity with other contemporary religious revivals that are visible throughout the world at the end of the twentieth century.

The use of terms like "democracy" and "fundamentalism" in contemporary Islamic discourse shows the dynamic diversity of the heritage of the Islamic resurgence. The conceptual continuity with the past is reflected in the use of terms like *tajdid*, *takfir*, and *jihad* and the transformation of the Islamic intellectual heritage as shown by the development of the concepts of *tawhid* and *jahiliyyah*, while contemporary Muslims also utilize the heritage from the recent experiences of interaction with the west. It is the Islamization of western concepts as well as the utilization of more traditional Islamic ones that point the way to a modern-but-not-western Islamic discourse for the twenty-first century.

CONCLUSION

The conceptual framework of thought in the contemporary Islamic world has undergone some significant changes as a result of the Islamic resurgence during the final quarter of the twentieth century. Although there definitely is not a monolithic similarity of ideas and positions, there has been a shift in the basic terms and formulations in all aspects of life, political, social, economic, and religious. The terms of debates have shifted from the older ones of westernizing modernization and the earlier pre-modern Islamic experiences. The new discourses represent a synthesis of the multiple heritages of contemporary Muslims.

This transformation of discourse has been discussed with specific reference to the Iranian experience by Afsaneh Najmabadi, but her analysis illustrates the developments in the broader Islamic world as well. She notes that "the revolution embodied a fundamental transformation in the terms of public discourse in Iran."[44] "Since the mid-19th century, Iranian politics can be said to have been shaped by an all-consuming preoccupation: *the concern with the material transformation of a backward society*....Political thinkers and activists of late 19th century Iran thought of their society as backward in comparison to western Europe. This view was dominant for over a hundred years. By the 1970s, however, political concerns had shifted from backwardness to decadence, from modernization to *the moral purification of a corrupt society.*"[45] This reflects the broader Islamization of significant discourse throughout the Muslim world. "In general terms, the political role of Islam has gone from being a support for other ideologies to providing the foundations for the current ideologies."[46]

The complex diversity of the new Islamized discourse can be seen by looking at key concepts that have emerged. Some reflect long continuities with past experiences of renewal in Islamic societies, while others represent re-orientations of older Islamic terms or western terms. Combined, these concepts become the foundation for a new discourse that is significantly both Islamic and modern. This new discourse is the heart of the literature of the contemporary resurgence.

Notes

1. Discussions of this tradition can be found in Fazlur Rahman, "Revival and Reform in Islam," *The Cambridge History of Islam*, ed. P.M. Holt, Ann K.S. Lambton, and Bernard Lewis, 2 vols. (Cambridge: Cambridge University Press, 1970), 2: 632-42, and John O. Voll, "Renewal and Reform in Islamic History: *Tajdid* and *Islah*," *Voices of Resurgent Islam*, ed. John L. Esposito (New York: Oxford University Press, 1983), 32-47.

2. Sayyid Abul A'la Maududi, *A Short History of the Revivalist Movement in Islam*, trans. al-Ash'ari, 3rd ed. (Lahore: Islamic Publications, 1976)

3. Maryam Jameelah, *Three Great Islamic Movements in the Arab World of the Recent Past* (Lahore: Mohammad Yusuf Khan, 1976), p. 13

4. Ibraheem Sulaiman, *The Islamic State and the Challenge of History* (London: Mansell, 1987), p.2.

5. Mawdudi, *Revivalist Movement,* 32-33.

6. Gilles Kepel, *Muslim Extremism in Egypt: the Prophet and Pharaoh,* trans. Jon Rothschild (Berkeley: University of California Press, 1985), 61-63.

7. Johannes J. G. Jansen, *The Neglected Duty: The Creed of Sadat's Assassins and Islamic Resurgence in the Middle East* (New York: Macmillan, 1986), p. 169.

8. For a discussion of the ruling of the Mufti, see Jansen, pp. 59-60; for al-Qaradawi's position, see Yusuf al-Qaradawi, *Islamic Awakening Between Rejection and Extremism* (Herndon, VA: International Institute of Islamic Thought, n.d.), pp. 18-20.

9. Sayyid Qutb, *Milestones,* rev. ed. (Cedar Rapids, Iowa: Unity Publishing, n.d.), 55, 57.

10. Abul A'la Maududi, *Khutubat (An English Version),* 2nd ed. (Chicago: Kazi, 1977), p. 243.

11. Abul A'la Mawdudi, *Towards Understanding Islam,* 6th ed. (Salimiah, Kuwait: International Islamic Federation of Student Organizations, 1982), 142.

12. Suzanne Haneef, *What Everyone Should Know About Islam and Muslims* (Chicago: Kazi, 1982), 118-119.

13. Abdulaziz Abdulhussein Sachedina, *The Just Ruler in Shi'ite Islam* (New York: Oxford University Press, 1988), 109.

14. See, for example, his analysis in Mawdudi, *Revivalist Movement,* 27-33.

15. Qutb, *Milestones,* 10-11.

16. Abd-al-Rahman 'Azzam, *The Eternal Message of Muhammad* (New York: New American Library, 1964), 53.

17. Muhammad Abduh, *The Theology of Unity,* trans. Ishaq Musa'ad and Kenneth Cragg (London: George Allen & Unwin, 1966), 29.

18. Muhammad Nejatullah Siddiqi, *"Tawhid*: The Concept and the Process," in *Islamic Perspectives,* ed. Khurshid Ahmad and Zafar Ishaq Ansari (Leicester, England: Islamic Foundation, 1979), 17.

19. Khurshid Ahmad and Zafar Ishaq Ansari, "Mawlana Sayyid Abul A'la Mawdudi: An Introduction to His Vision of Islam and Islamic Revival," in *Islamic Perspectives,* ed. Khurshid Ahmad and Zafar Ishaq Ansari (Leicester, England: Islamic Foundation, 1979), 365.

20. S. Abul Al'a Maududi, *Political Theory of Islam,* trans. Khurshid Ahmad (Lahore: Islamic Publications, 1976), 20. See also Maududi's *The Economic Problem of Man and Its Islamic Solution* (Lahore: Islamic Publications, 1978); *The Process of Islamic Revolution* (Lahore: Islamic Publications, 1977); *Nations Rise and Fall -- Why?* (Lahore: Islamic Publications, 1978).

21. Qutb, *Milestones,* 87.

22. Isma'il Raji al-Faruqi, *Tawhid: Its implications for Thought and Life* (Herndon, VA: International Institute of Islamic Thought, 1982), 11.

23. See, for example, the writings in Ayatullah Sayyid Mahmud Taleghani, *Society and Economics in Islam,* trans. R. Campbell (Berkeley, CA: Mizan Press, 1982), 54-56 and passim.

24. Hamid Enayat, *Modern Islamic Political Thought* (Austin, TX: University of Texas Press, 1982), 155.

25. Abdulaziz Sachedina, "Ali Shariati: Ideologue of the Iranian Revolution," in *Voices of Resurgent Islam,* ed. John L. Esposito (New York: Oxford University Press, 1983), 200. For Shariati's extended analysis, see Ali Shari'ati, *On the Sociology of Islam,* trans. Hamid Algar (Berkeley: University of California Press, 1979).

26. H.A.R. Gibb, *Modern Trends in Islam* (Chicago: University of Chicago Press, 1947), 119.

27. Jalal Al-e Ahmad, *Gharbzadegi (Weststruckness),* trans. John Green and Ahmad Alizadeh (Lexington, KY: Mazda, 1982).

28. Abdel Moghny Said, *Arab Socialism,* (New York: Barnes & Noble, 1972), 105. Part 3 of this book is a translation of the Egyptian National Charter.

29. Maududi, *Political Theory,* 23.

30. Ibid., 24-25.

31. Qutb, *Milestones,* 134.

32. Umar F. Abd-allah, *The Islamic Struggle in Syria* (Berkeley: Mizan Press, 1983), 143.

33. Ibid., 213-17.

34. Hassan Turabi, "The Islamic State," in *Voices of Resurgent Islam,* ed. John L. Esposito (New York: Oxford University Press, 1983), 244.

35. Mumtaz Ahmad, "Islamic Political Theory: Current Scholarship and Future Prospects," in *State, Politics, and Islam,* ed. Mumtaz Ahmad (Indianapolis, IN: American Trust Publications, 1986), 4.

36. See for example, the comments collected from a number of Muslim professionals and scholars in Karm B. Akhtar and Ahmad H. Sakr, *Islamic Fundamentalism* (Cedar Rapids, IA: Igram Press, 1982), 136-47.

37. See the discussion in Bruce B. Lawrence, "Muslim Fundamentalist Movements: Reflections Toward a New Approach," in *The Islamic Impulse,* ed. Barbara Freyer Stowasser (London: Croom Helm, 1987), 18-20.

38. Akhtar and Sakr, Chapter 11.

39. See Hamid Enayat, *Modern Islamic Political Thought* (Austin, TX: University of Texas Press, 1982), Chapter 3 and passim; Seyyed Hossien Nasr, "Islam in the Islamic World, An Overview," in *Islam in the Contemporary World,* ed. Cyriac K. Pullapilly (Notre Dame, IN: Cross Roads Books, 1980), 9-13.

40. See Fazlur Rahman, "Roots of Islamic Neo-Fundamentalism," in *Change and the Islamic World,* ed. Philip H. Stoddard, David C. Cuthell, and Margaret W. Sullivan (Syracuse, NY: Syracuse University Press, 1981), 23-39; Bassam Tibi, "The Renewed Role of Islam in the Political and Social Development of the Middle East," *Middle East Journal* 37, no. 1 (Winter 1983): 9-13; and Bassam Tibi, *The Crisis of Modern Islam,* trans. Judith von Sivers (Salt Lake City: University of Utah Press, 1988), 146 passim.

41. Rashid al-Ghanushi, *Mahawir Islamiyyah* (Cairo: Bayt al-Ma'rifah, 1989), 150.

42. Muhammad al-Hashimi al-Hamidi, *al-Ru'iyyah al-Fikriyyah wa al-Manhaj al-'Usuli li-Harakah al-Ittijah al-Islami bi-Tunis* (London: Dar al-Sahwah, 1987).

43. Hasan Hanafi, *al-Din wa al-Thawrah fi Masr, 1952-1981, 6: al-Usuliyyah al-Islamiyyah* (Cairo: Maktabah Madbuli, 1989), 3-6.

44. Afsaneh Najmabadi, "Iran's Turn to Islam: From Modernism to a Moral Order," *Middle East Journal* 41, no. 2 (Spring 1987): 216-17.

45. Ibid., 203.

46. John O. Voll, "Islamic Dimensions in Arab Politics," *American-Arab Affairs,* no. 4 (Spring 1983), 119.

3

Trailblazers of the Islamic Resurgence
John L. Esposito

The late nineteenth and early twentieth centuries constituted a singular challenge to Islam: politically, economically, and morally. European colonialism and imperialism threatened Muslim political and religio-cultural identity and history. The impact of western rule and modernization raised new questions and challenged time-honored beliefs and practices. Although modern Islamic history has often been characterized as static, retrogressive, or reactionary, in fact Muslim societies have undergone dynamic periods of change and development that have elicited a variety of responses within Islamic communities. Like many non-western societies, Muslims in many parts of the Islamic world have been caught up in a process of rapid and potentially far reaching change, impacting all areas of life. Modernity brought western governments, institutions, laws, education, cultural values, first through the direct or indirect rule or dominance of European colonialism in the nineteenth and first half of the twentieth centuries, and subsequently through the power and intervention of the superpowers (the United States and the Soviet Union) and multinational corporations. Muslim responses have varied from a wholehearted embrace of the west to rejection of the infiltration of foreign powers and alien cultures.

The experience of Muslim decline and western domination in the nineteenth century, as well as the fear of political subservience and unrestrained acculturation, moved a number of Muslims to seek to revitalize Islam and the Muslim community. Beginning with men like Jamal al-Din al-Afghani in the Middle East and Sayyid Ahmad Khan in South Asia, a movement often referred to as Islamic modernism produced a number of reformers (Muhammad Abdu, Rashid Rida, Muhammad Iqbal) who called for an Islamic reform which drew on the best in Islam's heritage while assimilating the accomplishments of western science and technology. Islam, they asserted, was a religion in perfect harmony with modernity.[1] However, by the 1930s others began to reflect the growing ambivalence towards the penetration of western culture. Two organizations in particular, the Muslim Brotherhood and the

Jamaat-i-Islami (Islamic Society), reflect this new movement. Their approach to reform may best be referred to as Islamic revivalism rather than modernism which they equated with westernization. The founders and ideologues of the Brotherhood and the Jamaat had a profound effect not only on their own societies but also on Muslim activists across the Islamic world to the present. Indeed, the contemporary resurgence of Islam, its leadership and organization, reflects and incorporates many of the themes and concerns of these trailblazers of Islamic modernism and revivalism.

Revivalism is integral to the fabric of Islamic faith and history, embodied in a host of individuals, organizations, and movements, from the time of the Prophet Muhammad to today.[2] Muhammad and his early community provided an inspirational paradigm for future generations. Though united by this common appeal to Islam and the example of Muhammad, Islamic revivalist movements have been remarkably diverse in their organization, leadership, tactics, and ideological agendas, due to different interpretations of Islam as well as to their varying sociopolitical contexts and issues. While Islam is firmly monotheistic, its interpretation and expression in history have been far from monolithic. A rich diversity of actors, forms, institutions and organizations is encompassed by that seemingly singular ascription, Islam. A study of the development of modern Islamic revivalist organizations reveals this unity-diversity motif.

THE MUSLIM BROTHERHOOD AND THE JAMAAT-I-ISLAMI

Though thousands of miles apart, two major Muslim organizations sprang up during the 1930s and 1940s in response to continued Muslim decline and western imperialism. Both had experienced British colonialism and with it the progressive westernization (Europeanization) of society. Both sought to counter this presence and influence through a revitalization of the Muslim community, advocating a process of Islamic renewal and reform. In Egypt Hasan al-Banna (1906-49), a school teacher, established the Muslim Brotherhood (Ikhwan al-Muslimun) in 1928, and in Pakistan Mawlana Abul 'A'la Mawdudi (1903-79) organized the Islamic Society (*Jamaat-i-Islami*) in 1941.[3] Both were pious educated men, with traditional Islamic backgrounds and a knowledge of modern western thought, who saw their societies adrift. They believed that the internal weakness of their societies stemmed from the guidance of leaders who, despite their anti-colonial politics, took the west as their model for development. They were, in effect, indigenous western cultural colonizers: "Until recently, writers, intellectuals, scholars and governments glorified the principles of European civilization... adopted western style and manner."[4] Like secular and Islamic modernists, they acknowledged the weakness of Muslim societies, the need for change and the value of science and technology. However, they criticized both secular and Islamic modernists for an excessive dependence upon the west. Secularists separated religion from society. Islamic modernists in their zeal to demonstrate the compatibility of Islam with modernity employed western criteria and values, producing a westernized Islam:

> All these people in their misinformed and misguided zeal to serve what they hold to be the cause of Islam, are always at great pains to prove that Islam contains within itself the elements of all types of contemporary social and political thought and action...this attitude emerges from an inferiority complex, from the belief that we as Muslims can earn no honor or respect unless we are able to show our religion resembles modern creeds and is in agreement with most of the contemporary ideologies.[5]

In contrast to modernists, these neo-revivalists were more sweeping in their indictment and condemnation of the west and their assertion of the total self-sufficiency of Islam. They maintained that Muslims should not look to western capitalism or marxism but solely to Islam, the divinely revealed foundation of state and society that offered a comprehensive framework of meaning, a guide for personal and public life. The goal was not a secular society or a process of modern Islamic reform which rendered Islam compatible with western culture but a more indigenously rooted, authentic re-creation of an Islamic state and society: "a return to the principles of Islam ...for initiating the reconciliation of modern life with these principles, as a prelude to a final Islamization (of society)".[6] Hassan al-Banna and Mawlana Abu al-'A'la al-Mawdudi appropriated and reapplied the vision and logic of the revivalist tradition in Islam to respond to the socio-historical conditions of 20th century Muslim society. They reinterpreted the paradigm of Muhammad and his first Islamic reformist movement as a process that has continued throughout Islamic history. They were inspired both by early Islamic history as well as by revivalist movements that flourished across the Muslim world in the 17th and 18th centuries: the Wahhabi in Arabia, the Mahdi in the Sudan, the Fulani in Nigeria, the Sanusi in Libya, the Padri in Indonesia.[7] Despite differences, Banna's and Mawdudi's reinterpretations of Islamic history and tradition produced a common ideological worldview which would legitimate and guide many modern Islamically oriented socio-moral reform movements. This worldview not only governed their organizations but also informed Islamic movements that sprang up throughout the Muslim world in future decades. Among its primary principles were the assertions that: (1) Islam constitutes a total all-embracing ideology for individual and corporate life, for state and society; (2) the foundations of Muslim life are the Quran, God's revelation, and the example *sunna* of the Prophet Muhammad which is the paradigm or model of humankind; (3) Islamic law (Shariah, the "path" of God), based upon the Quran and the Prophet's model behavior, is the sacred blueprint for Muslim life; (4) faithfulness to the Muslim's vocation to establish God's sovereignty or rule through implementation of God's law will be accompanied by success, power and wealth of the Islamic community *umma* as well as eternal reward in the next life; (5) the weakness and subservience of Muslim societies is due to the faithlessness of Muslims who have strayed from God's divinely revealed path and followed the secular, materialistic ideologies and values of the west or the east--capitalism or Marxism; (6) restoration of Muslim pride, power, and rule (the past glory of Islamic empires and civilizations) requires a return to Islam, the re-implementation of God's law and guidance for state and society; (7) science and technology must be harnessed and used within an Islamically oriented and guided context in order to avoid the westernization and secularization of Muslim society. Islam thus provides a divinely revealed and prescribed third alternative for modern Muslim societies.

Scripture and tradition were appealed to and reinterpreted by the founders of these modern religious societies. In this way, the inspiration and continuity of the past was coupled with their response to the demands and requirements of modernity. This combination of past and present is demonstrated by their organization and activities. Organizationally, the Brotherhood and the Jamaat followed the example of the Prophet Muhammad (which had been emulated by 17th and 18th century revivalist movements) in gathering together believers who were committed to establishing societies governed by God's rule and law. They were to be a vanguard that constituted the dynamic nucleus for a true Islamic reformation or revolution, returning society to the straight path of Islam. Followers were recruited from mosques, schools, and the marketplace--students, workers, merchants, and professionals. The goal was to produce a new generation of educated but Islamically oriented leaders prepared to take their place in every sector of society. They offered an "Islamic alternative" to conservative religious leaders and modern, western, secular-oriented elites. Religious commitment and modern learning/technology were combined as the Brotherhood and the Jamaat disseminated their interpretation of Islam through schools, publications, preaching, social services, student organizations. Their desire to transform society invariably led to involvement in politics and, at times, confrontation with their national governments. Both activists and national regimes accused one another of violence and sedition. At various times their leaders were arrested and their organizations suppressed. Hassan al-Banna was assassinated in 1949, Brotherhood leaders were executed and the Muslim Brotherhood was officially repressed and dissolved in the late 1960s. While Mawdudi and Jamaat leaders were imprisoned and even condemned to death on one occasion, members of the Jamaat-i-Islami were able to participate in the political process more freely than their Egyptian counterparts.

The significance of the Muslim Brotherhood and the Jamaat-i-Islami extended far beyond their national homelands and in time took on transnational significance. The Brotherhood inspired the establishment of similar organizations in the Sudan, Syria, Jordan, the Gulf, and Africa. The Jamaat developed sister organizations in India, Bangladesh, Afghanistan, and Kashmir. The writings of the Brotherhood's Hassan al-Banna and Sayyid Qutb and Mawlana Mawdudi of the Jamaat-i-Islami would in time become widely translated and disseminated throughout much of the Islamic world. Their vision of Islam as an alternative ideology for state and society as well as the example of their organizations and activities provided a model for future generations of Muslims. As such they constituted for many a link between their traditional religious heritage and the realities of modern life.

Despite the emergence of neo-revivalist groups, the post World War II period was dominated by political independence and the establishment of modern Muslim states. In general, nascent nations and their political leaders continued to be heavily influenced by the west in the development of national ideology and state institutions (parliamentary systems of government, legal codes, education), economics and the military. With few exceptions, nationalist leaders were more secular than religious in orientation. The United States and the Soviet Union emerged as superpowers; western capitalism, Marxism and socialism were contending forces in political development. From the late 1950s to the early 1970s nationalist and socialist slogans prevailed in the discourse and politics of many Muslim states: the Arab nationalism/socialism of Egypt's Gamal Abdul Nasser which also inspired the revolutions of Libya's Muammar al-Qadhafi and Sudan's Ja'far al-Numayri in the late 1960s; the socialism of the Baath Party in Syria and Iraq; the Algerian revolution; and Zulfiqar Ali Bhutto's Pakistan People's Party; local forms of nationalism in Turkey, Tunisia, Iran, and Afghanistan.

CONTEMPORARY RELIGIOUS REVIVALISM

Religion remained a presence in Muslim societies; governments continued to be sensitive to its potential force by seeking to control, coopt or restrict its role in society. However, in the 1970s what had seemed to be an increasingly marginalized force in the public life of modernizing states now reemerged often dramatically as a vibrant, dynamic socio-political reality. The resurgence of Islam in Muslim politics reflected a growing religious revivalism both in personal and public life which in time would sweep across much of the Muslim world.[8] The indices of Islamic reawakening in personal or individual life are many: increased religious observance (mosque attendance, prayer, fasting), more emphasis upon Islamic dress and values, proliferation of religious programming and publications, the revitalization of *Sufism* (mysticism). This broader based renewal has also been accompanied by the reassertion of Islam in public life: an increase in Islamically oriented governments, organizations, laws, banks, educational institutions, social welfare services. Both governments and opposition movements have turned to Islam to enhance their authority and muster support. Government leaders who have used Islam include

Sudan's Ja'far al-Numayri, Libya's Muammar al-Qadhafi, Egypt's Anwar al-Sadat, Iran's Ayatollah Khomeini, Pakistan's Zia ul-Haq, Bangladesh's Muhammad Ershad, Malaysia's Muhammad Mahathir. Most rulers and governments, aware of the potential strength of Islam, have shown increased sensitivity to Islamic issues and concerns, including more secular states such as Turkey and Tunisia. Indeed, revivalism has often proven to be strongest in more westernized states such as Egypt and Iran. At the same time, Islamic organizations and societies have mushroomed. Most (the Muslim Brotherhoods of Egypt and the Sudan, the Jamaat-i-Islami in Pakistan and India, Islamic Tendency Movement in Tunisia, the Islamic Youth Movement of Malaysia) have worked within the existing political system, while some (Lebanon's Hizbullah and al-Jihad, Egypt's Takfir wal Hijra and Jamaat al-Jihad, the Afghan Mujahideen, the Moro of the Philippines) have turned to armed struggle and violence to realize their revolutionary goals.

While contemporary Islamic revivalism is often associated with the Iranian Revolution of 1978-79, its seeds may be found in many parts of the Muslim world during the late 1960s and early 1970s. A combination of stunning setbacks, for example, in 1967, '69, '71 and remarkable successes in 1973 and '78-'79 served as important catalysts. The 1967 Arab-Israeli war proved a turning point in the Arab world. The decisive defeat of the combined Arab forces (Egypt, Jordan and Syria) by Israel in the Six Day War with its loss of the west Bank, Gaza, and the Sinai was a major blow to the charismatic leadership of Gamal Abdul Nasser and the banner of Arab nationalism/socialism. The loss of Jerusalem, the third holiest city of Islam, rendered the defeat a worldwide Islamic, not just Palestinian, issue, remembered in Arab literature as the "catastrophe". For many, the magnitude of the defeat struck at the heart of their sense of pride, identity, and history. Despite several decades of independence and modernization, Arab forces proved impotent. In the midst of the soul searching and disillusionment, a common critique of the military, political, and socio-cultural failures of western-oriented development and a quest for a more authentic, indigenously rooted society and culture emerged.

Similarly, Chinese-Malay communal riots in Malaysia in 1969 led the Malaysian government to address the socio-economic concerns of Malay Muslims who charged that the more urban based Chinese minority enjoyed disproportionate economic and educational advantages. This perceived threat to Malay status and identity fostered a government initiated plan (the *bhumiputra*, sons of the soil) to strengthen the economic and educational aspects of Malay Muslim life. Greater emphasis upon Malay identity, language, values, and community contributed to the attraction and growth of Islamic revivalism in a culture where many regard it as axiomatic that to be Malay is to be Muslim. In Lebanon Shi'i Muslims, long a minority in a Christian dominated system, called for greater political representation and socio-economic reforms to better reflect the demographic changes which had resulted in a Muslim majority. The Imam Musa Sadr appealed to Shi'i identity, history and symbols to organize and mobilize members of the Shi'i community into what would become in the mid 1970s the Movement for the Dispossessed, more commonly known today as AMAL.

The Pakistan-Bangladesh civil war in 1971 changed the map of South Asia when the Islamic Republic of Pakistan, a country established as a Muslim homeland in 1947, lost its eastern wing in a bloody slaughter of Muslims by their fellow Muslims and once more faced the question: "Why Pakistan?" In reestablishing Pakistan's identity and seeking greater economic ties with the Arab oil countries, Zulfiqar Ali Bhutto, a secular socialist, increasingly appealed to Islam to establish Pakistan's ties with its Arab Muslim brothers and to mobilize domestic political support. This unleashed a process in which Islam moved from the periphery to center stage as both the government and the opposition used Islam to legitimate their claims and gain popular support.

During the early 1970s, heads of state such as Muammar Qadhafi of Libya, who had seized power in a coup d'etat, and Egypt's Anwar Sadat, who struggled in the shadow of his dead predecessor Nasser, increasingly appealed to Islam to buttress their regimes. Qadhafi introduced Islamic laws and his *Green Book* to enhance his legitimacy and influence at home and abroad.[9] Sadat attempted to control and use Islamic groups such as the Muslim Brotherhood. Most significantly, he led Egypt in a "holy war" against Israel. In contrast to the 1967 Arab-Israeli war which was fought in the name of Arab socialism, the 1973 war was fought under the banner of Islam as Sadat generously employed Islamic symbols and history to rally his forces. Despite their loss of the war, the relative success of Egyptian forces led many Muslims to regard it as a moral victory since most believed that an Israel backed by the United States could not be beaten. Military vindication was accompanied by the economic power of the Arab oil boycott. For the first time since the dawn of colonialism, the power of the west had to contend with and acknowledge, albeit begrudgingly, its dependence on Middle Eastern powers. For many the new wealth, success and power of the oil rich countries seemed to be signs of a return of the power of Islam to a community whose rich history of centuries long political and cultural ascendence had been shattered by European colonialism and, despite independence, by second class status in a superpower dominated world. A number of factors enhanced the Islamic character of oil power. Most of the oil wealth was located in the Arab heartland, where Muhammad had received the revelation of the Quran and established the first Islamic community-state; its largest deposits were in Saudi Arabia, a self-styled Islamic state, which had asserted its role as a leader in the Islamic world as keeper of the holy cities of Mecca and Medina and protector of the annual pilgrimage *hajj*. As such it had used its oil wealth to establish numerous international Islamic organizations, promote the preaching and spread of Islam, support Islamic causes, and subsidize Islamic activities undertaken by Muslim governments.

No event demonstrated more dramatically the power of a resurgent Islam than the Iranian Revolution of 1978-79. For many in the west and the Muslim world the unthinkable became a reality. The powerful, modernizing and western oriented regime of the Shah came crashing down. This was an oil rich Iran whose wealth had been used to build the best equipped military in the Middle East and to support an ambitious White revolution, a modernization program that was supposed to rapidly bring Iran into the twenty first century. The Shah had long been regarded in the west as an enlightened, if somewhat autocratic, ruler who with strong support of the United States and Europe and assisted by western trained elites and advisers, governed the most stable western ally in the Muslim world. The fact that for a variety of reasons a revolution was effectively mounted in the name of Islam, organizing disparate groups under the banner of Islam and relying upon the mullah-mosque network for support, generated a euphoria among many in the Muslim world and convinced Islamic activists that the lesson was there to be emulated. Strength and victory would belong to those who pursued change in the name of Islam whatever the odds and however formidable the regime.

Post-revolutionary Islam influenced Islamic activists from Egypt to Malaysia. In the aftermath of the revolution Sunni and Shi'i delegates alike visited Iran. Quiescent Shi'i minority communities in Sunni dominated states like Saudi Arabia, the Gulf and Pakistan aggressively asserted their Shi'i identity and rights. In 1979 riots broke out among the 250,000 Shi'a in Saudi Arabia's oil rich Eastern Province. In 1980 Iraq executed Muhammad Baqr al-Sadr, paramount Shi'i cleric and the ideological inspiration of Iraqi Shi'i activism, in particular *Hizb al-Da'wa al-Islamiyya* (Islamic Call Society). Bahrain was rocked by a failed *coup d'etat* in 1981. In Lebanon Shi'i activism was dramatically affected by both the example of Iran and the exporting of its revolution.

Beneath the facade of Islamic revivalism is a richly textured reality whose seeming unity of purpose hides a diversity of expression and practice. The return to greater observance of Islam in private life and the reassertion of Islam in political life present a variety of common concerns and practices relating to Islamic laws, dress, and behavior. However, while many speak of an Islamic alternative for state and society what they mean and seek to bring about may in fact be quite different. The implementation of Islam by governments and the agendas and methods of Islamic organizations span the political and ideological spectrum. While all may agree upon their commitment to Islam, to the need for greater adherence to its principles, to the desire to live according to the Islamic law *Shariah*, and to the obligation to struggle *jihad* to restore Islam to its rightful place in society, their interpretations, leadership, and methods vary widely. Governments and opposition parties are often pitted against each other in the name of Islam. In 1979 the Grand Mosque in Mecca was seized by militants who called for the overthrow of an Islamically legitimated Saudi regime in the name of Islam.

Islam also proved to be a two edged sword in Egypt and Pakistan. After appealing to Islam to blunt his leftist opposition and legitimate policies such as the Camp David Accords, Anwar Sadat who had taken the title "the believer president" was judged by an Islamic yardstick and assassinated for his "unbelief".[10] Similarly, Pakistan's Bhutto soon found that his appeals to Islam resulted in an opposition, the Pakistan National Alliance, which united a cross section of political parties critiquing the government in the name of Islam and pledging themselves to the implementation of an Islamic system *nizam-i-Islam* of government. Bhutto's overthrow by General Muhammad Zia ul-Haq and subsequent execution were all justified by his alleged failure to adhere to Islamic standards. Islamically oriented governments (so called Islamic fundamentalist governments) themselves have proven to be quite diverse: from Libya's populist "peoples' state" *al-jamahiriya* to the conservative Saudi monarchy, from the clerically guided Islamic Republic of Iran to the martial law regime of Pakistan's Zia ul-Haq.

The common Islamic orientation of regimes reveals little unity of purpose in interstate relationships. Indeed, the opposite has often occurred due to conflicting national priorities and foreign policies. Qadhafi was a bitter enemy of Anwar Sadat and Jafar al-Numayri at the very time that all were projecting their "Islamic images". Khomeini's Islamic Iran has consistently called for the overthrow of the House of Saud on Islamic grounds, their rivalry even erupting during the annual pilgrimage to Mecca. Islamically identified governments also reflect differing relationships with the west. While much has been made of the confrontational relationship between Libya and Iran vis a vis the west, and the United States in particular, the U.S. at the same time has had strong allies in Saudi Arabia, Pakistan, and the Sudan.

Islamic organizations and movements, like Islamically oriented regimes, vary from moderate to radical, from traditionalist to modernizing. Their activities are rooted in the concepts of *da'wa*, calling to Islam, and *jihad*, striving or exerting oneself on God's path i.e. being a good Muslim. *Da'wa* not only means calling non-Muslims to the faith, i.e. propagating of the faith, but also calling those who are born Muslim to be more observant. *Jihad* has two general meanings: (1) the self-exertion or struggle to be virtuous, (2) the willingness to make the ultimate sacrifice and engage in armed struggle when necessary to defend Islam. Both concepts provide the rationale for a host of diverse contemporary Islamic organizations and societies which like the Muslim Brotherhood and the Jamaat-i-Islami seek to create more Islamic states and societies. For the moderate majority, the implementation of an Islamic system will indeed require a religio-social revolution or reformation but one that is achieved through peaceful means, working within the established system of government through such means as preaching, media, publishing, day-care clinics, hospitals, banks, youth centers, legal aid societies.

For a minority, armed struggle or revolution is seen as necessary and obligatory on theological and political grounds. Theologically, many would argue that an Islamic system is not simply an alternative but an imperative. If it is God's command, then it must be done now since God's will or command is for all times and places. The logic is similar to that of a Jew or Christian who might argue that the Ten Commandments must be obeyed at all times and that to postpone implementation or take a partial approach (eg. to postpone enforcement of the prohibition on adultery until the products of a permissive society have been properly prepared or reeducated) amounts to infidelity or heresy. Politically, radicals would maintain that the political reality in their countries requires armed struggle to defend Islam in the face of autocratic governments that repress and persecute those who advocate an Islamic alternative. They regard their governments as repressive and illegitimate and believe that all true believers have an obligation and duty to rise to the armed defense of Islam. Those Muslims who do not do so are seen not simply as sinners but as apostates, enemies of God. This was the rationale of the assassins of Anwar Sadat for whom *jihad* as armed struggle was the sixth pillar of Islam, requiring the death of a president whose policies they regarded as anti-Islamic.

Contrary to many stereotypes, the leaders of both moderate and radical Islamic organizations are not uneducated, anti-modern reactionaries. With the exception of *Shi'i* Islam where the ulama are prominent, most organizations are predominantly lay rather than clerical. Many of the activists combine traditional backgrounds with modern educations at major national universities and international centers of learning. They are graduates of Khartoum, Cairo, Alexandria, Teheran, Bandung and Kuwait universities as well as Harvard, MIT, Indiana, Wisconsin, Temple, Sussex, London, the Sorbonne. The majority are graduates of the faculties of science, engineering, law, and medicine rather than religion or the humanities. They come from lower middle class and middle class backgrounds, both village and city dwellers, and are pious and highly motivated. They are professionals from every walk of life: teachers, university professors, engineers, lawyers, doctors, government bureaucrats, the military. What one expert has said about the profile of an Egyptian radical group might be said for most moderates as well: "It is sometimes assumed in social science that recruits of 'radical movements' must be somehow alienated, marginal, anomic, or otherwise abnormal. Most of those we investigated would be considered model young Egyptians."[11] Participants in these Islamic groups are not simply victims of modernization, rejecting modernity and retreating to a seventh century haven. Unlike many of their peers, they are Muslims whose experience of modernization has led them not to embrace it but instead to criticize its political, economic, and religio-social excesses and to espouse a more indigenously rooted, Islamically oriented alternative to prevailing western forms of modernization. Consideration of several Islamic organizations in Egypt, Lebanon, and Malaysia will demonstrate their diversity.

EGYPT

Egypt provides an excellent context for the full range of revivalist organizations. Under Anwar Sadat the Muslim Brotherhood was again permitted to function during the 1970s; some of its members were released from prison while others returned from exile. However, the Brotherhood, which had once been regarded as a threat to state security, was now seen as a tired old guard whose mild mannered opposition was regarded as accommodationism by new militant groups that had sprung up after the 1967 Arab-Israeli war. By 1974 these clandestine groups, some of whose leaders had been young Brotherhood activists imprisoned and tortured during Nasser's suppression of the Brotherhood in the late 1960s, began attacking the Sadat government whose appeals to Islam were judged to be nothing more than political opportunism. In 1974 the Islamic Liberation Organization or Muhammad's Youth seized the technical military academy in a failed coup d'etat. In 1977 *Takfir wal Hijra* (Excommunication and Emigration), (i.e. those who condemned their society as guilty of unbelief, and following the example of Muhammad, withdrew to establish their own society of believers)[12] kidnapped a former Minister of Religious Endowments who had been critical of Takfir and killed him when their demand for the release of jailed compatriots was not met. Although the government cracked down, arresting militants and executing leaders of Takfir and the ILO, clandestine organizations like *Jund Allah* (the Army of God) and *Jamaat al-Jihad* (the Holy War Society) took up the struggle. These organizations recruited heavily from university mosques and private (non-government controlled) mosques. The leadership were well educated but disillusioned with and disaffected from a society judged to be politically autocratic and corrupt, economically unjust, and spiritually lax. They rejected the political and religious establishments, viewing the latter as puppets of the regime. Their ideological world view drew heavily on the writings of Hasan al-Banna, Mawlana al-Mawdudi and especially the more militant, revolutionary tracts of Sayyid Qutb, taking his statements quite literally and militantly. This approach was summarized effectively by Muhammad al-Farag of the Jamaat al-Jihad in his *The Forgotten Obligation (jihad* as armed struggle or holy war).[13] By the end of the 1970s secret, underground Islamic groups were among the most vocal and active participants in a growing opposition to Sadat's policies such as Camp David, the sheltering of the Shah of Iran, condemnation of Iran's Islamic revolution and of Khomeini as a "madman", Egypt's western oriented Open Door economic policy, and Muslim family law reforms. In 1981, in the midst of a turbulent period in which the government had arrested more than 1500 critics from former government ministers and journalists to leftist Islamic activists, Anwar Sadat was assassinated by members of Jamaat al-Jihad.

The complexity of Islamic revivalism can be seen clearly in the events of the 1980s. While violent clandestine extremist groups continue to exist and occasional confrontations between activists and the government have occurred, in fact the strength of Islamic revivalism is to be found in the quiet revolution represented by the proliferation of organizations engaged in religio-social and moral reform. Islamic activism has indeed become part of the mainstream. A Muslim Brotherhood that had been regarded as extremist in the 1960s and almost feeble in the Sadat years is now a vibrant political and social force in Egyptian society. Although the Brotherhood is not registered as a political party, it formed alliances with others and emerged from national elections as the leading opposition force. More importantly, the Muslim Brotherhood has widespread influence in education, publishing, social services and investment houses. Similarly, Egyptian society is served by numerous groups and societies who provide Islamically inspired alternative educational, legal, medical, banking, and social services often more conveniently, cheaply and efficiently than the government.

LEBANON

Lebanon provides an instructive example of the extent to which Islamic revivalism is the product of faith and experience. It demonstrates how religion interacts with sociopolitical reality, and therefore how even within one country two Shi'i movements, AMAL and Hizbullah, could develop in different directions. The disappearance of Imam Musa Sadr in 1978 and the Iranian revolution of 1978-79 reinforced the power and ability of Shi'i history and symbolism to provide a framework of meaning and social protest. In contrast to Sunni religious history, Shi'i history is not one of imperial success and rule but rather of frustration, betrayal, and defeat. From the early refusal of the Sunni majority to accept the claim of the party of Ali "shi'at al-Ali" to restrict leadership of the Islamic community to the descendants of the Prophet's family, the Shi'a developed a sense of history and belief which legitimated and gave meaning to their existence as a disenfranchised, diaspora community. Central to this understanding are the martyrdom of Husayn and the return of the Imam. Shi'a believe that Ali, the cousin and son-in-law of Muhammad, was designated by Muhammad as his successor and thus that his descendants should serve as the divinely guided religio-political leaders, Imams, of the community. The Sunni majority maintain that Muhammad died without designating his political heir and selected or elected a successor (caliph) to lead the community. In 680 Husayn, the son of Ali, challenged the leadership of the Sunni caliph Yazid whom he regarded as a usurper. He and his army were vanquished at Karbala in modern day Iraq. The martyrdom of Husayn became a paradigmatic event for Shi'a, providing a model for religious commitment, self-sacrifice and martyrdom, a "passion play" which is commemorated and ritually reenacted annually. The battle at Karbala coupled with belief in the eventual return of the hidden Imam (the twelfth Imam disappeared in 874 and his return from seclusion or occultation is awaited by believers), who will establish a reign of peace and justice, served as the ideological foundation for contemporary Shi'i politics. The forces of God are to wage war against those of Satan in the age-old battle against tyranny and oppression until the return of the Imam as the mahdi, a messianic figure, whose rule will usher in an age of righteousness and social justice. God is ultimately on the side of the disinherited and oppressed whom He will vindicate. This interpretation gave Shi'a Islam an ideological framework of protest and opposition to social injustice within which a variety of political and religious factions could function. It was this vision of the Imam's return and the spread of true Islamic rule that the Iranian revolution seemed to herald.

The euphoria which accompanied the return of the Ayatollah Khomeini to Iran and the establishment of the Islamic Republic of Iran soon proved a challenge to Nabih Berri's non-clerical leadership of AMAL, as Iranian inspired members pressed for a more militant Islamic orientation. AMAL which had developed in 1975 as the military wing or militia for Imam Musa Sadr's Movement for the Dispossessed, was sectarian in membership but pluralistic in outlook.[14] It had attracted upwardly mobile professionals and businessmen as well as clergy, demanding political and social reforms within Lebanon's pluralistic state which reflected the rights of a people who had become Lebanon's largest confessional group. However, Iran's post-revolutionary influence and the 1982 Israeli invasion of Lebanon radicalized the situation. Influenced by Iran, Husayn Musawi broke with Berri, rejecting his secular nationalist approach as un-Islamic, and created Islamic AMAL which advocated an Islamic Republic. He withdrew from Beirut to Baalbeck, which already served as a Shi'a center. More than 1000 Iranian Revolutionary Guards (Pasdaran) supported the militant Shi'i movement Hizbullah, the Party of God, which had emerged in the Beqaa Valley after the Iranian Revolution but came to prominence after the 1982 Israeli invasion. Its ideological outlook is closely aligned to that of Iran. In contrast to Amal's continued commitment to a multi-confessional state, Hizbullah's ultimate goal is an Islamic republic. It is anti-western and convinced that violence is the order of the day. Like Iran's Islamic movement, Hizbullah's ideology and leadership are heavily clerical. Its spiritual father and guide is Shaykh Muhammad Fadlallah, a prominent Shi'a preacher and leader who enjoys close links to Iran and whose reputation extends to the Gulf. In contrast to Amal which is organized as a unified political party and militia, Hizbullah is a more loosely structured confederation of groups. It serves as an umbrella organization for the activities of a variety of groups like Islamic AMAL, the Husayn Suicide Squadron, the Army of God, and the shadowy Islamic Jihad. While AMAL has tried to project a more moderate image (Nabih Berri accepted a cabinet position in a national unity government and mediated in the TWA hijacking of June 1985 and other hostage situations), Hizbullah has opted for a more extremist Shi'i Islamic alternative to AMAL, advocating a more general use of violence against all others: the Lebanese government and army, Christian militias, Israeli forces, foreign powers (European governments, conservative Arab States like Saudi Arabia and, in particular, the United States) and AMAL itself. It has been blamed for or claimed credit for attacks against foreign embassies, U.S. Marine and French military compounds, as well as for kidnappings and hijackings. Hizbullah has appealed to the most alienated and radicalized and, as such, has put indirect pressure upon Nabih Berri's AMAL to be more militant. Ironically, while Hizbullah is supported by Iran, AMAL has Syria, an ally of Iran, as its patron. Similarly, while Hizbullah often joined with returning Palestinian forces in fighting the Israeli army in South Lebanon, AMAL placed Palestinian camps in Beirut under siege. Thus, the mix of religion and politics among the Shi'a of Lebanon demonstrates not only the ability of Shi'i Islam to serve as a source of identity and mobilization, but also the extent to which contending differing political actors and forces can lead to the development of Islamic movements whose interpretation and use of Shi'i Islam result in quite different ideological orientations, competition and conflict.

MALAYSIA

The landscape of Islamic revivalism in Malaysia is less well known than that of the Middle East, but no less rich.[15] As indicated previously, Chinese-Malay riots in 1969 served as the catalyst for an Islamic revivalism that accompanied the government's attempt to improve the socio-economic status of Malays. Islam, already a fundamental element in Malay cultural identity, became an even more powerful ideological and political force and deeply reinforced previously existing communalism. Government quotas and subsidies for Malays in business, industry and education, and the promotion of Malay language and cultural values reinforced the bond between religion and ethnicity. This was particularly evident among the younger generation of Malay students and university graduates in the post 1969 period. As in Egypt and other Muslim countries, urban universities became centers for Islamic activism, replacing nationalist and socialist groups as the most effective actors. Thousands of Malays were admitted to universities at home or sent abroad for study. Uprooted from the integrated life and security of their rural environments and thrust into modern westernized cities dominated by Chinese, many Malay youth at campuses like the prestigious University of Malaya and the Kebangsaan (National) University turned to their Islamic heritage to preserve their sense of identity and to provide the context, language, and rationale for their reformism. This was further reinforced by Malay students returning from study in the United States and Great Britain, greatly influenced by their exposure to students from other Muslim countries and to the thinking of Islamic activists from the Arab world, Iran and Pakistan.

Events in the Muslim world also affected Malaysia's Islamic Revival. The Arab-Israeli war and oil embargo of 1973 brought an outpouring of popular Islamic sentiment and stronger governmental and non-governmental ties with the Arab world. Pakistan's Islamization program under General Zia ul-Haq and Iran's Islamic revolution were well known to Malaysian activist leaders who maintained contacts with fellow activists and participated in international conferences. At the same time, concern about the influence of Iranian and Libyan radicalism contributed to government sensitivity to Islamic sentiments and issues.

While Malaysia had a number of prominent organizations active in preaching Islam, the nature of post 1969 revivalism is reflected in the growth of what came to be called *dakwah* (Arabic, *da'wa*) movements. These organizations tended to condemn dependence on western and Chinese values which subvert Malay Muslim identity, integrity and solidarity. They advocate a return to Islam as a total way of life. However, the *dakwah* movements embrace diverse groups and interpretations of revivalist Islam with differing implications for matters of belief, ritual practice, dress and activity. Some simply emphasize greater attention to personal behavior: observance of prayer and fasting, the replacement of western styles with Islamic dress, avoiding dances, nightclubs, western music, drugs and alcohol. More militant activists agitate for the establishment of Islamic government and law, the separation of the sexes in education, sports, and public life in general, the banning of discotheques, alcohol, and other "western" or "yellow" cultural activities. The variety of *dakwah* organizations can be seen in three groups in particular: *Darul Arqam* (the House of Arqam), *ABIM* (the Islamic Youth Movement of Malaysia) and the Islamic Republic group. Darul Arqam fulfills some of the western stereotypes of fundamentalist movements, in particular the notion of a return to the seventh century. Established in 1969 by *Ustaz* (teacher) Ashaari Muhammad, it emphasizes the importance of establishing an Islamic society prior to creating an Islamic state. Arqam has been critical of most Muslim governments and Islamic organizations outside and within Malaysia, attributing their lack of success to a failure to focus sufficiently on Islamic education and to emulate the model Islamic society governed by the Prophet at Medina. Arqam has tended to be apolitical, focusing on the creation of ideal Islamic communities. Members live in groups that seek to emulate the communal life of the Prophet's time. Both western and traditional Malay forms of dress are eschewed. Although historically women have not been separated from males or veiled in Malay society, members of Darul Arqam practice total segregation of the sexes and women are completely veiled in public. Men wear green (the color of Islam) robes, a turban and beard in imitation of the Prophet. The Arqam communities run educational, agricultural, manufacturing, and social service projects, based strictly upon their interpretation of Islamic principles. Factories manufacture *halal* (permitted) foods, soap, and drinks.[16]

The most vital, effective, and politically successful *dakwah* movement in the 1970s was the Islamic Youth Movement of Malaysia (Angkatan Belia Islam Malaysia, or ABIM). It embodies the events, issues and concerns of the post 1969 period which fostered religious revivalism in general and the mobilization of youth in particular. ABIM was created specifically in 1971 to mobilize Muslim students and young professionals to spread Islam in Malaysia and to bring about socio-economic reforms. Much of the remarkable growths of ABIM was due to the charismatic leader Anwar Ibrahim, an activist student leader in the late 1960s. By the early 1970s Malay nationalism and social action were given an Islamic shape and idiom to mobilize disillusioned and disaffected students:

> [We were] disgusted by the hypocrisy in society. We were disillusioned with the leadership.... The leaders were condemning corruption, but they were enriching themselves. They talked about Malay nationalism, but they were alienated from the Malay masses. They were obsessed by the west. They were too accommodating to non-Malay sentiments. They were extremely slow in implementing national policies in education and language. We were impatient and angry about the plight of the Malays, their education, rural development, rural health. There was this huge University hospital, but no clinics in the rural areas. There were schools with no laboratories, no libraries and no qualified teachers. We were very angry, disgusted and critical of the government. There seemed to be no moral foundation and no spiritual guidance. We turned to Islam to fill this vacuum and to look for solutions.[17]

Ibrahim and his colleagues formed study groups, ran orientation programs for new students, conducted seminars and community projects, translated and distributed the writings of international activists like Hasan al-Banna, Sayyid Qutb and Mawlana Mawdudi into Malay, recast their nationalist concerns and commitment to social justice through socio-economic reform within an Islamic framework. Islam was offered to students as an alternative to prevailing nationalist and socialist options. For example, the program and activities of the Malay Language Society for implementation of Malay as the national language, as well as health and economic reforms, were now cast in a Malay nationalism clearly grounded in Islam. The aims of a consciousness raising program previously sponsored to foster Malay awareness and rights in national development were Islamized and rendered: "to establish justice, honesty, truth and understanding among the rural people to ensure their social, economic, political and educational development are linked to Islam".[18]

Although Anwar Ibrahim and ABIM were influenced by outside Islamic activists, movements and experiments in Pakistan (Zia ul-Haq and the Jamaat-i-Islami), Sudan (Jafar al-Numayri and the Sudanese Muslim Brotherhood), and to a lesser extent the creation of an Islamic republic in Iran, ABIM's ideology and goals were shaped to speak directly to Malaysia's history and context, a multi-ethnic, pluralistic society. Ibrahim recognized that the experience of other organizations and governments could be borrowed from but not duplicated in Malaysia's multi-ethnic and religious context. Advocacy of an Islamic state and implementation of the Sharia were accompanied by condemnation of racism, as well as by insistence upon the preservation of non-Muslim rights within a democratic society in a concerted effort to reassure the Chinese minority community in particular.[19] ABIM swept Student Union elections in 1974, signaling its rise to prominence. It reached the height of its power in the late 1970s both as a result of its leadership and activities and as an alliance with its chief political rival *PAS* (Parti Islam Se-Malaysia, Islamic Party of Malaysia). The government response was one of coercion and coaptation. It moved to contain and silence its Islamic opposition (in particular its most effective leader Anwar Ibrahim), but at the same time *UMNO* (United Malays National Organization), the ruling party's politicians, increasingly employed Islamic rhetoric and slogans to bolster their Islamic image.

By the early 1980s the newly elected Prime Minister, Muhammad Mahathir, placed UMNO and the government firmly on a more Islamically oriented path, giving greater emphasis to Islam both domestically and internationally. In moving to coopt the appeal of its Islamic opposition, the government was also testifying to the growth of the opposition and yielding to some of its demands. The government adopted a "Look East" (rather than west) policy and significantly expanded its involvement in Islamic affairs in a number of ways such as providing greater support for expanded coverage of Islam in the media and in school curricula; establishing a new International Islamic University, Islamic Studies faculties in existing universities, and an Islamic bank and insurance company; increasing funding for religious organizations and *dakwah* activities. Most significantly, Mahathir invited Ibrahim to join his government. Ibrahim's acceptance was read by many as cooptation; for Ibrahim it was the opportunity to work for Islamization from within the system. His resignation as president of ABIM in 1982 was the beginning of his rapid rise to power through several ministries to his current position as Minister of Education and status as the man most believed to be Mahathir's choice to be his successor. However, ABIM has not faired as well. By the late 1970s, it was already being challenged by more militant Islamic activist students and professionals recently returned from Britain. The loss of its charismatic leader in 1982 and the subsequent move of other ABIM leaders into the government as well as ABIM's moderation of its criticism of the government made ABIM more vulnerable to critics' charges of cooptation and accommodation. ABIM's changing image and role was signaled by PAS's return as the leading Islamic opposition group and ABIM's loss of dominance on the campuses to the more radical voices of the Islamic Republic group, a close ally of PAS, which in 1983 wrested control of the Islamic Student Society, the most important student *dakwah* organization.

PAS was established in 1951 by defectors from UMNO who believed that UMNO's vision for a recently independent Malaysia was too secular. PAS advocated an Islamic state in which all aspects of life would be affected by the state's Islamic orientation. In contrast to ABIM's more moderate image as an urban- based, Islamic reformist pressure group for Islamically rooted socio-economic change, PAS has often been regarded as a more strident, confrontative, Islamically conservative or traditionalist, religiously chauvinistic political party, whose strongest support was in the rural areas. While most of its early leaders came from more traditional religious educational backgrounds, the late 1970s and 1980s brought significant changes in its orientation and leadership. As a result of its alliance with ABIM in 1977, PAS and ABIM strengthened each other and made UMNO's Islamic opposition far more formidable. Both groups joined together in the 1978 elections with ABIM campaigning for PAS candidates and a number of ABIM members joining PAS to run for office. By 1980, PAS began to be transformed as its old guard leadership was challenged by younger voices. Ex-ABIM members and more Islamically militant activists newly returned from study in Britain pressured the PAS leadership to adopt a purer, more systematic Islamic stance with less emphasis on Malay nationalism and to devote more emphasis to organization, cadre training and political action. These demands set up a struggle for power between the older leadership of PAS's president Mohammed Asri and the new guard.[20] Among the key figures in the new guard was Hajji Abdul Hadi Awang, the traditionally raised son of a religious leader who was educated at Medina University and al-Azhar University in Cairo. His fluency in Arabic, training at leading Islamic universities, and ability as a preacher enhanced his credibility with the ulama and contributed to his popularity. His simple lifestyle and sermons which drew heavily upon Islamic sources and symbols in calling for sociopolitical reforms proved popular. In language reminiscent of Iran's Islamic revolution he denounced the government's un-Islamic colonialist policies and called for the creation of a true Islamic state, a struggle whose realization might require martyrdom. Here was an ABIM leader who had contested the 1978 elections as a PAS candidate and possessed the background, training, and rhetorical approach attractive to a PAS constituency. In 1982 the new guard joined with the ulama and Hadi Awang captured the PAS party leadership.

The ranks of PAS had increasingly attracted more militant students, in particular those students, professors and young professionals who returned from study in Britain in the late 1970s and early '80s. They were influenced by radical interpretations of the teachings of Mawlana Mawdudi and Sayyid Qutb, introduced by Muslim faculty members or fellow students from other Muslim countries. In Britain they had formed two organizations: *Saura Islam* (Voice of Islam), influenced by the Jamaat-i-Islami and the Islamic Representative Council, drawn to the example of the Egyptian Muslim Brotherhood. Saura Islam believed that an Islamic state could only be realized by a revolution led by an Islamic party composed of a trained, Islamically committed elite. The IRC sought to create a mass movement, organized as the Egyptian Brothers into secret cells *usra*. IRC's militant, underground organizational approach and straightforward unambiguous revolutionary message proved the most attractive:

Their black and white approach to the Islamic struggle -- you are either a Muslim practicing Islam as a complete way of life or you are an infidel, you either fight for Islam or you are irreligious, you either join an Islamic group or you are not part of the movement -- appealed, in particular, to the science students.[21]

Having returned from Britain to take up positions in the universities, schools, government bureaucracy and professions, these activists were more attracted to the militant Islamic political language of PAS, which mirrored their own, than to the more moderate approach of ABIM. This language called for the condemnation of an "infidel" secular government, anti-western rhetoric, a true and all encompassing Islamic state, and admiration and support for revolutionary Iran. Whereas ABIM and PAS had both been early supporters of the Iranian revolution, ABIM's enthusiasm had cooled while PAS continued its support. The young guard in a PAS that seized the banner of Islamic opposition from ABIM and formed the Islamic Republic group, committed to the establishment of an Iranian type Islamic government in Malaysia, replaced ABIM as the dominant Islamic student organization in the 1980s. Their ideology and political activism is radical in its rigid worldview, confrontational politics and agenda. There are no grey areas. The individual as well as the state is either Muslim or not, Islamically committed or un-Islamic, believer or infidel, saved or damned. Malaysia's man-made constitutional government must be replaced by one based upon the Qur'an and *Sunnah* (model example) of the Prophet Muhammad and guided by Islamic law the *Sharia*. Organizationally emulating the Egyptian Muslim Brotherhood and the Jamaat-i-Islami, their chief means for achieving their goals are the *usra*, study-support groups and religious activism. Their strength lies in the level of their ideological commitment and organization which often enables a minority to influence or dominate the majority. Students are organized into small cells *usra* which meet regularly to study (religious talks, discussions, debates) and pray together as well as provide a social support system, thus developing and reinforcing a strong sense of religious identity and solidarity. Student activists, who see themselves as guardians of Islam and community morality, seek to quietly spread their message through distribution of publications, organization of orientation programs and religious courses for new students, gaining control of student organizations and hostels, and confronting university administrators and other students in order to ban "un-Islamic" activities such as dances, parties, concerts, mixed socials.

Islamic activist organizations have had a significant impact upon Malaysian society, transforming a government sponsored program for Malay uplift into a potentially far reaching process of Islamization of state and society. The more moderate Islamic reformism of ABIM proved a catalyst for Prime Minister Mahathir's government sponsored Islamization program and the incorporation of Anwar Ibrahim and other ABIM members in the government. At the same time, a pronounced turn to Islam has included the more strident voices of a new PAS which has tried to combine its traditional rural base of support with a new generation of members, modern educated but militantly Islamically oriented. ABIM and PAS demonstrate the extent to which faith and sociopolitical realities combine to determine the make-up, ideology and political activism of Islamic organizations as well as influence their changing configuration and fortunes.

Finally, the experience of Anwar Ibrahim and ABIM highlights an interesting problem. Moderate Islamic activists seek to bring about change from within the system. However, what are they to do when invited to join an incumbent government? They have not come to power directly or elected their own candidate. As a result, they run the risk of being coopted or being perceived as having been coopted. The case of Ibrahim and of Dr. Hasan al-Turabi, the leader of Sudan's Muslim Brotherhood who joined the Numayri government in 1977 as Attorney General, reflect the positive and negative aspects of cooperation. While a government portfolio presents the opportunity to influence Islamization measures and affect change, activists are identified with (and are used to give legitimacy to) all government policies, good and bad, even in situations over which they have little control. Moreover, their new position requires compromises that they never would have made when out of government, undermining their former role as social critics. Indeed, the strength of ABIM and the Sudanese Brotherhood were greatest when they were viewed as independent pressure groups or members of the opposition.

CONCLUSION

As we have seen, Islamic governments and organizations have ranged from the military regimes (Qadhafi, Numayri, Zia ul-Haq) to monarchy (the House of Saud) to clergy (Khomeini), from relatively conservative religious states (Saudi Arabia and Pakistan) to Libya's experiment with a "people's state". Governments have used Islam to enhance their authority and legitimacy, strengthen nationalism, and legitimate or mobilize popular support for their programs and policies. Islamic organizations manifest an even richer range of orientations: apolitical educational and social service groups, moderate socio-political societies and parties, violent revolutionaries. Islam has provided the rationale for social action and political dissent, attempts to foster social reform, political change and the overthrow of Muslim rulers. While many have appealed to Islam and called for an Islamic alternative, their interpretations of Islam have varied widely. There has been unity neither of purpose nor of action and agenda. In many Muslim countries (Egypt, Pakistan, Malaysia) both the government and its opposition have appealed to Islam. Often Muslim organizations have proven more capable of agreement and cooperation in opposition to a government than of implementing their Islamic vision. Unity in opposition quickly dissolved into ideological and political infighting in Pakistan and post-revolutionary Iran as anti-Bhutto and anti-Shah forces grappled for power and influence. Not only did religious and secular parties fight among themselves, but also religious leaders and parties. Khomeini's clerically dominated state has silenced secularists, communists, socialists and Islamically oriented (former) allies and critics alike. The Islamic Republic's first elected president, Abul Hasan Banisadr fled to France; its first prime minister, Mehdi Bazargan resigned; its foreign minister, Sadeq Gobtzadeh was executed; a revered senior cleric, Ayatollah Shariatmadari was defrocked. All had been strong supporters of the revolution. The Pakistan National Alliance, a coalition of political parties which spanned the political spectrum but was united in opposition to Ali Bhutto and in calling for an Islamic system of government, fell apart over support for Zia ul-Haq and his Islamization policies. A tendency to divide rather than unite can also be seen in the relationship of PAS and ABIM in Malaysia AMAL and Hizbollah in Lebanon. Questions of political power, strong leadership personalities and differing interpretations of Islam have generally divided rather than united those who make common use of Islam.

Among the major questions that have grown out of contemporary Islamic revivalism and remain important issues for the foreseeable future are those of leadership and interpretation. If the state is to implement Islam, who shall do it and how? Is Islam to be imposed from above by monarchs, military leaders, the clergy? Or is Islamic government to come from below, to be the product of an electoral process? Many who have witnessed the use of Islam to ban political parties, to silence dissent, to impose unpopular laws and measures increasingly emphasize the importance of traditional notions of consultation *shura* and community consensus *ijma*. They regard these as safeguards against both secular and Islamically legitimated authoritarianism. While many Muslims remain wary of the excesses that have accompanied the reassertion of Islam in politics, the tendency in many countries is not simply to advocate secularism or secular forms of nationalism but rather to urge some kind of accommodation or synthesis of Islam and society. Most Muslims emphasize the role of representative bodies such as parliaments in charting an Islamic path for state and society. The role of the *ulama* in this process remains unclear. In many Muslim societies the more established *ulama* are regarded as pawns of the state as well as retrogressive thinkers. Thus, in contrast to Shi'i Islam, in Sunni majority (85% of the world of Islam) societies most Islamic movements and societies are run by the laity. At best the ulama are regarded as those who should play an advisory role to organizations and to parliamentary bodies. Indeed some reform minded Muslims emphasize that Islam knows no clergy and that the ulama were merely a class of scholars who emerged during the early Islamic centuries. Thus, they stress that given the nature of many modern day political, social and economic problems, the notion of expert must be broadened to include those that possess the knowledge and experience required, including economists, historians, lawyers, sociologists. All will be necessary to undertake appropriate reforms.

Islamic interpretation or orientation is the second major issue facing contemporary revivalists. Is a more authentic return to Islam to be a process of restoration or reformation? For many of the more traditional *ulama* and their followers, the renewal of Islamic society means a re-implementation of classical Islam, its laws and institutions. In contrast, Islamic reformers distinguish between the immutable sources of Islam and the socio-historically conditioned forms and regulations developed by the ulama of the past. Islamic reformers emphasize the need for reconstruction, substantial reinterpretation and reform. It should be emphasized that the issue is not whether there should be change but how much and what kind. Modernization as science and technology is not rejected; modernization as westernization of state and society is. The issue is one of culture and values. All Muslims accept much of modern technology; they differ as to how that technology is to be utilized. Those who paint pictures of retrogressive anti-modern fundamentalists often forget that they travel by jet and automobile, rely heavily on modern communications (press, video and audiotapes, the telephone, telex and fax), obtain modern educations and training, and often advocate parliamentary systems of government. Radicals have no religious qualms about using the most up to date weapons. Perhaps the best way to appreciate the differing orientations towards change is to briefly consider the issue of Islamic law. The first thing that Islamic revivalists demand, regardless of their differences, is the implementation of Islamic law *shariah*, the ideal blueprint for the good society. However, they differ in what they wish to implement. Conservatives tend to regard much of the corpus of traditional Islamic law as binding. Reformers note that the law is a combination of revelation and human interpretation and that the later is subject to reinterpretation *ijtihad* and reform. Many of the issues that have accompanied the revival of Islam such as the status and role of women, relations between the sexes, and the rights of minorities spring from this difference of opinion.

The contemporary revival of Islam has been a dynamic period of implementation and experimentation. Like all experiments, some have succeeded and many have failed. The excesses have caused many to reject what they regard as a negative Islam, one which often seems to emphasize penalties, taxes, and restrictions rather than true liberation. However, while the retrogressive hold of tradition is often emphasized in reports on revivalism, a great deal of change is taking place, often supported by both conservative and reform minded Muslims: Islamic banks, insurance companies, money markets, schools, social services and development projects have been introduced. The vast majority of Muslims, secularists and Islamic revivalists abhor the exploitation of Islam by some governments and movements. A minority continue to espouse violence as the necessary means for change. They will continue to disrupt society from time to time. However, the strength of contemporary revivalism remains with a growing moderate majority of Islamic activists whose activities have become part of mainstream Muslim life. These are the apolitical and political *da'wa* organizations who seek to call all to a religious renewal which combines prayer observance with social action. Their vision of Islam is holistic. They believe that a faithful, righteous Islamic community is one that observes God's mandate to worship Him and to create a socially just society. This long term process, which is weaving its way into political and social institutions, will have significance both for the development of Muslim societies and for their relationship with the west.

Notes

1. John O. Voll, *Islam: Continuity and Change in the Modern World* (Boulder, Colorado: Westview Press, 1982), 93ff; Albert Hourani, *Arabic Thought in the Liberal Age* (London: Oxford University Press, 1980), chs. 5-6.

2. John O. Voll, "Renewal and Reform in Islamic History: *Tajdid* and *Islah*," in *Voices of Resurgent Islam*, ed. John L. Esposito (New York: Oxford University Press, 1983), ch. 2.

3. Richard Mitchell, *The Society of Muslim Brothers* (New York: Oxrford University Press, 1969); and Charles J. Adams, "Mawdudi and the Islamic State," *Voices....,* ed. John L. Esposito, ch. 5.

4. Hassan al-Banna, "The New Renaissance," *Islam in Transition: Muslim Perspectives*, ed. John J. Donohue and John L. Esposito (New York: Oxford University Press, 1982), 78.

5. Abul Ala Mawdudi, "Political Theory of Islam", in *Islam in Transition*, 78.

6. Hassan al-Banna, "The New Renaissance," 78.

7. Voll, *Islam....,* ch. 3; and John L. Esposito, *Islam and Politics* (Syracuse, New York: Syracuse University Press, 2d rev. ed. 1987), 30-39.

8. James P. Piscatori, *Islam in a World of Nation States* (Cambridge: Cambridge University Press, 1986), ch. 2; and Esposito, *Islam and Politics*, ch. 5.

9. Lisa Anderson, "Qaddafi's Islam" in *Voices....,* ch. 6; and Ann Elizabeth Mayer, "Islamic Resurgence or New Prophethood: The Role of Islam in Qaddafi's Ideology," in *Islamic resurgence in the Arab World,* ed. Ali E. Hillal Dessouki (New York: Praeger, 1982), ch. 10.

10. Hamied N. Ansari, "The Islamic Militants in Egyptian Politics," *International Journal of Middle East Studies* 16, no. 1 (March 1984), 123-444.

11. Saad Eddin Ibrahhim, "Egypt's Islamic Militants," *MERIP Reports* no. 103 (February 1982), 11.

12. Johannes J. G. Jansen, *The Neglected Duty* (New York: Macmillan, 1986), ch. 1 and Appendix.

13. Richard Augustus Norton, *Amal and the Shia: Struggle for the Soul of Lebanon* (Austin, Texas: The University of Texas Press, 1987).

14. Judith Nagata, *The Reflowering of Malaysian Islam: Modern Religious Radicals and Their Roots* (Vancouver: University of British Columbia Press, 1984); and Fred R. von der Mehden, "Malaysia: Islam and Multiethnic Polities," in *Islam in Asia: Religion, Politics and Society,* ed. John L. Esposito (New York: Oxford University Press, 1987), ch. 8.

15. Zainah Anwar, *Islamic Revivalism in Malaysia: Dakwah Among the Students* (Selangor: Pelanduk Publications, 1987), 37.

16.   Ibid., 12-13.

17.   Ibid., 16.

18.   Fred R. von der Mehden, "Islamic Resurgence in Malaysia" in *Islam and Development: Religion and Sociopolitical Change*, ed. John L. Esposito (Syracuse: Syracuse University Press, 1980), 174-75.

19.   Jomo Kwame Sundaram and Ahmad Shabery Cheek, "The Politics of Malaysia's Islamic Resurgence," *Third World Quarterly* 10, no. 2 (April 1988), 852-53.

20.   Anwar, 29.

21.   John L. Esposito, *Islam the Straight Path* (New York: Oxford University Press, 1988), ch. 5.

4

Bibliography of the Islamic Revival

Yvonne Yazbeck Haddad,
Kathleen Moore, and David Sawan

I. GENERAL STUDIES

A. INTERPRETIVE STUDIES

0001 ABU-LUGHOD, JANET L. "The Islamic City-Historic Myth, Islamic Essence, and Contemporary Relevance." *IJMES*, 19 (May 1987), 155-76.

0002 ABU-SULAYMAN, ABDUL HAMID A. *The Islamic Theory of International Relations: New Directions for Islamic Methodology and Thought*. Introduction Isma'il al Faruqi. Herndon, VA: The International Institute of Islamic Thought, 1987, 184 p.
  Contributes to an understanding of the Muslim perception of an Islamic paradigm for the study of international relations within the 'Islamization of Knowledge' school of thought, founded by Ismail al-Faruqi. Provides the essentials of an Islamic world order: commitment to work for world peace even if it requires martyrdom; elimination of war; rejection of distinctions on race, income, wealth, and language; individual liberty; equality of opportunity; and just treatment of minorities.

0003 _____. "Islamization of Knowledge with Special Reference to Political Science." *AJISS*, 2 (1985), 263-89.

0004 ABUN-NASR, JAMIL N. "Militant Islam: a Historical Perspective." In *Islamic Dilemmas: Reformers, Nationalists and Industrialization*. Ed. Ernest Gellner. New York: Mouton Publishers, 1985, 73-93.

0005 AHMAD, EQBAL. "Islam and Politics." In *The Islamic Impact*. Eds. Haddad, Yvonne, Haines, Byron, and Findly, Ellison. Syracuse, NY: Syracuse University Press, 1984, 7-26.

0006 AHMED, MANZOORUDDIN. *Islamic Political Systems in the Modern Age: Theory and Practice*. Karachi: Saad Publications, 1983, 360 p.

0007 AHMED, AKBAR. *Discovering Islam: Making Sense of Muslim History and Society*. London: Routledge & Kegan Paul, Ltd., 1988, 251 p.
A Pakistani anthropologist and civil servant tries to offset the western negative coverage and image of Islam and to provide a "Muslim perspective" on the nature and history of Islamic belief and society. The book is the product of personal reflections from a South Asian perspective. Drawing on some previously published materials, the volume ranges widely from a theory of Islamic history and studies on Sufis and scholars to chapters on Muslim society such as Saudi Arabia, Muslim scholarship, and the impact of colonialism in the Muslim world. The author gives much attention to western perceptions of Islam and, conversely, less attention to Muslim perceptions of the west.

0008 _____. "Toward Islamic Anthropology." *AJISS*, 3 (1986), 181-230.

0009 AL-AHSAN, 'ABDULLAH. *The Organization of the Islamic Conference: An Introduction to an Islamic Political Institution*. Herndon, VA: The International Institute of Islamic Thought, 1988, 141 p.
As part of the 'Islamization of Knowledge' series published by the IIIT, this book is intended to be used as an undergraduate Islamic textbook on international organizations. Throughout the text the concept of *ummah* is emphasized in an attempt to demonstrate its centrality to the structure and functions of the OIC. At the outset the book provides a brief review of the philosophy and history of the OIC, in the light of an Islamist interpretation, and then describes at length its organization and operation. A chapter focuses on the Muslim struggle for self-determination in Palestine and Afghanistan, the plight of Muslim minorities and the OIC's stance with regard to these issues. The Charter of the Islamic Conference is provided in the appendix.

0010 ALI, ABD AL-RAHIM. "The Islamic Revolution: Its Impact on the Islamic Movement." In *The Islamic Revolution: Achievements, Obstacles and Goals*. Eds. K. Siddiqui, et al. London: The Muslim Institute, 1980, 37-43.

0011 AMIN, SAYED HASSAN. *Islamic Law in the Contemporary World*. Glasgow: Royston; Tehran: Vahid Publications, 1985, 190 p.

0012 ANDERSEN, ROY R., ROBERT SIEBERT, and JON D. WAGNER. *Politics and Change in the Middle East: Sources of Conflict and Accommodation*. 2d ed. Englewood Cliffs, NJ: Prentice-Hall, Inc., 1987, 334 p.
Discussion of *Kharijites*, *Ismailis* and *Qarmatians*, *Mahdi*, Twelver Shiism, and the *Wahhabi* Movement. The Muslim Brotherhood is discussed in the context of Egyptian independence. A chapter is devoted to Islamic revival, in which revival movements in Egypt, Saudi Arabia, Iran, Turkey, the Levant, and Libya, are discussed. Also discussed at length is the religio-political theory of an Islamic state, and the specific example of the Islamic Republic of Iran.

0013 ARJOMAND, SAID AMIR, ed. *From Nationalism to Revolutionary Islam.* Foreward by Ernest Gellner. Albany, NY: State University of New York Press, 1985, 256 p.

A collection of conference papers that address various aspects of nationalism and Islamic revivalism in the contemporary Muslim world. The general thesis is that nationalism is giving way to "revolutionary" Islam as the appropriate paradigm to use in understanding politics in selected Muslim countries, including Pakistan, Egypt, Algeria, Syria and Turkey.

0014 ARMAJANI, YAHYA. *Middle East: Past and Present.* 2d ed. Englewood Cliffs, NJ: Prentice-Hall, Inc., 1986, 466 p.

Provides a brief but thorough introduction to the Muslim Brotherhood, the factors which contributed to its rise, its ideology and organization. In a chapter on Iran, the role of Shi'ite religious organization is highlighted as "the only outlet the people had to protest their economic misery, which practically everyone felt..." (p. 438)

0015 ASHRAF, SYED ALI. "Islam in the Contemporary World." *MEQ*, 5 (1988), 1-4.

0016 ASKARI, HASAN. "Christian Mission to Islam: A Muslim Response." *JIMMA*, 7 (1986), 314-29.

0017 AL-ATTAS, SYED MUHAMMAD NAQUIB. *Islam, Secularism and the Philosophy of the Future.* New York: Mansell Publications, 1985, 240 p.

A compilation of monographs originally published between 1975 and 1980, this volume is an exposition of Islam, Islamic ethics and education, and the effort to 'de-westernize' knowledge from a proponent of Islamization. Islam is compared favorably to Christianity in the context of the global hegemony of western secularism and is validated as a better alternative. The author criticizes Muslim traditionalists and modernists for having distorted Islam by aiding in the process of secularizing it.

0018 AYOOB, MOHAMMAD. *The Politics of Islamic Reassertion.* New York: St. Martin's Press, 1981, 298 p.

A wide ranging collection of studies by historians and social scientists on the reassertion of Islam in contemporary politics, spanning the Muslim world from the Middle East to Southeast Asia, particularly useful on Southeast Asia.

0019 AYOUB, MAHMOUD M. "Islam Between Ideals and Ideologies: Toward a Theology of Islamic History." In *The Islamic Impulse.* Ed. Barbara F. Stowasser. London: Croom Helm, 1987, 297-319.

0020 _____. "Martyrdom in Christianity and Islam." In *Religious Resurgence, Contemporary Cases in Islam, Christianity, and Judaism.* Eds. Richard T. Antoun and Mary E. Hegland. Syracuse, NY: Syracuse University Press, 1987, 67-77.

0021 EL-BANNA, GAMAL. "The Crisis of Unionism Between Contemporary Ideologies and Islam." *IQ*, 30 (1986), 5-19.

0022 BASSIOUNI, M. CHERIF. "A Search for Islamic Criminal Justice: An Emerging Trend in Muslim States." In *The Islamic Impulse.* Ed. Barbara F. Stowasser. London: Croom Helm, 1987, 244-54.

0023 BIGGAR, NIGEL, JAMIE S. SCOTT, and W. SCHWEIKER, eds. *Cities of God: Faith, Politics and Pluralism in Judaism, Christianity and Islam*. Contributions to the Study of Religion Series: no. 16. Westport, CT: Greenwood Press, 1986, 244 p.

A collection of essays analyzing the nexus between religious faith and political action in the heritage of Jews, Christians, and Muslims. Essays on Islam suffer from the relative absence of an historical approach; they tend to emphasize the current Islamic resurgence, perhaps due to its topical appeal. Authors include Fazlur Rahman, Charles J. Adams, Marvin Zonis, and Khalid Bin Sayeed.

0024 BINDER, LEONARD. *Islamic Liberalism: A Critique of Development Ideologies*. Chicago: University of Chicago Press, 1988, 399 p.

Essentially a Foucaultian analysis of the 'discursive shaping' of the liberal Islamic paradigm. Beginning with an exposition of liberalism and the premise that "the reduction of western cultural pressure" has weakened the position of Muslim liberals vis-a-vis traditionalists and fundamentalists, the author turns his attention to the dialectic in contemporary Islamic revival texts between 'western' ideas, such as those contained in liberalism, and the Islamists' world view. He devotes a chapter to the secularist position, represented by the writings of Ali Abd al-Raziq; a chapter to Sayyid Qutb; a chapter to several Marxist interpretations of Islam; and a chapter to the works of Tariq al-Bishri.

0025 BOUTALEB, ABDELHADI. "Information Policy in Islam." *IT*, 4(1986), 7-11.

0026 AL-BRAIK, NASSER AHMED M. "Islam and World Order: Foundations and Values." Ph.D. diss., American University, 1986, 302 p.

0027 CARRE, OLIVIER, ed. *Islam and the State in the World Today*. New Delhi: Manohar Publishers, 1987, 279 p.

French scholars, representing a variety of disciplines, look at the impact of Islam on the state in Egypt, Syria, Lebanon, Turkey, Iran, Southeastern Europe, the Soviet Muslim Republics, China, Niger, Senegal, and the Malay Archipelago. While there are a number of useful studies, some, in fact, only provide the historical background, (up to the mid-1970s) for the contemporary period.

0028 CHATTY, HABIB. "Islam Finds Itself." In *The Islamic Impulse*. Ed. Barbara F. Stowasser. London: Croom Helm, 1987, 217-25.

0029 COLE, JUAN R., and NIKKI R. KEDDIE, eds. *Shi'ism and Social Protest*. New Haven, CT: Yale University Press, 1986, 325 p.

Offers a comparative approach to the study of Shi'ite social protest movements. The collection of essays demonstrates that the Iranian experience, while a major example, is not the only manifestation of a nexus between Shi'ism and politics. Variations in ideological interpretation and practice arise from different social, economic, and political contexts. Countries covered are Iran, Iraq, Lebanon, Saudi Arabia, the Gulf States, and Afghanistan.

0030 COWARD, HAROLD. "Religious Pluralism and Islam." In *Pluralism: Challenge to World Religions*. Maryknoll, NY: Orbis Books, 1985, 46-62.

This chapter of Coward's book on world religions concentrates on the encounter of Islam with other faiths, the Islamic view of Judaism, Christianity, Buddhism and Hinduism, and assesses whether Muslims have succeeded in understanding other religious traditions. A section deals with militant responses in modern Islam in which the writings of Sayyid Qutb (about Christians and Jews in particular) are of special interest.

0031 CUDSI, ALEXANDER S., and ALI E. DESSOUKI, eds. *Islam and Power.* Baltimore, MD: John Hopkins University Press, 1981, 204 p.
A collection of essays dealing largely with theoretical issues, containing titles such as "The Ideologization of Islam" (Ali Merad) and "Towards a Muslim Theory of History" (Thomas Naff). Other essays, such as Alexandre Bennigsen's "Official Islam and Sufi Brotherhoods in the Soviet Union Today" attempt to provide some insight into the origins of current resurgence of Islam in specific countries and the goals of Islamic reform movements.

0032 DAVIS, ERIC. "The Concept of Revival and the Study of Islam and Politics." In *The Islamic Impulse.* Ed. Barbara F. Stowasser. London: Croom Helm, 1987, 37-58.

0033 DAWISHA, ADEED, ed. *Islam in Foreign Policy.* New York: Cambridge University Press, 1984, 250 p.
Eleven articles plus an introduction to the role of Islam in foreign policy. Covers Iran, Saudi Arabia, Pakistan, Libya, Egypt, Morocco, Nigeria, Iraq, Indonesia, and the Soviet Union.

0034 DEGENHARDT, HENRY W., ed. *Revolutionary and Dissident Movements: An International Guide.* 2d ed. Detroit, MI: Gale, 1988, 600 p.

0035 DEKMEJIAN, R. HRAIR. "The Anatomy of Islamic Revival: Legitimacy Crises, Ethnic Conflict and the Search for Islamic Alternatives." *MEJ*, 34 (Winter 1980), 1-12.

0036 _____. "Charismatic Leadership in Messianic and Revolutionary Movements: The Mahdi (Muhammad Ahmad) and the Messiah (Shabbatai Zevi)." In *Religious Resurgence, Contemporary Cases in Islam, Christianity, and Judaism.* Eds. Richard T. Antoun and Mary E. Hegland. Syracuse, NY: Syracuse University Press, 1987, 78-107.

0037 _____. "Islamic Revival: Catalysts, Categories, and Consequences." In *The Politics of Revivalism: Diversity and Unity.* Ed. Shireen T. Hunter. Bloomington and Indianapolis, IN: Indiana University Press, 1988, 3-22.

0038 _____. "The Islamic Revival in the Middle East and North Africa." *CH*, 78 (April 1980), 169-74.

0039 DOBBIN, CHRISTINE. *Islamic Revivalism in a Changing Peasant Economy.* London: Curzon Press, 1987, 328 p.

0040 DONOHUE, JOHN J., and JOHN L. ESPOSITO, eds. *Islam in Transition: Muslim Perspectives.* New York: Oxford University Press, 1982, 322 p.
Selected primary texts by Muslim thinkers that reflect a variety of modern Islamic perspectives on a wide range of issues. This volume surveys Muslim responses to the challenge of modernity, which emphasize the need to revive and renew the strength of the global Muslim community. A section presents writings by leading figures of the contemporary Islamic resurgence from Egypt, Pakistan, and Iran.

0041 EICKELMAN, DALE F. "Changing Interpretations of Islamic Movements." In *Islam and the Political Economy of Meaning*. Ed. William R. Roff. Berkeley, CA: University of California Press, 1987, 13-30.

0042 ENAYAT, HAMID. *Modern Islamic Political Thought*. Modern Middle East Series: no. 8. Austin, TX: University of Texas Press, 1982, 220 p.
A discussion of the major trends in twentieth-century Muslim political thought. It examines the ways in which traditional Islamic heritage impinges on modern thought, especially with regard to the political differences and areas of convergence between Sunnism and Shi'ism; the concept of the Islamic state; and Muslim responses to the "alien" ideologies of nationalism, democracy, and socialism. The author looks at the writings of Muslim intellectuals primarily in Egypt and Iran but also in Pakistan, India, Lebanon, Syria and Iraq. The last chapter discusses Shi'i modernism including the roles of constitutionalism, *taqiyya* and martyrdom in Iranian politics.

0043 _____. "The Resurgence of Islam, 1: The Background." *HT*, 30 (February 1980), 16-22.

0044 ENGINEER, ASHGAR ALI. *Islam and Revolution*. Flushing, NY: Asia Book Corporation, 1984, 268 p.

0045 ESPOSITO, JOHN L. *Islam and Politics*. rev. 2d ed. Contemporary Issues in the Middle East Series. Syracuse, NY: Syracuse University Press, 1987, 302 p.
A revised edition of a study of Islamic resurgence, this book begins with a review of the historical relationship of Islam to politics and revival and reform movements in Islamic history. The main focus of the book is an analysis of major recent developments in the Muslim world. While attempting to give a general overview, the author draws examples from various parts of the Muslim world: Africa, Arabia, the Arab East, Iran, Turkey and South Asia. Among the topics considered are modernization, law, education, women, *jihad*, Shi'i Islam and political protest, the Muslim Brotherhood, and the *Jama'at-i Islami*. Includes discussion of the works of Jamal al-Din Afghani, Hassan al-Banna, Sayyid Qutb, Mawlana Mawdudi, Muhammad Iqbal, Ali Shar'iati, and Ruhollah Khomeini. This edition adds the Sudan and Lebanon to the discussion of countries experiencing Islamic revival.

0046 _____. "Islamic Resurgence." *PMVB*, no. 109 (1987), 2-21.

0047 _____. *Islamic Revivalism*. Occasional Paper, no. 3. Washington, DC: American Institute for Islamic Affairs, 1986, 17 p.
A presentation of Islamic revivalism for the non-specialist reader. Includes recent history, ideology, country profiles and descriptions of major fundamentalist groups.

0048 _____, ed. *Islam and Development: Religion and Socio-Political Change*. Syracuse, NY: Syracuse University Press, 1980, 268 p.

0049 _____, ed. *Voices of Resurgent Islam*. New York: Oxford University Press, 1983, 294 p.
The introduction of this edited volume provides a brief overview of the Islamic world-view and religion and politics in the modern Muslim world. Sections I and II contain essays by scholars of contemporary Islam and include studies of such

Muslim activists as Sayyid Qutb, Mawlana Mawdudi, Muammar al-Qadhafi, Ruhollah Khomeini, Muhammad Iqbal and Ali Shar'iati. The third section presents selections of writings by Muslims who have been active in the Islamic movement: Khurshid Ahmad, Al-Sadiq al-Mahdi, Hassan al-Turabi, Isma'il al-Faruqi, Khalid Ishaque and Kemal Faruki. Issues covered in this section range from the question of change and adaptation, the modern Islamic state, democracy, Zionism, economic development and the present and future implications of the Islamic trend.

0050 AL FARUQI, ISMA'IL R. "Islam and the Social Sciences." *Itt*, 14 (1977).

0051 _____. "The Islamic Critique of the Status Quo of Muslim Society." In *The Islamic Impulse*. Ed. Barbara Stowasser. London: Croom Helm, 1987, 226-43.

0052 _____. *Tawhid: Its Relevance for Thought and Life.* Muslim Training Manual, vol. 2. Kuala Lumpur: The International Institute of Islamic Thought, 1982, 367 p.

0053 AL FARUQI, ISMA'IL R. and ABDULLAH OMAR NASSEEF, eds. *Social and Natural Sciences: The Islamic Perspective.* Sevenoaks, Kent: Hodder and Stoughton, 1981, 177 p.

0054 AL-FARUQI, LAMYA. "Islamization Through The Sound Arts." *AJISS*, 3 (December 1986), 171-81.

0055 FERDINAND, KLAUS and MEHDI MOZAFFARI, eds. *Islam: State and Society*. Studies on Asian Topics: no. 12. London: Curzon Press; Riverdale, MD: Riverdale, 1988, 219 p.

0056 FISCHER, MICHAEL M.J. "Islam and the Revolt of the Petit Bourgeoisie." *Daedalus*, 111 (Winter 1982), 101-25.

0057 *From Muslim to Islamic*. Proceedings of the Fourth Annual Convention of the Association of Muslim Social Scientists, Indianapolis, Indiana, 1976, 72 p.

0058 GILSENAN, M. *Recognizing Islam: Religion and Society in the Modern World*. New York: Pantheon Books, 1983, 287 p.
A discussion of Islam in culture and society, this book is an anthropological study of the distinctive forms and functions of Islamic institutions in different Arab societies. It illustrates the various ways similar Islamic beliefs and institutions manifest themselves from one community to another. The author shows how people have reformulated Islam to respond to the pressures of western penetration.

0059 HADDAD, YVONNE YAZBECK, BYRON HAINES and ELLISON FINDLY, eds. *The Islamic Impact*. Syracuse, NY: Syracuse University Press, 1984, 249 p.
A collection of ten essays plus an introduction on the development of Islam-- in both its historical and contemporary settings -- focusing on how the faith permeates many aspects of Muslim life. Topics include Islam and politics, education and science, economics, law, women, mysticism, art and music.

0060 HALLIDAY, FRED, and HAMZA ALAVI, eds. *State and Ideology in the Middle East and Pakistan*. London: MacMillian, 1988, 267 p.

0061 HANAFI, HASSAN. "The Origin of Modern Conservatism and Islamic Fundamentalism." In *Islamic Dilemmas: Reformers, Nationalists and Industrialization.* Ed. Ernest Gellner. New York: Mouton Publishers, 1985, 94-103.

0062 HAQ, M. "The Muslim World League: A New Trend in Panislamism." *Encounter,* no. 54 (April 1979), 9 p.

0063 HUNTER, SHIREEN T. "Islamic Fundamentalism: What it Really is and Why it Frightens the West." *SAIS Review,* 6 (Winter-Spring 1986), 189-200.

0064 _____, ed. *The Politics of Islamic Revivalism: Diversity and Unity.* Bloomington, IN: University of Indiana Press, 1988, 303 p.
An edited volume of working papers by the Middle East Program of the Center for Strategic and International Studies which includes excellent papers on the west Bank and Gaza Strip, Kuwait, Bahrain, Morocco, Tunisia, Algeria as well as other Muslim nations. It updates prior studies on revival in different countries and places them in historical and developmental context.

0065 HUSSAIN, ASAF. "Islamic Awakening in the Twentieth Century: An Analysis and Selective Bibliography." *TWQ,* 10 (April 1988), 1005-23.

0066 _____. *Islamic Movements in Egypt, Pakistan, and Iran: an Annotated Bibliography.* New York: Mansell, 1983, 182 p.
A guide to English-language literature on Islamic movements in three countries.

0067 _____. *Political Perspectives on the Muslim World.* New York: St. Martin's Press, 1984, 220 p.
This book discusses the five approaches the author suggests exist for studying the Muslim world: modernization theory, Marxist theory, the elite approach, the ideologies (democracy, nationalism, and socialism), and the Islamic perspective. Each approach is accompanied by brief case studies.

0068 HYMAN, ANTHONY. *The Muslim Fundamentalism.* Conflict Studies no. 174. London: The Institute for the Study of Conflict, 1985, 27 p.

0069 IQBAL, JAVED. "The Concept of State in Islam." *AJIS,* 1 (1984), 11-26.

0070 *Islam and Contemporary Society.* London: Longman in Association with The Islamic Council of Europe, 1982, 279 p.

0071 ISMAEL, TAREQ Y. and JACQUELINE S. ISMAEL. *Government and Politics in Islam.* New York: St. Martin's Press, 1985, 177 p.
Except for introductory chapters on classical Islamic political thought and nineteenth and twentieth century reformers, this book is devoted to a discussion of contemporary Islamic political activism in the Middle East. It traces the evolution of two interrelated themes -- political legitimacy and accountability-- that have been central in Islamic political thought generally and take on a particular urgency in the context of the contemporary resurgence of Islam in politics. In short, in the analysis of Islamic revivalist groups, modern political institutions are judged to have failed to realize unity, while existing regimes have found it necessary to legitimate their rule officially via Islamic symbols.

0072 ISRAELI, RAPHAEL. "The New Wave of Islam." *IJ*, 34 (Summer 1979), 369-90.

0073 JANSEN, JOHANNES J.G. "Tafsir, Ijma', and Modern Muslim Extremism." *Orient*, 27 (1986), 642-46.
Provides the "four groups of passages from the Koran" from which Muslim radicals of today find justification for political violence.

0074 JITMOUD, JAMILAH. "Principles of Jihad in the Qur'an and Sunnah." In *State Politics and Islam*. Ed. Mumtaz Ahmed. Indianapolis, IN: American Trust Publications, 1986, 133-48.

0075 JITMOUD, LINDA KAY KOLOCOTRONIS. "An Intellectual Historical Study of Islamic Jihad During the Life of Muhammad and in the Twentieth Century." Ph.D. diss., Ball State University, 1985, 279 p.
Attempts to clarify the definition and to determine the proper application of the Islamic concept of *jihad*. Instances of *jihad* in the life of Muhammad and in twentieth-century Islamic thought are examined. Contemporary manifestations of *jihad* arise from the Islamic revival movement, and are used as a means of implementing basic Islamic principles, whether in the battlefield, the legislature or the print media. Examples of contemporary *jihad* included in the study are: the establishment of Pakistan; the Islamic Republic of Iran; the revivalist movement in Egypt; and the Islamic rebellion against Soviet occupation of Afghanistan.

0076 KARPAT, KEMAL H. "Elites and the Transmission of Nationality and Identity." *CAS*, 5, (1986), 5-24.

0077 KERIMOV, G.M. OGLY. "The Socio-Political Aspects of the Modern Islamic Mission." In *Islam: State and Society*. Eds. Klaus Ferdinand and Mehdi Mozaffari. London: Curzon Press, 1988, 39-50.

0078 KERN, HARRY F. "The Organization of the Islamic Conference." *AAA*, no. 20 (Spring 1987), 96-106.
There is a correction to the article in no. 22.

0079 KETTANI, M. ALI. *Muslim Minorities in the World Today*. London and New York: Mansell, 1986, 267 p.
This book includes chapters on Muslim minorites in Europe, the USSR, China, Asia, Africa, and North and Latin America. Provides information of demography, political organization, local institutions, and relations with the majority community. The author insists that for Muslim minorities to flourish, they need to be isolationists.

0080 KHADDURI, MAJID. "Revival of Islam." Chap. in *Political Trends in the Arab World. The Role of Ideas and Ideals in Politics*. Baltimore, MD: Johns Hopkins Press, 1970, 55-88.

0081 KHALL-AF, 'ABD AL-MUNI'IM MUHAMMAD. *Islamic Materialism and its Dimensions*. Trans. Hussein M. ed Gayyar. Cairo: Supreme Council for Islamic Affairs, A.R.E., 1971, 293 p.

0082 AL-KHATIB, N.A. "Islamic Thought and Political Parties." *IT*, 4 (1986), 12.

0083 KHURI, FUAD I. "The Ulama: A Comparative Study of Sunni and Shi'a Religious Officials." *MES*, 23 (July 1987), 291-312.

0084 KRAMER, MARTIN S. *Political Islam*. Beverly Hills, CA: Sage Publications, 1980, 88 p.

0085 LAFFIN, JOHN. *Holy War, Islam Fights*. London: Grafton, 1988, 240 p.
A sensationalist account of the hostile confrontation between American power and the Muslim, largely Iranian, call to *jihad*. Reduces Islam and "Islamic" power to terrorism. Dramatizes the significance of Islamic militantism in the late twentieth century, and capitalizes on western insecurity.

0086 LAPIDUS, IRA M. *A History of Islamic Societies*. Cambridge: Cambridge University Press, 1988, 1002 p.
A comprehensive survey of Islamic history. The author provides an overview of the development of Islamic history and culture from the advent of Islam to the present and from Africa to Asia.

0087 LAWRENCE, BRUCE B. "Muslim Fundamentalist Movements: Reflections Toward a New Approach." In *The Islamic Impulse*. Ed. Barbara F. Stowasser. London: Croom Helm, 1987, 15-36.

0088 LEWIS, BERNARD. "The Return of Islam." *Commentary*, 1 (January 1974), 39-49. Reprinted in *Middle East Review*, 12 (1979), 17-30.

0089 LINGAWI, WAHEEB ABDALLAH. "Modernization and Preservation of the Islamic Urban Heritage." Ph.D. diss., Claremont Graduate School, 1988, 274 p.

0090 LIPPMAN, THOMAS W. *Islam: Politics and Religion in the Muslim World*. Foreign Policy Association Headline Series, no. 258. (March/April 1982) New York: Foreign Policy Association, Inc., 64 p.
This pamphlet is designed for use in classrooms, seminars, discussion groups, etc. The author identifies what he considers to be the salient factors contributing to Muslim political activism and alienation from the west. The pervasive tone is that "militant" Islam, which he considers to be a growing menace, is jeopardizing western ideals and interests.

0091 LITTLE, DAVID, ABDULAZIZ SACHEDINA, and JOHN KELSAY. *Human Rights and the Conflicts of Culture: Western and Islamic Prespectives on Religious Liberty*. Columbia, SC: University of South Carolina Press, 1988, 112 p.
A thought-provoking exercise in comparative ethics. The authors provide a comparative study of the western and Islamic traditions on the relationship between religion and human rights, focusing on freedom of religion and conscience. Through understanding and culturally sensitivity, the authors provide a critical analysis.

0092 MacEOIN, DENIS and AHMED AL-SHAHI, eds. *Islam in the Modern World*. New York: St. Martin's Press, 1983, 148 p.

0093 MITCHELL, RICHARD P. "The Islamic Movement: Its Current Condition and Future Prospect." In *The Islamic Impulse*. Ed. Barbara F. Stowasser. London: Croom Helm, 1987, 75-86.

0094 MOINUDDIN, HASAN. *The Charter of The Islamic Conference: The Legal and Economic Framework.* New York: Oxford University Press, 1987, 322 p.

A legal analysis of the Charter of the Islamic Conference and selected economic agreements. The purpose is to illustrate the legal bases of inter-regional cooperation among Islamic states in international relations. The book describes Islamic concepts of *jihad,* property rights, treaties, sovereignty, abrogation and investment in the context of global politics and international law.

0095 MORTIMER, EDWARD. *Faith and Power: The Politics of Islam.* New York: Random House, 1982, 432 p.

The author claims to look at an "Islamic" approach to politics, past and present, and provides, in a lengthy introduction, a overview of Islamic civilization. He points to seventh-century *Kharijites* as rebels against the Islamic establishment and argues that they serve as prototypes for today's Islamic militants. Presents six case studies: Turkey; Saudi Arabia; Pakistan; the Muslim Brotherhood; Iran; and Soviet Central Asia.

0096 MOZAFFARI, MEHDI. *Authority in Islam, from Muhammad to Khomeini.* Trans. Michel Vale. Armonk, NY and London: M.E. Sharpe, 1987, 127 p.

0097 MROUE, HUSSEIN. "A Study of Islamic Organizations." *WMR,* 30 (April 1987), 88-94.

0098 MUZAFFAR, CHANDRA. "Islamic Resurgence: A Global View." In *Islam and Society in Southeast Asia.* Eds. Taufik Abdullah and Sharon Siddique. Singapore: Institute of Southeast Asian Studies, 1986, 5-39.

0099 AN-NA'IM, ABDULLAHI A. "Religious Minorities Under Islamic Law and the Limits of Cultural Relativism." *HRQ,* 9 (1987), 1-18.

0100 NAHAS, MARIDI. "State-Systems and Revolutionary Challenge: Nasser, Khomeini, and the Middle East." *IJMES,* 17 (November 1985), 507-27.

0101 NASR, SEYYED HOSSEIN. *Islam and the Plight of Modern Man.* London: Longman, 1975, 161 p.

This well-written philosophical account focuses on the dilemma of the present-day Muslim: the tension between faith (*iman*) and materialistic modernism, between two contradictory world views. Having witnessed the west excel in economic and military fields, the contemporary Muslim is, according to the author, susceptible to the strong pull of everything else coming from the west and prone to venerate western ideals and aesthetics over those of his own Islamic tradition. To offset this condition he posits Islamic spiritual heritage, specifically mysticism and Sufism, as providing solutions to the problems of modernity for Muslims and non-Muslims alike.

The author gives some attention to Islam in historical and contemporary settings in Iran and the Arab world.

0102 _____. *Traditional Islam in the Modern World.* New York: Rutledge, Chapman & Hall, 1989, 320 p.

0103 _____. "Islam in the Islamic World, An Overview." In *Islam in the Contemporary World.* Ed. Cyriac K. Pullapilly. Notre Dame, IN: Cross Roads Books, 1980, 1-20.

0104 _____, ed. *Islamic Spirituality: Foundations.* World Spirituality Series. New York: Crossroad, 1987, 450 p.

Presents the foundations of Islamic spirituality from its roots in the Qur'an, the Hadith, and the Pillars to the basic theologies of Sunni, Shi'ite and Isma'ili sects. Female spirituality, Sufism, the Islamic doctrines of God, the natural order, and eschatology are explored in depth.

0105 PETERS, RUDOLPH. *Islam and Colonialism: the Doctrine of Jihad in Modern History.* Religion and Society Series. The Hague; Hawthorne, NY: Mouton de Gruyter, 1979, 245 p.

Begins with a review of the classical doctrine of *jihad* and then examines the religiously-inspired reactions of Sunni Muslims against European colonialism and secular nationalism in modern history. Characterizes *jihad* literature as (1) mobilizing and/or (2) instructional. The book treats Muslim resistance to British colonialism in India; Algerian resistance to French colonialism; the Mahdist movement in the Sudan; the Urabi revolt in Egypt; Sanusi resistance to Italian colonialism in Libya; the Ottoman declaration of *jihad* in World War I; and Muslim opposition to the British mandate in Palestine, Zionism and the state of Israel. A very thorough yet concise and well-written survey of scriptural bases for and political aspects of the doctrine of *jihad.*

0106 PIPES, DANIEL. *In the Path of God: Islam and Political Power.* New York: Basic Books, 1983, 373 p.

This book attempts to provide a scholarly historical analysis of Muslim civilization as a primer for those who want to understand and prepare for conflict in the Muslim world. The approach is disparaging of Muslim history. The author distorts events as well as the work of other scholars.

0107 _____. "'This World is Political!!' The Islamic Revival of the Seventies." *Orbis,* 24 (Spring 1980), 9-41.

0108 PISCATORI, JAMES P. *Islam in a World of Nation-States.* New York: Cambridge University Press, 1986, 193 p.

Author argues that the modern nation-state and its authority have become legitimate in Muslim public discourse, the Islamic theory of the *umma* notwithstanding. While contemporary Islamic revival movements emphasize the universalism of Islam and often denounce the divisiveness of nationalism, many Muslims consider the nation-state to be the current appropriate milieu that provides the proper set of institutions to govern the Muslim community as an intermediate step toward forming a global Islamic order.

0109 _____, ed. *Islam in the Political Process.* New York: Cambridge University Press, 1983, 240 p.

Dealing essentially with contemporary politics and the movement toward Islamization, this collection of essays covering several countries attempts to explore the political relevance of Islam. A brief introduction sets out two general approaches to the study of Islamic politics and the difficulties of identifying and studying something commonly recognized as 'Islamic' politics.

Countries studied are: Algeria, Egypt, Iraq, Saudi Arabia, the Sudan, Syria, Senegal, Turkey, Iran, Pakistan and Indonesia. The concluding chapter, written by Albert Hourani, identifies some common themes in the country studies: the search for beliefs and symbols in a rapidly changing world and the political language of Islam; the appearance of new actors in the political process; urbanization; and the impact of mass communications.

0110 POLONSKAYA, L.R., ed. *Islam in the Modern Politics of Oriental Countries (the late 1970s and the early 1980s)*. Moscow: Nauka Publishers, 1986, 27 p.

0111 PRIMAKOV, YE. M. "Dialectics of Social Development and Ideological Struggle. The Wave of 'Islamic Fundamentalism': Problems and Lessons." *SOS*, (Moscow), (1987), 7-20.

0112 PULLAPILLY, CYRIAC K., ed. *Islam in the Contemporary World*. Notre Dame, IN: Cross Roads Books, 1980, 420 p.

0113 QADRI, ANWAR AHMAD. *Justice in Historical Islam*. Lahore; Chicago: Kazi Publications, 1968, 145 p.

0114 AL-QARADAWI, YUSUF. *Islamic Awakening Between Rejection and Extremism*. Issues of Islamic Thought Series, no. 2. Herndon, VA: International Institute of Islamic Thought, 1987, 123 p.

0115 QUDDUS, SYED ABDUL. *The Challenge of Islamic Renaissance*. Karachi: Royal Book Company, 1987, 243 p.

0116 QURAISHI, M. TARIQ, ed. *Islam: A Way of Life and a Movement*. Indianpolis, IN: American Trust Publications, 1984, 221 p.
  Presents Islam as the remedy to the problems of contemporary, amoral times. Most of the writings appeared in *al-Ittihad*, the journal of the Muslim Students' Association of North America, between 1969 and 1982. Among the topics covered are Muhammad's prophethood, the Islamic state and the welfare state, political rights, gender roles, Islamic dress and Islamic art. Selections by Maududi are included.

0117 RAHMAN, FAZLUR. *Islam & Modernity: Transformation of an Intellectual Tradition*. Publications of the Center for Middle Eastern Studies: no. 15. Chicago: University of Chicago Press, 1982, 172 p.
  A study of the development of Islamic education and intellectualism, including an assessment of their deficiencies and strengths, and of modernization efforts of the past century. The author stresses what he sees as the unity, sense of direction, or *weltanschauung* embodied in the Qur'an and the Sunna which has been obscured by centuries of exegesis, a dysfunctional educational system, foreign accretion and Islamic jurisprudence. Discusses the varying impact of western influence and modernism in different regions of the Muslim world and the nature of the Muslim responses, as well as the altered circumstances following political independence at the middle of this century. Included is a discussion of the thought of Sir Sayyid Ahmad Khan, Jamal al-Din al-Afghani, Namik Kemal, Muhammad Abdu and the society of *Jama'at-i Islami*. The book ends with the author's suggestions for rejuvenating Islamic education and sciences and reinvigorating creativity.

0118 _____. "Islam and Political Action: Politics in the Service of Religion." In *Cities of Gods: Faith, Politics, and Pluralism in Judaism, Christianity and Islam*. Eds. Nigel Biggar, Jamie S. Scott, and William Schweiker. Westport, CT: Greenwood Press, 1986,

0119 _____. "Islamic Modernism: Its Scope and Alternatives." *IJMES*, 1 (1970), 317-33.

0120 _____. "Non-Muslim Minorities in an Islamic State." *JIMMA*, 7 (1986), 13-24.

0121 RATHMANN, LOTHAR and HOLGER PREISLER. *Tradition in Movement: The Islamic Revival in the Countries of the Near East and North Africa.* Berlin: Akademie Verlag, 1986, 32 p.

0122 ROFF, WILLIAM R., ed. *Islam and the Political Economy of Meaning.* Berkeley, CA: University of California Press, 1987, 295 p.
A collection of essays by sociologists, historians and anthropologists which explore the nature of Muslim social and political action as well as the interaction between belief systems and the exigencies of daily living. It places into the historial context of capitalist global relations the local efforts to create and sustain shared understandings of what it means to 'be Muslim.' Complexities of meanings and objectives, as well as the impact of various structural determinants on the evolution of Muslim discourse, are illuminated in many of these essays.

0123 RUTHVEN, MALISE. "Islamic Politics in the Middle East and North Africa." In *The Middle East and North Africa 1988.* London: Europa Publications, 1987, 138-152.

0124 SACHEDINA, ABDULAZIZ ABDULHUSSEIN. *Islamic Messianism: The Idea of the Mahdi in Twelver Shi'ism.* Albany, NY: State University of New York Press, 1980, 230 p.
This book presents one of the major doctrinal components of Shi'a Islam, the belief that the Twelfth Imam disappeared in the ninth century A.D., and will return at the end of time to bring justice to the world. The prevailing legal and political conditions which influenced the development of Shi'ite messianic doctrine, as well as Shi'ite traditions concerning the functions of the Imam, are taken into consideration in the author's analysis.

0125 SAIEDI, NADER. "What is Islamic Fundamentalism?" In *Prophetic Religions and Politics: Religion and the Political Order.* vol. 1. Eds. Jeffrey K. Hadden and Anson Shupe. New York: Paragon House Publishers, 1986, 173-95.

0126 SAIKAL, AMIN. "Islam: Resistance and Reassertion." *WT*, 43 (1987), 191-94.

0127 SALAHUDDIN, M. "Political Obligation: Its scope and Limits in Islamic Political Doctrine." *AJISS*, 3 (1986), 247-64.

0128 SARDAR, ZIAUDDIN. *Islamic Futures: The Shape of Ideas to Come.* London: Mansell Publishing, 1985, 367 p.
Considers options for Muslims in the modern world, and rejects the late nineteenth and early twentieth century "modernist" model in favor of an Islamic paradigm which is less accommodating of western values. The author argues that Muslims need to assess the "Islamicity" of available options in light of a "matrix of Islamic concepts" before making choices that will shape their future. Principally, technologies adopted from the west are suspect.

0129 SAYEED, KHALID BIN. "Islamic Resurgence and Societal Change." *IC*, 60 (January 1986), 45-60.
Author argues that Islam is not like any other religion, and that Islamic resurgence is not like the revival of fundamentalism in western societies. Islam

differs in that it does not allow the separation of religion and politics, and offers a different model of development. Islamic resurgence is a continuing effort to shape Islamic society in line with its own unique ideology, to create a Muslim community (*umma*) which serves as a model for all mankind. Article discusses three types of Muslim response to western encroachment, represented by Saudi Arabia, Iran, and Pakistan.

0130 SAYEED, S. M. "Human Rights In Islam." *HamdIs*, 9 iii (1986), 67-75.

0131 SERAJUDDIN, ALAMGIR MUHAMMAD. "Shari'ah Law and Society: Continuity and Change in the World of Islam." *IMA*, 18 (May-August 1987), 119-32.

0132 SHEPARD, WILLIAM. "'Fundamentalism' Christian and Islamic." *Religion*, 17 (October 1987), 355-78.

0133 _____. "Islam and Ideology: Towards a Typology." *IJMES*, 19 (August 1987), 307-36.

0134 SIDDIQUI, DILNAWAZ A. "Human Resource Development: A Muslim World Perspective." *AJISS*, 4 (December 1987), 277-94.
    This article examines different conceptions of development, including the Islamic one, and asserts that the Muslim model of human resource development is the appropriate means for achieving necessary changes in less developed countries. The Muslim model entails, in part, the restoration of the mosques as the central intstitution in society, and of Islamic learning in education, as well as the "de-westernization of the Muslim psyche."

0135 SIDDIQUI, KALIM. "Nation-States as Obstacles to the Total Transformation of the Ummah." In *The Impact of Nationalism on the Muslim World*. Ed. G. Ghayasuddin. London: The Open Press and Al-Hoda Publishers, 1986, 1-22.

0136 _____, ed. *Issues in the Islamic Movement: 1984-85 (1405-06)*. London: Open Press, 1986, 462 p.

0137 SIDDIQUI, K., et. al. *The Islamic Revolution: Achievements, Obstacles, and Goals*. London: The Muslim Institute, 1980, 48 p.

0138 SONN, TAMARA. "Secularism and National Stability in Islam." *ASQ*, 9 (Summer 1987), 284-305.

0139 STODDARD, PHILIP H., DAVID C. CUTHELL and MARGARET W. SULLIVAN, eds. *Change and the Muslim World*. Syracuse, NY: Syracuse University Press, 1981, 187 p.

0140 STOWASSER, BARBARA FREYER, ed. *The Islamic Impulse*. London: Croom Helm; Washington, DC: Center for Contemporary Arab Studies, 1987, 329 p.
    A collection of conference papers that organizes a range of issues in contemporary Islam and Muslim responses in terms of secularist and normative or Islamic reformist analyses. As such it presents a useful blend of Muslim and non-Muslim reflections.

0141 SYED, ANWAR H. "Revitalising the Muslim Community." *RC*, 28 (Winter 1987), 41-54.

0142 SYEED, SAYYID MUHAMMAD. "The Islamization of Linguistics." *AJISS*, 3 (1986), 77.

0143 TAHERI, AMIR. *Holy Terror: Inside the World of Islamic Terrorism*. Bethesda, MD: Adler & Adler, 1987, 332 p.

The sensationalist title of this work reveals something of the author's bias against the current resurgence of Islam. Written by a former editor of Iran's largest newspaper, this book reduces Islamic revival to a bellicose rejection of the west generated and sustained by religious zeal.

From Egypt to Lebanon to Iran, the author paints all Islamic movements with the same brush: terroristic and anti-rational, they promote the long-term objective of conversion of all humanity to Islam. Terrorism is characterized as the means preferred by 'fundamentalists' to create an Islamic state and spread the rule of Islam worldwide. Further, the author distinguishes the 'Islamic' variety of terrorism from all other forms by virtue of its uncompromising and zealous nature. While the author argues that Islam is innately violent -- terror is "directly traceable to the basic teachings of Islam" (p. 9) -- he also maintains that Khomeini's brand of Islam does not represent the popular understanding of Islam in Iran or elsewhere. He finds that the current phenomenon of Islamic terrorism is analogous to the Inquisition; both are steeped in strict interpretations of religion but are not the only possible manifestations of religious feeling. Much of the discussion focuses on Iran, Southern Lebanon and Palestinian guerrilla groups.

0144 TALBI, MOHAMED. "Religious Liberty: A Muslim Perspective. *Islamochristiana*, 11 (1985), 99-113.

0145 TAMADONFAR, MHERAN. "The Islamic Polity and Political Leadership: A Conceptual and Theoretical Assessment." Ph.D. diss., University of Colorado at Boulder, 1986, 428 p.

Examines the question of leadership and authority in contemporary Muslim nation-states.

0146 TIBI, BASSAM. *The Crisis of Modern Islam: A Preindustrial Culture in the Scientific-Technological Age*. Trans. Judith von Sivers. Salt Lake City, UT: University of Utah Press, 1988, 192 p.

The author critiques the efforts of modern Muslims to combine Islam and politics and calls for the adoption of secular institutions.

0147 VATIKIOTIS, P.J. *Islam and the State*. London and New York: Croom Helm, 1987, 136 p.

A study prompted by current events and the recent "return" of Islam to politics in the Middle East. The author stresses the antagonisms betweeen Islam and the nation-state in this exposition of the relation between religion and politics in Islam. He compares Islamic and European history, particularly with regard to orientations toward political order, and delineates what he considers to be obstacles to pluralist politics in Islam. Of topical interest but presents nothing new.

0148 _____. "Islamic Resurgence: A Critical View." In *Islam and Power*. Eds. Cudsi and Dessouki. Baltimore, MD: Johns Hopkins University Press, 1981, 169-96.

0149 VOLL, JOHN OBERT. *Islam: Continuity and Change in the Modern World*. Boulder, CO: Westview Press, 1982, 398 p.
An authoritative study of the history and experience of the Muslim community from the eighteenth century. The length and breadth of the Muslim world are covered in what is arguably the best single volume coverage to date.

0150 _____. "Islamic Renewal and the 'Failure of the West.'" In *Religious Resurgence, Contemporary Cases in Islam, Christianity, and Judaism*. Eds. Richard T. Antoun and Mary Elaine Hegland. Syracuse, NY: Syracuse University Press, 1987, 127-44.

0151 _____. "Revivalism and Social Transformations in Islamic History." *MW*, 76 (July-October 1986), 168-80.

0152 WAARDENBURG, JACQUES. "Islam as a Vehicle of Protest." In *Islamic Dilemmas: Reformers, Nationalists and Industrialization*. Ed. Ernest Gellner. New York: Mouton Publishers, 1985, 22-48.
This article surveys recent trends in which Islam has served as a means of political and social protest, particularly in the Arab world.

0153 WAHEED-UZ-ZAMAN. "Doctrinal Position of Islam Concerning Inter-State and International Relations." *HamdIs*, 9 (1986), 81-91.

0154 WATT, W. MONTGOMERY. *Islamic Fundamentalism and Modernity*. New York and London: Routledge, Chapman and Hall, 1988, 158 p.
Repetitious of the author's earlier work. Reviews Islamic history, the beginnings of Islamic resurgence -- with mention of Abdu, al-Banna, Mawdudi, and Qadhafi -- and liberalism in Islam. In the epilogue the author makes the case for greater efforts toward intercultural reconciliation and understanding.

0155 WAUGH, EARLE H. "Islam an International Value System?" *JIMMA*, 7 (1986), 32-34.

0156 WINKEL, ERIC A. "The Ontological Status of Politics in Islam and the Epistemology of the Islamic Revival." Ph.D. diss., University South Carolina, 1988, 369 p.

0157 WRIGHT, ROBIN B. "The Islamic Resurgence: A New Phase?" *CH*, 87 (1988), 53-56.

0158 _____. *Sacred Rage: The Wrath of Militant Islam*. Touchstone Edition. New York: Simon & Schuster, 1986, 336 p.
A journalist provides an analysis of the Islamic resurgence in the Middle East, which is enlivened by biographical sketches and stories from her first hand experience, especially in Lebanon and Iran.

0159 YADEGARI, MOHAMMAD. *Ideological Revolution in the Muslim World*. Indianapolis, IN: American Trust Publication, 1983, 95 p.
The author provides his explanation for the events leading to the Iranian Revolution of 1978/79, discussing largely the motives and leadership of the

Islamic movement in Iran. The focus of this book is on the life and works of Ali Shariati.

0160 ZAMAN, S. "Place of Man in the Universe in the World-View of Islam." *Isl Std*, 25 (1986), 325-331.

0161 ZUBAIDA, SAMI. *Islam, The People and the State.* London: Routledge, 1989, 192 p.

B. ECONOMICS

0162 AHMAD, KHURSHID, et al. "Problems of Research in Islamic Economics with Emphasis on Research Administration and Finance." In *Problems of Research in Islamic Economics.* Research Papers and Proceedings. Amman: Royal Academy for Islamic Civilization Research (Al-Albait Foundation) 1987, 75-105.

0163 AHMAD, ZIAUDDIN. "Interest-Free Banking". *JIBF*, 4 (January- March 1987), 8-30.

0164 ALI, ABDEL-FATAH DIAB. "Toward an Islamic Managerial Alternative: An Analysis of Faisal Islamic Bank of Egypt." Ph.D. diss., Claremont Graduate School, 1986, 248 p.
Focuses on an Islamic managerial alternative in the resolution of administrative problems in Islamic countries, with emphasis of Egypt. Proposes an "Islamic" organizational structure, based on Islamic principles, which is aimed at creating an ideal Muslim society. Includes a case study of the Faisal Islamic Bank of Egypt.

0165 ANWAR, MUHAMMAD. "A Macroeconomic Model for Interest-Free Economies: An Integrative Study of Western and Islamic Economic Systems." Ph.D. diss., University of New Hampshire, 1985, 159 p.
Attempts to offer a macroeconomic model for economic planning and development which is consistent with interest-free financing. Compares the roles of profit-sharing and interest rates in Islamic and western economies, respectively, and finds the former, Islamic model to be better suited to developing economies.

0166 _____. *Modelling an Interest-Free Economy: A Study in Macro-Economics and Development.* Islamization of Knowledge Series, no. 4. Herndon, VA: International Institute of Islamic Thought, 1987, 140 p.

0167 _____. "Reorganization of Islamic Banking: A New Proposal." *AJISS*, 4 (December 1987), 295-304.
Presents a dual banking system model and its Islamic justifications, recommending it as the appropriate financial system for Islamic, interest-free societies.

0168 AL-ATAS, SYED FARID. "An Islamic Common Market and Economic Development." *IC*, 61 (1987), 28-38.

0169 BEININ, JOEL. "Islamic Responses to the Capitalist Penetration of the Middle East." In *The Islamic Impulse*. Ed. Barbara F. Stowasser. London: Croom Helm, 1987, 87-105.

0170 BURKI, SHAHID JAVED. "Economic Management within an Islamic Context." In *Islamic Reassertion in Pakistan*. Ed. Anita M. Weiss. Syracuse: Syracuse University Press, 1986, 49-58.

0171 CHAPRA, M. UMER. "Mokhtar M. Metwally: Role of the Stock Exchange in an Islamic Economy." (Comments) *JRIE*, 3 (1985), 75-82.

0172 _____. *Towards a Just Monetary System: A Discussion of Money, Banking and Monetary Policy in the Light of Islamic Teachings*. Islamic Economic Series, no. 8. Leicester: The Islamic Foundation, 1985, 292 p.

0173 CHOUDHURY, MASUDUL. "Micro-Economic Foundations of Islamic Economics: A Study in Social Economics." *AJISS*, 3 (1986), 231-45.

0174 HASAN, ZUBAIR. "Determination of Profit and Loss Sharing Ratios in Interest-Free Business Finance." *JRIE*, 3 (1985), 13-30.

0175 "Islamic Banking in Pakistan." (Appendix). In *Directory of Islamic Financial Institutions*. Ed. John R. Presley. London: Croom Helm, 1988, 254-97.

0176 "Islamic Banking Operations." In *Directory of Islamic Financial Institutions*. Ed. John R. Presley. London: Croom Helm, 1988, 20-36.

0177 "The Islamic Republic of Iran. Appendix: Islamic Banking Law in Iran". In *Directory of Islamic Financial Institutions*. Ed. John R. Presley. London: Croom Helm, 1988, 217-53.

0178 JOHANSEN, BABER. *The Islamic Law on Land Tax and Rent*. London: Croom Helm, 1988, 143 p.

0179 KHAN, MOHSIN S. and ABBAS MIRAKHOR, eds. *Theoretical Studies in Islamic Banking and Finance*. Houston, TX: The Institute for Research and Islamic Studies, 1987, 245 p.
Includes chapters on: "An Economic Model of a PLS Model for the Financial Sector."; "The Framework and Practice of Islamic Banking."; "The Financial System and Monetary Policy in an Islamic Economy."; and "Islamic Interest-Free Banking: A Theoretical Analysis."

0180 KHAN, MUHAMMAD AKRAM. "Islamic Banking in Pakistan." *IJIAS*, 2 no. 2 (1985), 21-35

0181 KURAN, TIMUR. "The Economic System in Contemporary Islamic Thought: Interpretation and Assessment." *IJMES*, 18 (May 1986), 135-64.

0182 MANNAN, MUHAMMAD ABDUL. *Islamic Economics: Theory and Practice*. Boulder, CO: Westview Press, 1987, 448 p.

0183 NASSER, EL-GHARIB. "The Role of Islamic Banks for Initiating an Islamic Common Market". *JIBF*, 5 (January-March 1988), 119-38.

0184 NIEBAUS, VOLKER. "An Islamic Common Market? Problems and Strategies of Economic Co-operation Among Islamic Countries." *Economics*, 5 (1987), 21-41.

0185 PRESLEY, JOHN R., ed. *Directory of Islamic Financial Institutions*. London: Croom Helm, 1988, 353 p.
The book discusses the major issues in Islamic banking and proposes an Islamic Financial System. It includes a selected bibliography on Islamic economics and banking and appendixes of Islamic banking in Malaysia and Turkey.

0186 QADRI, S.M. "The Quranic Approach to the Problem of Interest in the Context of Islamic Social System." *IC*, 60 (January 1981), 35-47.

0187 AL-SADR, MUHAMMAD BAQUIR. *Islam and Schools of Economics*. Trans. M.A. Ansari. Woodside, NY: Islamic Seminary, 1983, 160 p.

0188 SHAAELDIN, ELFATIH and RICHARD BROWN. "Toward an Understanding of Islamic Banking in Sudan: The Case of the Faisal Islamic Bank." In *Sudan: State, Capital and Transformation*. Eds. Tony Barnett and Abbas Abdelkarim. London: Croom Helm, 1988, 121-40.

0189 SIDDIQI, MUHAMMAD NEJATULLAH. "Public Expenditure in an Islamic State." *JIBF*, 4 (October-December 1987), 7-34.

0190 _____. "Muslim Economic Thinking: A Survey of Contemporary Literature." In *Studies in Islamic Economics*. Ed. Khurshid Ahmad. London: Islamic Foundation, 1980, 191-316.

0191 TALEQANI, SEYYED MAHAMMOD. *Islam and Ownership*. Lexington, KY: Mazda Publishers, 1981, 203 p.

0192 ZAIM, SABAHUDDIN. "Contemporary Turkish Literature on Islamic Economics" In *Studies in Islamic Economics*. Ed. Khurshid Ahmad. London: Islamic Foundation, 1980, 317-50

0193 ZARQA, ANAS. "Islamic Economic: An Approach to Human Welfare." In *Studies in Islamic Economics*. Ed. Khurshid Ahmad. New Delhi: Amar Prakashan, 1983, 3-18.

C. WOMEN

0194 AFSHAR, HALEH. "Women and the State: Women, Marriage and the State in Iran". In *Women, State and Ideology: Studies from Africa and Asia*. Ed. Haleh Afshar. Albany, NY: SUNY Press, 1987, 70-86.

0195 ALI, PARVEEN SHAUKAT. *Status of Women in the Muslim World: A Study in the Feminist Movement in Turkey, Egypt, Iran and Pakistan*. Lahore, Pakistan: Aziz Publishers, 1975, 248 p.

0196 ALTORKI, SORAYA. *Women in Saudi Arabia: Ideology and Behavior Among the Elite.* New York: Columbia University Press, 1986, 183 p.

A study of women of thirteen elite families in Jeddah, Saudi Arabia, belonging to three generations, by a western-educated, female anthropologist of Saudi Arabian background. Fieldwork was conducted periodically between 1971 and 1984. Describes family relationships, marriage customs, religious practices, homes and households, veiling, and official Saudi policy, especially with regard to *Wahhabi* teachings, and policy implementation. Makes reference to the works of other anthropologists who have done fieldwork in Muslim societies, such as Hildred and Clifford Geertz and Fatima Mernissi, and to scriptural bases for religiously prescribed roles and behavior. Heavy emphasis is on the significance of change in ideology and social relations.

0197 ATA, A.W. "The Impact of Westernizing and Other Factors in the Changing Status of Muslim Women (II)." *IQ*, 31 (1987), 38-56.

0198 AZ. "The Women's Struggle in Iran." *MonR*, 32 (March 1981), 22-30.

0199 AZARI, FARAH, ed. *Women of Iran: The Conflict with Fundamentalist Islam.* London: Ithaca Press, 1983, 225 p.

This volume of essays is the product of expatriate Iranian feminists who visited Iran, formed connections with women's groups there, and continued discussions of feminism and Iran upon their return to London. The essays attempt to explain Islam's appeal to women and women's participation in the Iranian revolution by describing its cultural, religious and political features.

0200 AZEREDO, SANDRA MARIA DE MATA. "Representations of Sexual Identity and Domestic Labor: Women's writings from the United States, Morocco, and Brazil." Ph.D. diss., University of California at Santa Cruz, 1986, 273 p.

Studies social relations in domestic work, specifically, the relationship between maids and housewives, as represented in the feminist writings of Fatima Mernissi (Morocco) and Grupo Ceres (Brazil). The works of Nancy Chodorow and Angela Davis are representative of the U.S.

0201 BAHRY, L. "The New Saudi Women: Modernizing in an Islamic Framework." *MEJ*, 36 (1982), 502-15.

0202 BAKHASH, HALEH E. "Veil of Fears: Iran's Retreat from Women's Rights." *NRep*, no. 3693 (28 October 1985), 15-16.

0203 BECK, LOIS and NIKKI KEDDIE, eds. *Women in the Muslim World.* Cambridge, MA: Harvard University Press, 1978, 712 p.

An early but still useful collection of studies on the status and roles of Muslim women, covering Africa to South Asia, by historians, social scientists, and legal scholars. Will need to be supplemented by studies which measure the impact of Islamic revivalism during the past decade.

0204 BOOTH, MARILYN. "Prison, Gender, and Praxis: Women's Prison Memories in Egypt and elsewhere." *MERIP*, no. 149 (November-December 1987), 35-41.

0205 CALLAWAY, BARBARA J. *Education and Emancipation of Hausa Muslim Women in Nigeria.* Publications on Women in International Development, no. 129. East Lansing, MI: Michigan State University, 1986, 29 p.

0206 _____. *Muslim Hausa Women in Nigeria: Tradition and Change*. Syracuse, NY: Syracuse University Press, 1987, 264 p.

0207 CILARDO, AGOSTINO. "The Evolution of Muslim Family Law in Egypt." *OM*, 65 (1985), 67-124.

0208 COLES, CATHERINE H. *Urban Muslim Women and Social Change in Northern Nigeria*. Publications on Women in International Development, no. 19. East Lansing, MI: Michigan State University, 1983, 28 p.

0209 ESPOSITO, JOHN L. *Women in Muslim Family Law*. Syracuse, NY: Syracuse University Press, 1982, 172 p.
    A study of Muslim family law (marriage, divorce, and inheritance) in classical and modern times. This volume delineates the development of Islamic law, presents a synthesis of classical Muslim family law, and analyzes the sources, methodology, and modern reform of family law with particular attention to Egypt and Pakistan.

0210 FATHI, ASGHAR, ed. *Women and the Family in Iran*. Leiden: E.J. Brill, 1985, 239 p.

0211 FERNEA, ELIZABETH WARNOCK, ed. *Women and the Family in the Middle East: New Voices of Change*. Austin, TX: University of Texas Press, 1985, 368 p.
    Complements Fernea's earlier anthology, *Middle Eastern Muslim Women Speak*. A collection of documents, life histories, essays, and poems drawn from ten Middle Eastern countries. The volume reflects the changing realities of women in Arab societies: the growing criticism of western models of development, the return to more indigenous traditions, issues of law, health and education, war and revolution.

0212 HADDAD, YVONNE. "Islam, Women and Revolution in Twentieth-Century Arab Thought." *MW*, 74 (July-October 1984), 137-60.

0213 HAERI, SHAHLA. "Contracts as Models for Sexual Unions: Temporary Marriage, "Mut'a," in Contemporary Iran." Ph.D. Diss., UCLA, 1985, 350 p.
    The author uses an anthropological approach to study the law of temporary marriage and examines its content in contemporary Iran. It explores the complexity of the institution, its meaning for men and women who use it, and the social implications. The data was collected in Iran in 1981-2. The analysis highlights the underlying Shi'ite conceptions concerning men, women, sexuality and marriage, and describes, the institution as administered under the Islamic Republic.

0214 HALE, SONDRA. "The Wing of the Patriarch: Sudanese Women and Revolutionary Parties." *MERIP*, no. 138 (January-February 1986), 25-30.

0215 HALL, MARJORIE and BAKHITA AMMIN ISMAIL. *Sisters under the Sun: The Story of Sudanese Women*. London: Longman Publishers, 1981, 264 p.

0216 HEGLAND, MARY ELAINE. "Political Roles of Iranian Village Women." *MERIP*, no. 138 (January-February 1986), 14-19.

0217 AL-HIBRI, AZIZAH, ed. *Women and Islam.* Elmsford, NY: Pergamon Press, 1982, 197 p.

This collection of nine essays attempts to show that sex discrimination is not a by-product of Islam but a social construct. Essays treat such topics as the representation of Eve in the Qur'an, feminist movements in Turkey, Egypt, Algeria and Yemen, laws of divorce and polygamy, and prominent women in Islamic history.

0218 HIJAB, NADIA. *Womanpower: The Arab Debate on Women at Work.* Cambridge: Cambridge University Press, 1988, 176 p.

Provides important information on legislation regarding women's rights in various Arab countries. It also discusses issues related to women's work which have been central to the debate, such as the politics surrounding family law, the polemics of nationalism, anti-colonialism, secularism, Islamic Marxism, and feminism, as well as employment opportunities for women in the Arab world. This concise study is thorough, containing information on several countries including Tunisia, South Yemen, Bahrain, Kuwait, the Arab Gulf states, Algeria, Egypt, Lebanon, and Jordan.

0219 HOFFMAN-LADD, VALERIE. "The Religious Life of Muslim Women in Contemporary Egypt." Ph.D. Diss., University of Chicago, 1986, n.p.

0220 HUSSAIN, AFTAB. *Status of Women in Islam.* Lahore: Law Publishing House, 1987, 47 p.

As Chairman Chief Justice of the Federal Shariah Court, Justice Aftab Hussain was an important participant in General Zia ul-Haq's Islamization program (1977-88) which included controversy over the implementation of Islamic laws which affected the status and role of women. This volume, written after his retirement from the bench, examines many of these issues, discussing the legal status and rights of women in Islamic jurisprudence: equality of the sexes; women's right to hold public office; marriage, divorce, and inheritance; family planning and abortion; segregation of the sexes.

0221 HUSSAIN, FREDA, ed. *Muslim Women: The Ideal and Contextual Realities.* New York: St. Martin's Press, 1984, 240 p.

A collection of essays covering a wide geographic area including Egypt, the Sudan, Tunisia, Turkey, Iran, Pakistan, and Malaysia. Looks at the role of women in society as represented in North African literature, Tunisian legal codes, and Islamic *Shari'a*; and by feminist movements in Egypt and Turkey, women's participation in revolutionary Iran, and the nationalist movement in Pakistan. Emphasis is on the discussion of the "contextual realities" the editor wants to illuminate through case studies, as opposed to theoretical understandings of the Islamic ideal for women. Most articles focus on the life conditions of women, providing information on education, employment and health care. With the exception of the article on Iran, there is no discussion of the impact of the current Islamic resurgence on Muslim women.

0222 JANSEN, WILLY. *Women without Men: Gender and Marginality in an Algerian Town.* London: E.J. Brill, 1987, 249 p.

Study of women who are widowed, divorced, or orphaned. Field work done in 1981/82 in a growing town in northern Algeria where women without men are especially plentiful. Collected data from fifty women. Women engage in activities which defy the gender hierarchy that would place them in seclusion, i.e. as religious intermediaries who facilitate communication between women and the supernatural, as assistants in fertility and birthing, etc.

0223 JENNINGS, ANNE MARGARET. "Power and Influence: Women's Associations in an Egyptian Nubian Village." Ph.D. diss., University of California at Riverside, 1985, 215 p.

Field work done in the Nubian village of Gharbaswan, with the purpose of investigating the model of Muslim society as one in which the male sphere is the dominant one, and women are excluded from important decision-making. This study challenges the validity of such a model, contending that women are actively engaged in influence, persuasion, and other attempts at control. Women use their social networks to transmit information and influence decisions in areas in which, ideologically, they have no power. Concludes that sexual segregation does not exclude women from important decision-making, but gives both sexes control over various aspects of village life. They have different areas of knowledge and expertise, which provide them alternate sources of power, self-esteem, and control.

0224 JOSEPH, SUAD. "Women and Politics in the Middle East." *MERIP*, no. 138 (January-February 1986), 3-8.

Introductory essay to special issue of *MERIP* Reports on women.

0225 KEDDIE, NIKKI. "Pakistan's Movement Against Islamization." *MERIP* no. 148 (September-October 1987), 40-41.

Keddie's observations after trips to Pakistan in 1985 and 1986 to investigate groups that have worked against Zia ul-Haq's attempts to "Islamize" Pakistan's legal system. Many of these groups are women's organizations.

0226 MASAUD, SAMAR F. "The Development of Women's Movements in the Muslim World." *HamdIs*, 8 (1985), 81-86.

0227 MASKILL, MICHELLE. *The Impact of Islamization Policies on Pakistani Women's Lives*. Publications on Women in International Development, no. 69. East Lansing, MI: Michigan State University, 1984, 23 p.

0228 MERNISSI, FATIMA. *Beyond the Veil: Male-Female Dynamics in Modern Muslim Society*. 2d ed. Bloomington, IN: Indiana University Press, 1987, 200 p.

The new introduction to this revised edition of the study (first published in 1975) discusses fundamentalism and Muslim women. The book examines the sexual lives of men and women, and the bearing Islamic law and social customs have upon them, in Muslim countries.

0229 _____. *Doing Daily Battle, Interviews with Moroccan Women*. Trans. Mary Jo Lakeland. New Brunswick, NJ: Rutgers University Press, 1989, 224 p.

The author, a Moroccan feminist, uses transcripts of taped interviews with women from a variety of walks of life providing a critical evaluation of the heritage which she describes as "obscurantist and mutilating." Most interviews are conducted among women of low-income Moroccan families. The book presents the woman's view of Moroccan society and the exigencies that have brought about fundamental changes in her social relations and access to employment and education. The introduction argues that the words of women, found in the interviews, differ substantially from the dominant male discourse, where Islamic ideology is located. Generally the interviews share three subjects in common: sex roles, the marital couple, and contraception. Mernissi suggests that a wide gap separates Islamic law and debates in religious circles about these subjects from the needs and perceptions of women.

0230 _____. "Professional Women in the Arab World: The Example of Morocco." *FI*, 7 (1987), 47-65.

0231 MINAI, NAILA. *Women in Islam, Tradition and Transition in the Middle East.* New York: Seaview Books, 1981, 283 p.
Contains a chapter on women and the Islamic revival.

0232 MOGHADAM, VAL. "Women, Work and Ideology in the Islamic Republic." *IJMES*, 20 (May 1988), 221-43.
An analysis of Islamic ideology and female employment in Iran today. Examines the Iranian regime's ideology regarding women's roles and contrast it to women's employment patterns. Also compares women's current employment patterns with those before the revolution. Concludes that much of the revolution's rhetoric discouraging female employment and encouraging domesticity has been unsuccessful. The female share of the urban labor force has not changed, and government employment for women has actually increased since 1979. The author suggests that there is a discrepancy between ideological prescriptions and economic imperatives.

0233 MOJAB, SHAHRZAD. *The Islamic Government's Policy on Womens' Access to Higher Education and its Impact on the Socio-economic Status of Women.* Publications on Women in International Development, no. 156. East Lansing, MI: Michigan State University, 1987, 20 p.

0234 MUMTAZ, KHAWAR and FARIDA SHAHEED, eds. *Women of Pakistan: Two Steps Forward, One Step Back?* London: Zed Press, 1988, 196 p.
Covers the evolution of Islam in politics; profiles on Pakistani women from 1896 to 1947 and women's organizations; veiling and seclusion of women in Pakistan; the impact of Zia ul-Haq's rule on woman's status in Pakistan; and the creation of the Women's Action Forum.

0235 MUNIR, ZAHRA. "Being Muslim and Female." *JIMMA*, 5 (1983-1984), 77-80.

0236 MUTAHHARI, MURTAZA. *On the Islamic Hijab.* Tehran: Islamic Propagation Organization, 1987, 106 p.

0237 MYNTTI, CYNTHIA. "Yemeni Workers Abroad: The Impact on Women." *MERIP*, no. 124 (June 1984), 11-16.

0238 NASHAT, GUITY, ed. *Women and Revolution in Iran.* Boulder, CO: Westview Press, 1983, 301 p.
Focuses on the role of women in the 1979 Iranian revolution and their subsequent conditions. Emphasizes the lives of elite women, and uses primary sources which are written largely by men.

0239 NAZZAL, LAILA AHMED. "The Role of Shame in Societal Transformation Among Palestinian Women on the West Bank." Ph.D. diss., University of Pennsylvania, 1986, 428 p.
Examines the moral and social order of Palestinian women on the West Bank through the concept of shame and its role in the transformation of society. Field

work was conducted from September 1984 to May 1985, among Palestinian girls and women, both Christian and Muslim, in a Palestinian community in Lebanon. The institution of shame is examined through the perceptions of these girls and women as it relates to their daily lives.

0240 OLSON, E. "Muslim Identity and Secularism in Contemporary Turkey: The Headscarf Dispute." *Anthr Q*, 58 (1985), 161-70.

0241 PEETS, LEONORA. *Women of Marrakesh*. London: C. Hurst and Company, 1988, 215 p.
A western view of Moroccan society that reflects the author's genuine fondness of the people of Morocco and her antipathy towards their religion and culture.

0242 PETEET, JULIE. "No Going Back: Women and the Palestinian Movement." *MERIP*, no. 138 (January-February 1986), 20-24.

0243 RAMAZANI, NESTA. "Arab Women in the Gulf." *MEJ*, 39 (1985), 258-76.

0244 _____. "Behind the Veil: Status of Women in Revolutionary Iran." *JSAMES*, 4 (Winter 1980), 27-36.

0245 _____. "Islamization and the Women's Movement in Pakistan." *JSAMES*, 8 (Summer 1985), 53-64.

0246 ROYANIAN, SIMIN. "A History of Iranian Women's Struggle." *RIPEH*, 3 (Spring 1979), 17-29.

0247 RUGH, ANDREA B. *Reveal and Conceal: Dress in Contemporary Egypt*. New York: Syracuse University Press, 1986, 185 p.
This study examines the significance of contemporary Islamic dress in Egypt (especially women) and its use in constructing socially meaningful categories. Includes a short discussion of the relation of modesty norms and religion to attire.

0248 SAYIGH, ROSEMARY. "Review Essay: Looking Across the Mediterranean." *MERIP*, no. 124 (June 1984), 22-26.
Reviews *Femmes de la Mediteranee*. (Monique Gadant, ed.), *Peuples Mediterraneens/Mediterranean Peoples*. no. 22/23 (Jan-June 1983), as well as briefly mentioning other related works. Discusses women in authoritarian states (Turkey, Tunisia, and brief reference to Algeria), in political movements (Palestine, Lebanon, Algeria, and Iran), the power of the family, the impact of migration, and women and culture.

0249 SHAABAN, BOUTHAINA. *Both Right and Left Handed, Arab Women Talk About Their Lives*. London: The Women's Press, 1988, 242 p.
Looks at women's situations in Lebanon, Syria, Palestine, and Algeria. Relates women's personal lives and perspectives through interviews.

0250 SMITH, JANE I. "Islam." In *Women in World Religions*. Ed. Arvin Sharma. Albany, NY: State University of New York Press, 1987, 235-50.

0251 _____, ed. *Women in Contemporary Muslim Societies*. Lewisburg, PA: Bucknell University Press, 1980, 259 p.

A collection of essays originally presented in 1975 at a workshop at the Center for the Study of World Religions at Harvard University. Topics covered include the role of women as described in contemporary Arab Islamic literature; the situations of rural women in India and Morocco; women's access to property according to Islamic law; and women, law, and social change in Iran.

0252 STOWASSER, BARBARA FREYER. "Liberated Equal or Protected Dependent? Contemporary Religious Paradigms on Women's Studies in Islam." *ASQ*, 9 (Summer 1987), 260-83.
An analysis of published material on the viewpoints of contemporary "fundamentalists" and "conservatives" concerning the status of women in present day Islamic Middle Eastern society.

0253 _____. "Religious Ideology, Women, and the Family: The Islamic Paradigm." In *The Islamic Impulse*. Ed. Barbara F. Stowasser. London: Croom Helm, 1987, 262-96.

0254 TABARI, AZAR and NAHID YEGANEH, eds. *In the Shadow of Islam: The Women's Movement in Iran*. London: Zed Press, 1983, 239 p.

0255 TAPPER, NANCY. "Gender and Religion in a Turkish town: a Comparison of Two Types of Formal Women's Gatherings." In *Women's Religious Experience*. Ed. P. Holden. London: Croom Helm, 1983, 71-88.

0256 TOUATI, FETTOUMA. *Desperate Spring: Lives of Algerian Women*. London: The Women's Press, 1987, 156 p.

0257 UTAS, BO, ed. *Women in Islamic Societies: Social Attitudes and Historical Perspectives*. Brooklyn, NY: Olive Branch Press, 1988, 252 p.
This collection of essays, mostly by Scandinavian scholars, attempts to show the complexities of women's lives in Muslim countries and the differing degrees to which women play public roles from one setting to the next. Included is discussion of the circumstances of women in Iran, Afghanistan, Albania, the western Sahel countries of Africa, Malaysia, Indonesia, Palestine, Algeria, and Turkey.

0258 WEISS, ANITA M. "Implications of the Islamization Program for Women." In *Islamic Reassertion in Pakistan*. Ed. Anita M. Weiss. Syracuse, NY: Syracuse University Press, 1986, 97-114.

0259 _____. *Women in Pakistan: Implication of the Current Program of Islamization*. Publications on Women in International Development, no. 78. East Lansing, MI: Michigan State University, 1985, 23 p.

II. AFRICA

0260 ABU-LUGHOD, IBRAHIM. "The Islamic Factor in African Politics." *Orbis*, 8 (1964), 425-44.

An article written before the resurgence of Islam which has received much attention. It was an early statement that Islam was not a spent force and deserves attention.

0261 AUSTEN, RALPH A. "Islam in African History." In *Islam in the Contemporary World*. Ed. C.K. Pullapilly. Notre Dame, IN: Cross Roads Books, 1980, 274-83.

The author gives a brief summary of the history of Islam in Africa, noting the special characteristics of African Islamic societies. He believes that with modern global communications and the current Islamic revival, Islamic societies in Africa will become increasingly closer to Islamic societies in the Middle East.

0262 BROWN, GODFREY and MERVYN HISKETT. *Conflict and Harmony in Education in Tropical Africa*. Rutherford, NJ: Fairleigh Dickinson University Press, 1976, 496 p.

0263 DADA, EBRAHIM. *The Challenge of Dawah in Southern Africa*. Durban: Islamic Dawah Movement, 1984.

0264 ESACK, FARID. "Three Islamic Strands in the South African Struggle for Justice." *TWQ*, 10 (April 1988), 473-98.

The author is a South African Muslim activist who describes the emergence of three contemporary revivalist groups in South Africa, the Muslim Youth Movement (influenced by the international Sunni Islamist groups), the Iranian-influenced Qiblah organization, and the more nationalist Call of Islam group.

0265 HARON, MUHAMMAD. "Islamic Dynamism in South Africa's Western Cape." *JIMMA*, 9 (July 1988), 366-72.

This is an article written by an important young South African Muslim scholar who is active in Islamic organizations. It provides important insight into the nature of the South African Muslim community and into the thinking of a moderate but committed Muslim.

0266 IMRAN, MUHAMMAD. "Muslim Liberation Movements in Africa." *IL*, 17 (May 1971), 35-58.

0267 KING, NOEL. "Encounters between Islam and the African Traditional Religions." In *Islam: Past Influence and Present Challenge*. Eds. A. Welch and P. Cachia. Edinburgh: Edinburgh University Press, 1979, 296-311.

This analysis starts with African Traditional Religions and shows how they interacted with Islam in the medieval, pre-European, and modern eras through short case studies. The modern case is the experience in Uganda. The author notes the continuing influence of African traditions.

0268 KRITZINGER, J.N.J. "Islam as Revival of the Gospel in Africa." *Missionalia*, 8 (1980), 89-104.

0269 MAZRUI, ALI A. "African Islam and Competitive Religion: Between Revivalism and Expansion." *TWQ*, 10 (April 1988), 499-518.

Mazrui discusses the role of Islam in the context of the "Triple Heritage" of African religious legacies - the indigenous, Christian, and Islamic. He stresses the important dimension of tolerance given to Islam and Christianity by African traditions. He also examines the two aspects of contemporary Islam, its rapid expansion and its revivalist movements.

0270 _____. "Islam, Political Leadership and Economic Radicalism in Africa." *CSSH*, 9 (1967), 274-91.

0271 MOSIMANE, M. "The Silent Swing to Islam." *Pace*, (October 1982), 33-37.

0272 McKAY, VERNON. "The Impact of Islam on Relations Among the New African States." In *Islam and International Relations*. Ed. J. Harris Proctor. New York: Praeger, 1965, 158 p.
This is a comprehensive survey of the status of Islam in most of the major African countries in the mid-1960s. The author, at that time, sees Islam as primarily a local force rather than a national or international one. Emphasis is given to the importance of more secular ideologies. This is an important example of the type of analysis that was possible in the 1960s.

0273 NAUDE, J.A. "Islam in South Africa: A General Survey." *JIMMA*, 6 (January 1985), 21-33.
This article provides a general description of the history and composition of the Muslim communities in the Union of South Africa. The author notes that in recent years new organizations have been established which reflect some of the goals of the global Islamic resurgence.

0274 NYANG, SULAYMAN S. *Islam, Christianity and African Identity*. Brattleboro, VT: Amana Books, 1984, 106 p.

0275 OASTUIZEN, G.C. *The Muslim Zanzibaris of South Africa*. Durban: University of Durban-Westville, 1982.

0276 O'BRIEN, DONALD B. CRUISE. "Islam and Power in Black Africa." In *Islam and Power*. Eds. Alexander S. Cudsi and Ali E. Hillal Dessouki. Baltimore, MD: Johns Hopkins University Press, 1981, 158-68.
The author emphasizes the role of the *tariqahs* or brotherhoods in Islamic societies in sub-Saharan Africa. One conclusion is that more formal fundamentalist-type movements are limited by the lack of knowledge of Arabic in these societies.

0277 PEEL, J.D.Y. and C.C. STEWART, eds. *Popular Islam South of the Sahara*. Manchester: Manchester University Press, and *Africa* (Journal of the International African Institute), 4 (1986), 363-464.
This is an important collection of essays on a variety of subjects related to Islam in Africa. The focus is not clear but in addition to articles on west African Islamic languages, Senegalese literature and films, there are chapters on a populist Islamic revolt in northern Nigeria, Mahdism in western Sudan, and an analysis of Islam and politics during the era of Numayri in the Sudan.

0278 PETERSEN, KIRSTEN HOLST, ed. *Religion, Development and African Identity*. Seminar Proceedings No. 17. Uppsala: Scandinavian Institute of African Studies, 1987, 163 p.

0279 VON SICARD, SIGVARD. "Islam in South Africa." *IMA*, 11 (February 1980), 58-81.

0280 _____. "The Zanzibaris in Durban." *JIMMA*, 2 (1982), 128-36.

0281 WESTERLUND, DAVID. *From Socialism to Islam? Notes on Islam as a Political Factor in Contemporary Africa*. Scandinavian Institute of African Studies, Research Report No. 61. Uppsala: Scandinavian Institute of African Studies, 1982.

0282 WINTERS, CLYDE AHMED. "The African Ummah al-Muslimin fi Brazil." *IMA*, 10 (November 1979), 1-12.

A. EAST AFRICA

0283 BONE, DAVIS S. "The Muslim Minority in Malawi and Western Education." *JIMMA*, 6, (July 1985), 412-19.
The author shows the importance of Muslim schools for the small community of Muslims in Malawi. Muslims have been slow to participate in the governmental schools.

0284 CONN, HARVIE M. "Islam in East Africa: An Overview." *IS*, 17 (1978), 75-91.

0285 ESMAIL, A. "Satpanth Ismailism and Modern Changes Within It: With Special Reference to East Africa." Ph.D. diss., Edinburgh University, 1972.

0286 KASOZI, ABDU B.K. "The Uganda Muslim Supreme Council: An Experiment in Muslim Administrative Centralization and Institutionalization. 1972-1982." *JIMMA*, 6 (January 1985), 34-52.

0287 KOKOLE, OMARI H. "The 'Nubians' of East Africa: Muslim Club or African 'Tribe'? The View from Within." *JIMMA*, 6 (July 1985), 420-48.

0288 LEWIS, I.M. *A Pastoral Democracy: A Study of Pastoralism and Politics Among the Northern Somali of the Horn of Africa*. New York: African Publishing Company, 1982, 320 p.

0289 NANJI, AZIM. "Modernization and Change in the Nizari Ismaili Community in East Africa - a Perspective." *JRA*, 6 (1974), 123-39.

0290 NIMTZ, AUGUST H., Jr. *Islam and Politics in East Africa: The Sufi Order in Tanzania*. Minneapolis: University of Minnesota Press, 1980, 234 p.
This is a useful monograph. Its primary focus is an examination of the reasons for the continuing importance in the context of modernization of a traditional Islamic organization. The author is interested in the political dimensions of the subject. Although the work does not primarily discuss a movement of the Islamic resurgence, it provides a sound introduction to the background of the resurgence.

0291 OMARI, C.K. "Christian-Muslim Relations in Tanzania: The Socio-Political Dimension." *JIMMA*, 5 (July 1984), 373-90.

B. NORTH AFRICA

0292 AN-NA'IM, ABDULLAHI AHMAD. "The Elusive Islamic Constitution: The Sudanese Experience." *Orient*, 26 (September 1985), 329-40.
Highlights aspects of the debate over Islamization in the Sudan, with emphasis on the Islamic modernist perspective.

0293 ANDERSON, LISA. "Qadhdhafi and His Opposition." *MEJ*, 40 (Spring 1986), 225-37.
A clear and relatively comprehensive discussion of the groups who represented some kind of organized opposition to Qadhafi. It appeared shortly before the U.S. attack on Tripoli, which tended to change the dynamics of opposition, but Anderson's analysis provides an important understanding of the possibilities of opposition in Libya.

0294 _____. "Qaddafi's Islam." In *Voices of Resurgent Islam*. Ed. John L. Esposito. New York: Oxford University Press, 1983, 134-49.
This article provides an introduction to the life and personality of Qaddafi as well as a summary of his major ideas. It notes that Qadhafi began as an admirer of Nasser but developed an increasingly personal interpretation of Islam which diverged significantly from the mainstream of Islamic thought.

0295 _____. "Religion and State in Libya: The Politics of Identity." *AAAPSS*, 483 (January 1986), 61-72.

0296 _____. *The State and Social Transformation in Tunisia and Libya 1830-1980*. Princeton Studies on the Near East. Princeton, NJ: Princeton University Press, 1986, 320 p.
This is an important work in developing the definition of the relationship between the state and religion in North Africa. It provides an excellent introduction to the eccentric policies of Qadhafi and to the rise and decline of secularism in Tunisia.

0297 ARKOUN, MOHAMMAD. "Algeria." In *The Politics of Islamic Revivalism: Diversity and Unity*. Ed. Shireen T. Hunter. Bloomington, IN: Indiana University Press, 1988, 171-86.
The author is himself an important contributor to the efforts by Muslims to reinterpret the foundations of the Islamic experience. In this chapter, Arkoun provides a historical summary of the major Islamic movements in Algeria during the twentieth century and an analysis of the nature of relations among state, society, and Islam in contemporary Algeria.

0298 AYOUB, MAHMOUD M. *Islam and the Third Universal Theory: The Religious Thought of Mu'ammar al-Qadhdhafi*. London: Routledge, Chapman & Hall, 1987, 200 p.

0299 BARCLAY, HAROLD B. "Sudan (North): On the Frontier of Islam." In *Religions and Societies: Asia and the Middle East*. Ed. Carlo Caldarola. Hawthorne, NY: Mouton de Gruyer, 1982, 147-70.
This chapter provides a good summary of the Islamic background in the Sudan but was written before the Islamization program of Numayri and is optimistic about the prospects of the development of religious pluralism in the Sudan.

0300 BATRAN, AZIZ A. *Islam and Revolution in Africa*. Brattleboro, VT: Amana Books, 1984, 51 p.

0301 BAUMANN, GERD. *National Integration and Local Integrity: The Miri of the Nuba Mountains in the Sudan*. Oxford: Oxford University Press, 1987, 232 p.

0302 BEARMAN, JONATHAN. *Qadhafi's Libya*. London: Zed Books, 1986, 298 p.
This study is sympathetic to the efforts of Qadhafi to create a radical transformation of Libyan society and generally believes that such a transformation has taken place. The author argues that the transformation has not created a socialist society, rather it has created significant contradictions which remain to be resolved.

0303 BENOMAR, JAMAL. "The Monarchy, the Islamist Movement and Religious Discourse in Morocco." *TWQ*, 10 (April 1988), 539-55.
The author provides an account of the development of the political structure of Morocco during the past two centuries, with an emphasis on the role of Islamic forces. The monarchy is itself a major Islamic institution and during the 1980s was able to overcome major threats from the Left and secularist parties. However, by the late 1980s, the author feels that a new radical Islamist movement has emerged which provides an important challenge to the monarchy.

0304 BOULBY, MARION. "The Islamic challenge: Tunisia since Independence." *TWQ*, 10 (April 1988), 590-614.
This article presents a history of the Islamic Tendency Movement in Tunisia, showing how it parallels the evolution of the Bourguiba regime. The Islamist tendency is seen as being an important force in the post-Bourguiba era.

0305 CHRISTELOW, ALLAN. "Ritual, Culture and Politics of Islamic Reformism in Algeria." *MES*, 23 (July 1987), 255-73.

0306 DE FEYER, KOEN. "Unveiling a Hidden Painting: Islam and North African Constitutions." *Verfassung und Recht in Ubersee*, 21 no. 1 (1988), 17-39.

0307 DURAN, KHALID. "The Centrifugal Forces of Religion in Sudanese Politics." *Orient*, 26 (1985), 572-600.

0308 DWYER, KEVIN. *Moroccan Dialogues: Anthropology in Question*. Baltimore, MD: Johns Hopkins University Press, 1982, 297 p.

0309 ESPOSITO, JOHN L. "Sudan's Islamic Experiment." *MW*, 76 (July-October 1986), 203-18.

0310 FLUEHR-LOBBAN, CAROLYN. *Islamic Law and Society in the Sudan*. London: Frank Cass, 1987, 320 p.
A comprehensive study of the history and implementation of Islamic law in the Sudan. The author combines a treatment of legislation and judicial practice, utilizing an analysis of legal texts and cases as well as the development of the women's movement to illustrate the dynamic character of the Sudanese Shari'a.

0311 HARRIS, LILLIAN CRAIG. *Libya: Qadhafi's Revolution and the Modern State*. Boulder, CO: Westview Press, 1986, 157 p.

This is a general introduction to Libya with five of the seven chapters concentrating on the Qadhafi era. It is highly critical of Qadhafi's policies but willing to recognize some accomplishments.

0312 HEGGOY, ALF ANDREW, ed. *Through Foreign Eyes: Western Attitudes Toward North Africa.* Washington, DC: University Press of America, 1982, 194p.

0313 JACOBS, SCOTT H. "The Sudan's Islamization." *CH*, 84 (May 1985), 205.
This is a critical and pessimistic analysis of Sudanese politics written in the time just before the overthrow of the Numayri regime.

0314 JOFFE, GEORGE. "Islamic Opposition in Libya." *TWQ*, 10 (April 1988), 615-31.

0315 KEDDIE, NIKKI. "The Islamic Movement in Tunsia." *MR*, 11 (1986), 26-39.

0316 MAYER, ANN E. "Islamic Resurgence or a New Prophethood: The Role of Islam in Qadhdafi's Ideology." In *Islamic Resurgence in the Arab World.* Ed. Ali E. Hillal Dessouki. New York: Praeger, 1982, 196-220.
Mayer provides a relatively detailed analysis of Qadhafi's ideas as presented in the *Green Book*, showing how these diverge significantly from the normal Sunni Muslim interpretations of Islamic Law.

0317 MELASUO, TUOMO. "Culture and Minorities in the Arabo-Islamic Identity of Algeria." In *Islam: State and Society.* Eds. Klaus Ferdinand and Mehdi Mozaffari. London: Curzon Press, 1988, 183-94.

0318 MUNSON, HENRY Jr. "Islamic Revivalism in Morocco and Tunisia." *MW*, 76 (1986), 203-18.

0319 _____. "The Social Base of Islamic Militancy in Morocco." *MEJ*, 40 (Spring 1986), 267-84.
Provides a relatively detailed analysis of the Islamist groups in Morocco, showing how they have interacted with the general political evolution in recent years.

0320 PLATT, KATIE. "Island Puritanism." In *Islamic Dilemmas: Reformers Nationalist and Industrialization.* Ed. Ernest Gellner. Berlin: Mouton Publishers, 1985, 169-86.
A comparative study of traditionalist and activist Puritanism in the Tunisian islands of Kerkennah.

0321 AL-QADHAFI, MUAMMAR. *The Green Book, Part 1- the Solution to the Problem of Democracy.* See also *The Green Book, Part 2- the Solution of the Economic Problem.* Tripoli: Rublis Establishment for Publishing, n.d., 120 p.
This is the primary presentation of the ideas of Qadhafi and represents the basic foundations of the effort of social transformation that has taken place in Libya. It is the essential source for Qadhafi's ideology. Also published seperately.

0322 ROBERTS, HUGH. "Radical Islamism and the Dilemma of Algerian Nationalism: the Embattled Arians of Algiers." *TWQ*, 10 (April 1988), 556-98.

0323 SALEM, NORMA. "Islam and the Politics of Identity in Tunisia." *JAA*, 5 (1986), 194-216.
This article examines the use of Islamic symbols in political mobilization and legitimation efforts in Tunisia during three consecutive phases of Tunisian political history: (1) struggle for independence from the French; (2) independence; and (3) the rise of active opposition to President Bourguiba. The emphasis is on the speeches and writings of Bourguiba.

0324 SEDDON, DAVID. "Popular Protest and Political Opposition in Tunisia, Morocco and Sudan, 1984-1985." In *Urban Crisis and Social Movements in the Middle East: Proceedings of the C.N.R.S.E.S.R.C. Colloquium in Paris, May 23-27, 1986.* Paris: Editions L'Harmattan.

0325 TAHA, MAHMOUD M. *The Second Message of Islam.* Trans. Abdullahi Ahmed AnNa'im. Contemporary Issues in Middle East Series. Syracuse, NY: Syracuse University Press, 1987, 313 p.
Taha's controversial thesis, that the "First Message" of Islam was appropriate to Muslims of the Seventh Century, was the cause of his execution in 1985. The translator provides an excellent introduction which clarifies basic concepts and presents biographical information which elucidate the radical reinterpretation of the Islamic tradition for the contemporary era.

0326 TURABI, HASSAN. "Principles of Governance, Freedom and Responsibility in Islam." *AJISS*, 4 (September 1987), 1-12.
The author is the major leader of the Muslim Brotherhood in the Sudan. This article is a clear expression of Turabi's renewalist approach to Islam and was originally published in *Voices of Resurgent Islam*, edited by John L. Esposito.

0327 VATIN, JEAN CLAUDE. "Religious Resistance and State Power in Algeria." In *Islam and Power.* Ed. Cudsi and Dessouki. Baltimore, MD: Johns Hopkins University Press, 1981, 119-57.
The author discusses both the history of Islamic institutions and the methods for studying them. Vatin goes beyond the older approaches which concentrate on marabouts and examines Muslim organizations as sources of resistance to centralized state control. Early Sufi and *ulama* movements may have been superseded in the 1970s by a puritanism of the deprived classes as a source of Islamic opposition.

0328 VIKOR, K.S. "Al-Sanusi and Qadhafi: Continuity of Thought?" *MR*, 12 (1987), 78-83.

0329 VINCENT, ANDREW W. "Religion and Nationalism in a Traditional Society: Ideology, Leadership and the Role of the *Umma* Party as a Force for Social Change in the Northern Sudan." Ph.D. diss., University of Pennsylvania, 1988, 330 p.

0330 VOLL, JOHN. "Mahdis, Walis, and New Men in the Sudan." In *Scholars, Saints and Sufis: Muslim Religious Institutions in the Middle East Since 1500.* Ed. Nikki Keddie. Berkeley, CA: University of California Press, 1972, 367-84.

0331 WALTZ, SUSAN. "Islamist Appeal in Tunisia." *MEJ*, 40 (Autumn 1986), 651-70.
The author sees the emergence of significant Islamist sentiments in Tunisia as being deeply rooted in the social and psychological crises of the society. The

Islamist appeal involves important political issues but is not seen as purely a matter of political opposition to the secularist regime.

0332 WARBURG, GABRIEL. *Islam, Nationalism and Communism in a Traditional Society: The Case of Sudan*. London: F. Cass; Totowa, NJ: Distributed by Biblio Distribution Centre, 1978, 253 p.
This collection of studies provides important discussions of the evolution of Mahdist politics in the twentieth century, the development of Sudanese nationalism, and an extensive discussion of history of the Sudanese Communist Party and its programs. Warburg shows how Muslim organizations adapt to modern contexts.

0333 WARBURG, GABRIEL R. and URI M. KUPFERSCHMIDT, eds. *Islam, Nationalism and Radicalism in Egypt and the Sudan*. New York: Praeger, 1983, 416 p.
A collection of seventeen papers from a conference sponsored by the Institute of Middle Eastern Studies, the University of Haifa. The papers address four themes: Islam, Nationalism, and the State; Fundamentalism, Militant, and Ethnic Minorities.

C. WEST AFRICA

0334 ABUBAKER, R.D. "The Role of Muslim Youth in the Propagation of Islam in Nigeria." *IMA*, 17 (November 1986), 257-70.

0335 AMSELLE, JEAN-LOUP. "A Case of Fundamentalism in West Africa: Wahabism in Bamako." In *Studies in Religious Fundamentalism*. Ed. Lionel Caplan. Albany, NY: State University of New York Press, 1987, 79-94.

0336 BIENEN, HENRY. "Religion, Legitimacy and Conflict in Nigeria." *AAAPSS*, 483 (January 1986), 50-60.

0337 CHAN, MBYE B. "Islam and the Creative Imagination in Senegal." *AJIS*, 1 (1984), 1-22.

0338 CHRISTELOW, ALLAN. "Religious Protest and Dissent in Northern Nigeria: From Mahdism to Qur'anic Integralism." *JIMMA*, 6 (1985), 375-93.
This is an analysis of the revolt led by Mai Tatsine in 1980 in northern Nigeria. It presents the uprising in a broad historical and social context, seeing the movement as a product of the pressures and tensions of the time and also of the personal development of the leader and his followers.

0339 _____. "Three Islamic Voices in Contemporary Nigeria." In *Islam and the Political Economy of Meaning*. Ed. William R. Roff. Berkeley, CA: University of California Press, 1987, 226-53.
The author discusses the careers and ideas of Abubakar Gumi (a conservative Islamist), Ibraheem Sulaiman (a radical intellectual Islamist), and Abdulmalik Bappa Mahmud (an active Muslim judge). The analysis places these people in the context of social change and religious diversity in Nigeria.

0340 CLARKE, PETER B. "Islamic Millenarianism in West Africa: A 'Revolutionary' Ideology?" *RelSt*, 16 (1980), 317-39.

0341 _____. "Islamic Reform in Contemporary Nigeria: Methods and Aims." *TWQ*, 10, (April 1988), 519-38.
The author shows that Islamic reform has moved from being a northern Nigerian issue to a national one. Many different groups are mentioned, with the author distinguishing between moderate and radical ("fundamentalist") Muslim reformers.

0342 _____. *West Africa and Islam: A Study of Religious Development from the 8th to the 20th Century*. London: Edward Arnold Publishers, Ltd., 1982, 275 p.
A general history textbook of West African Islam which uses four typologies, placing events, figures and movements within either a pluralistic, accommodationist, quietist or militant Islamic paradigm. It covers history from the earliest advance of Islam in West Africa, in 1000 A.D., to 1980.

0343 COMSTOCK, G.L. "The Yoruba and Religious Change." *JRA*, 10 (1979), 1-12.

0344 CREEVEY, LUCY E. "Religion and Modernization in Senegal." In *Islam and Development*. Ed. John L. Esposito. Syracuse, NY: Syracuse University Press, 1980, 207-21.
This chapter presents an analysis of the continuing importance of the major Islamic organizations in Senegal. It is noted, however, that the social transformations of the twentieth century have had a major impact, shifting the nature of the influence of Islam but not necessarily reducing its importance.

0345 GBADAMOSI, G.O. "The Imamate Question Among the Yoruba Muslims." *JHSN*, 6 (1971-1972), 229-37.

0346 GELLAR, SHELDON. *Senegal: An African Nation Between Islam and the West*. Profiles - Nations of Africa Series. Boulder, CO: Westview, 1982, 128 p.

0347 GILLILAND, DEAN STEWART. *African Religion Meets Islam: Religious Change in Northern Nigeria*. Lanham, MD: University Press of America, 1986, 250 p.

0348 HISKETT, MERVYN. "The 'Community of Grace' and its Opponents the 'Rejecters': a Debate about Theology and Mysticism in Muslim West Africa with Special Reference to its Hausa Expression." *AfLS*, 17 (1980), 90-140.

0349 _____. *The Development of Islam in West Africa*. Studies in African History Series. Harlow, Essex: Longman, 1984, 353 p.

0350 HODGKIN, T. "The Radical Tradition in Muslim West Africa." In *Essays on Islamic Civilization Presented to N. Berkes*. Leiden: E.J. Brill, 1976, 103-17.
This is a well-known essay which examines the traditions of Islamic activism as being movements of radical revolution.

0351 HUNWICK, J.O. "Black Africans in the Islamic World: An Understudied Dimension of the Black Diaspora." *Tarikh*, 5 (1977-8), 20-40.

0352 ISICHEI, ELIZABETH. "The Maitatsine Risings in Nigeria 1980-85: A Revolt of the Disinherited." *JRA*, 17 Fasc. 3 (October 1987), 194-208.

0353 JOHNSON, LEMUEL. "Crescent and Consciousness: Islamic Orthodoxies and the West African Novel." *RAL*, 11, i(1980), 26-49.

0354 KABA, LANSINE. *The Wahhabiyya; Islamic Reform and Politics in French West Africa*. Studies in African Religion. Evanston, IL: Northwestern University Press, 1974, 320 p.
This is a study of the impact of Middle East Islamic revivalism in West Africa in the twentieth century.

0355 KRAUS, J. "Islamic Affinities and International Politics in Sub-Saharan Africa." *CH*, 78 (1980), 154.

0356 LUBECK, PAUL M. *Islam and Urban Labor in Northern Nigeria: The Making of a Muslim Working Class*. African Studies Series, 52. New York: Cambridge University Press, 1987, 368 p.
This study concentrates on a particular region, Kano, between 1966 and 1979, but also provides a basic perspective for a class analysis of major social transformations. It illustrates the role of Islam as an oppositional force that shaped class consciousness.

0357 _____. "Islamic Political Movements in Northern Nigeria: The Problem of Class Analysis." In *Islam, Politics, and Social Movements*. Eds. Edmund Burke, III, and Ira M. Lapidus. Berkeley, CA: University of California Press, 1988, 244-60.

0358 _____. "Structural Determinants of Urban Islamic Protest in Northern Nigeria." In *Islam and the Political Economy of Meaning: Comparative Studies of Muslim Discourse*. Ed. William R. Roff. Berkeley, CA: University of California Press, 1987, 79-107.

0359 MAZRUI, ALI A. "Islam, Political Leadership and Economic Radicalism in Africa." *CSSH*, 9 (April 1967), 274-91.

0360 MOTIN, A. RASHID. "Political Dynamism of Islam in Nigeria." *IS*, 26 (Summer 1987), 179-90.

0361 MUHAMMAD, AKBAR. "Islam and National Integration Through Education in Nigeria." In *Islam and Development*. Ed. John L. Esposito. Syracuse, NY: Syracuse University Press, 1980, 181-205.
The author provides a general introduction to the political history of Nigeria and then examines the potential divisions created by different educational systems in Nigeria. Islam is seen as an important part of the broader Nigerian national culture which is emerging as a result of national educational policies. The author is optimistic about the prospects for effective national unity in Nigeria.

0362 NYANG, SULAYMAN S. "A Contribution to the Study of Islam in Gambia." *JPHS*, 25 (1977), 125-38.

0363 _____. "West Africa." In *The Politics of Islamic Revivalism*. Ed. Shireen T. Hunter. Bloomington, IN: Indiana University Press, 1988, 204-25.

The author places present Islamic revivalism in the historical context of precolonial traditions and the later anti-imperialist struggle. After independence, he feels that a critical issue has been the relationship between Islam and the new states. Influences from Libya, Saudi Arabia and Egypt as well as local issues are seen as affecting the emergence of movements rejecting secularism and affirming an Islamic identity.

0364 O'BRIEN, DONALD B. CRUISE. "A Versatile Charisma: The Mouride Brotherhood 1967-1975." *AES*, 18 (1977), 84-106.

0365 QUADRI, Y.A. "A Study of the Izalah: A Contemporary Anti-Sufi Organization in Nigeria." *Ibadan Journal of Religious Studies*, 17 (1985), p. 95.

0366 QURESHI, TUFAIL AHMAD. "Courses for Islamic Law Teaching." In *Islamic Law in Nigeria (Application & Teaching)*. Ed. Syed Khalid Rashid. Lagos: Islamic Publications Bureau, 1988, 165-70.

0367 RYAN, PATRICK J. "Islam and Politics in West Africa: Minority and Majority Models." *MW*, 77 (January 1987), 1-15.
    The author provides a wide ranging account of the different conceptualization used by Muslim thinkers to define the nature of pluralistic societies and minority-majority statuses in Islamic terms. This is historical in approach, bringing the account to the 1980's.

0368 SALAMONE, FRANK A. "Competitive Conversion and its Implications for Modernization (Nigeria)." *Anthropos*, 75 (1980), 383-404.

0369 SANNEH, LAMIN O. "Christian Experience of Islamic Da'wah, with Particular Reference to Africa." *IRM*, 65 (October 1976), 410-26.

0370 _____. "The Islamic Education of an African Child: Stresses and Tensions." In *Conflict and Harmony in Education in Tropical Africa*. Eds. Gedfrey Brown and Mervyn Hiskett. Rutherford, NJ: Farleigh Dickinson University Press, 1976, 168-86.

0371 SIMMONS, WILLIAM S. "Islamic Conversion and Social Change in a Senegalese Village." *Ethnology*, 18 (1979), 303-23.

0372 TABI'U, MUHAMMAD. "Application of Islamic Law in Nigeria: Constraints in the Application of Islamic Law in Nigeria." In *Islamic Law in Nigeria (Application & Teaching)*. Ed. Syed Khalid Rashid. Lagos: Islamic Publications Bureau, 1988, 75-85.

0373 WINTERS, CLYDE AHMED. "Koranic Education and Militant Islam in Nigeria." *IRE*, 33 (1987), 171-85.

0374 YADUDU, AUWALU HAMISU. "Islamic Law and Law Reform Discourse in Nigeria: A Comparative Study and Another Viewpoint." J.D. thesis, Harvard University, 1985, 261 p.

III. AMERICA

0375 ABU-LABAN, BAHA. "Canadian Muslims: The Need for a New Survival Strategy." *JIMMA*, 2-3 (Winter 1980-Summer 1981), 98-109.

0376 _____. *An Olive Branch on the Family Tree: The Arabs in Canada.* Toronto: McClelland & Stewart, 1980, 259 p.

0377 ALI, KAMAL. "Islamic Education in the United States: An Overview of Issues, Problems, and Possible Approaches." *AJIS*, 1 (1984), 127-32.

0378 AYATOLLAH, S.M.T. "Reflections of the Islamic Revolution of Iran in the Caribbean." *IR*, 1 (January 1980), 8-11.

0379 BIN-SAYEED, KHALID. "The Predicament of Muslim Professionals in Canada and its Resolution." *JIMMA*, 3 (Winter 1981),104-19.

0380 DARRAT, ALI F. "Are Checking Accounts in American Banks Permissible Under Islamic Laws?" *AJISS*, 2 (1985), 101-4.

0381 AL FARUQI, ISMA'IL RAJI. "Islamic Ideals in North America." In *The Muslim Community in North America.* Eds. Earle H. Waugh, et al. Edmonton, Alberta: University of Alberta Press, 1983, 259-78.

0382 _____. *The Path of Da'wah in the West.* London: The UK Islamic Mission, 1986, 28 p.

0383 HADDAD, YVONNE YAZBECK. *A Century of Islam in America.* The Muslim World Today Occasional Paper, no. 4. Washington DC: American Institute for Islamic Affairs, 1986, 13 p.

0384 _____. "Arab Muslims and Islamic Institutions in America: Adaptations and Reform." In *Arabs in the New World: Studies on Arab American Communities.* Eds. Sameer Y. Abraham and Nabeel Abraham. Detroit, MI: Wayne State University Press, 1983, 64-81.

0385 _____. "The Impact of the Islamic Revolution in Iran on the Syrian Muslims of Montreal." In *The Muslim Community in North America.* Eds. Earle Waugh, et al. Edmonton, Alberta: University of Alberta Press, 1983, 165-81.

0386 _____. "The Muslim Experience in the United States." *The Link*, 2 (September/October 1979), 1-11.

0387 _____. "Muslims in the United States." In *Islam: The Religious and Political Life of a World Community.* Ed. Marjorie Kelly. New York: Praeger Press, 1984, 258-74.

0388 _____. "Muslims in Canada: A Preliminary Study." In *Religion and Ethnicity.* Eds. Howard Coward and Leslie Kawamura. Waterloo, Ontario: Wilfred Laurier University Press, 1978, 71-100.

0389 _____. "Nationalist and Islamist Tendencies in Contemporary Arab-American Communities." In *Arab Nationalism and the Future of the Arab World.* Ed. Hani A. Farris. Belmont, MA: Association of Arab-American University Graduates, Inc., 1987, 141-60.

0390 HADDAD, YVONNE YAZBECK and ADAIR T. LUMMIS. *Islamic Values in the United States: A Comparative Study.* New York: Oxford University Press, 1987, 196 p.

0391 HAMDANI, D.H. "Muslims and Christian Life in Canada." *JIMMA,* 1 (Summer 1979), 51-59.

0392 _____. *Muslims in Canada: A Century of Settlement 1871-1976.* Ottawa: Council of Muslim Communities of Canada, 1978.

0393 _____. "Muslims in the Canadian Mosaic." *JIMMA,* 5 (1983-1984), 7-16.

0394 HANEEF, SUZANNE. *What Everyone Should Know About Islam and Muslims.* Chicago: Kazi Publications, Inc., 1982, 202 p.
Written by an American convert, it outlines the basic teachings of Islam with chapters on values and morals, the observance of Islamic festivals, family life, relations between the sexes, and relations with Jews and Christians.

0395 HASSAN, UMAR A. "African-American Muslims and the Islamic Revival." In *Islam in the Contemporary World.* Ed. Cyriac K. Pullapilly. Notre Dame, IN: Cross Road Books, 1980, 284-95.

0396 KASULE, OMAR HASAN. "Muslims in Trinidad and Tobago." *JIMMA,* 7 (January 1986), 195-213.

0397 MAMIYA, LAWRENCE H. "From Black Muslim to Bilalian: The Evolution of a Movement." *JSSR,* 21 (1982), 138-52.

0398 MARSH, JAMES A. *The Canadian Encyclopedia.* 2d ed. Edmonton: Hurtig Publishers, 1988. S.v. "Islam: Islam in Canada," by Yvonne Y. Haddad.

0399 MUHAMMAD, AKBAR. "Muslims in the United States: An Overview of Organizations, Doctrines, and Problems." In *The Islamic Impact.* Eds. Haddad, Haines, and Findly. Syracuse, NY: Syracuse University Press, 1984, 195-217.

0400 _____. "Some Factors Which Promote and Restrict Islamization in America." *AJIS,* 1 (1984), 41-50.

0401 MUHAMMAD, WALLACE D. *As the Light Shineth from the East.* Chicago: WDM Publications Co., 1980.

0402 _____. *The Teachings of W.D. Muhammad (Elementary Level).* Chicago: Elijah Muhammad Mosque no. 2, 1976, 198 p.

0403 _____. *The Teachings of W.D. Muhammad (Secondary Level).* Chicago: Elijah Muhammad Mosque no. 2, 1975, 198 p.

0404 MUHAMMAD, IMAM WARITHUDDIN. *Prayer and al-Islam.* Chicago: Muhammad Islamic Foundation, 1982, 297 p.

Designed to initiate African-American converts into the basic teachings, rituals, and regulations of Islamic life.

0405 NADWI, SYED ABUL HASAN ALI. *Muslims in the West: The Message and Mission.* Leicester, England: The Islamic Foundation, 1983, 191 p.
A collection of the author's speeches delivered in Europe and America.

0406 NAZIM, ZAHEER UDDIN. *Manual of Da'wah.* Montreal: Islamic Circle of North America, 1983.
A manual for the propagation of Islam among Muslims and non-Muslims in North America prepared by the Islamic Circle in North America which teaches that full time missionary activity is a divine obligation placed on each individual Muslim.

0407 NIJIM, BASHEER K., ed. *American Church Politics and the Middle East.* AAUG Monograph Series: no. 15. Belmont, MA: Association of Arab-American University Graduates, 1982, 156 p.

0408 NYANG, SULAYMAN S. "Islam in the United States of America: A Review of the Sources." *The Search*, 1 (Spring 1980), 164-82.

0409 NYANG, SULAYMAN S. and MUMTAZ AHMAD. "The Muslim Intellectual Emigre in the United States." *IC*, 59 (1985), 277-90.

0410 PIPES, DANIEL. "Fundamentalist Muslims Between America and Russia." *FA*, 64 (Summer 1986), 939-59.

0411 POSTON, LARRY ALLAN. "Islamic Da'wah in North America and the Dynamics of Conversion to Islam in Western Societies." Ph.D. diss., Northwestern University, 1988, 495 p.
Examines Islamic missionary activity in North America and constructs a profile of the 'typical' convert. Reviews contemporary thought on the religious duty of *da'wah*.

0412 POWER, JONATHAN. *Migrant Workers in Western Europe and the United States.* London: Pergamon Press, 1979, 167 p.

0413 RASHID, A. *The Muslim Canadians, A Profile.* Ottawa: Ministry of Supply and Services Canada, 1985, 75 p.
A socio-demographic and economic description of the Muslim Community in Canada based on the statistics gathered in the 1981 census.

0414 SALEM, JAMIL R. "The Impact of Socio-Cultural Factors Upon the Assimilation of Lebanese Moslem Groups in Metropolitan Detroit." Ph.D. diss., Wayne State University, 1988, 177 p.

0415 SHAD, ABDUR RAHMAN. *The Duties of an Imam.* rev. by Abdul Hamid Siddiqui. Chicago: Kazi Publications, 1978, 67 p.
Provides guidelines for qualities desired in an Imam, the leader of prayer at the mosque as well as instructions for matrimonial and funeral rites.

0416 SHARAFELDIN, IBNOMER MOHAMED. "Human Resource Management: An Islamic Perspective, a Study of the Islamic Academic Institutions in the United States." Ph.D. diss., Claremont Graduate School, 1987, 244 p.

0417 AL-TALAL, FAISSAL FAHD and KHALID ABDULLAH TARIQ AL-MANSOUR. *The Challenges of Spreading Islam in America and Other Essays.* San Francisco: by the authors, 1980, 213 p.

The authors conclude that a major successful campaign for Islam is not only feasible within the United States but should be initiated without delay. They outline a strategy for the conversion of Americans to Islam.

0418 TURNER, RICHARD BRENT. "Islam in the United States in the 1920s: The Quest for a New Vision in Afro-American Religion." Ph.D. diss., Princeton, 1986, 234 p.

Analyzes the impact of the *Ahmadiyya* movement and Marcus Garvey's Universal Negro Improvement Association on African-American religious consciousness in the 1920s. The final chapter analyzes developments in the *Ahmadiyya* movement in the U.S. since the 1930s with some attention to other contemporary Muslim movements in American culture.

0419 WAUGH, EARLE H. "The Imam in the New World: Models and Modifications." In *Transitions and Transformation in the History of Religions.* Eds. Frank E. Reynolds and Theodore M. Ludwig. Leiden: E.J. Brill, 1980, 124-49.

0420 WAUGH, EARLE H., BAHA ABU-LABAN, and REGULA B. QURESHI. *The Muslim Community in North America.* Edmonton, Alberta: University of Alberta Press, 1983, 316 p.

Essays on immigrant and indigenous Muslims which help to illustrate manifestations of Islam in particular areas of the United States and Canada. Draws on a variety of approaches to study the growth and identity of selected North American Muslim communities.

0421 WOMEN'S COMMITTEE OF MSA. *Parents' Manual: A Guide for Muslim Parents Living in North America.* Indianapolis, IN: American Trust Publications, 1976, 152 p.

Provides an overview of the Islamic personality, the goals and orientation of the Muslim home and the methods of initiating children into such a system. The second section deals with practical aspects such as guidance and discipline, western standards, the problems of adolescence, sex and marriage, and the means of maintaining an Islamic life in the American milieu.

IV. ASIA

0422 ESPOSITO, JOHN L., ed. *Islam in Asia: Religion, Politics and Society.* New York: Oxford University Press, 1987, 272 p.

A collection of studies on Islamic revivalism which encompass the Muslim world from Iran to the southern Philippines. Historians, social scientists, lawyers, and Islamicists examine the multifaceted reassertion of Islam in public life: in Islamic republics (Iran and Pakistan), in liberation movements (Afghanistan and the Philippines), among Muslim minorities (China, Soviet Union and India), and in the Southeast Asian Muslim majority states of Malaysia and Indonesia.

0423 METCALF, BARBARA DALY, ed. *Moral Conduct and Authority: The Place of "Adab" in South Asian Islam*. Berkeley, CA: University of California Press, 1984, 350 p.

0424 MOGNI, A. "Islamic Renaissance in Modern Times." *Radiance*, (8 February 1981), 3.

0425 PISCATORI, JAMES P. "Asian Islam: International Linkages and Their Impact on International Relations." In *Islam in Asia: Religion, Politics and Society*. Ed. John L. Esposito. New York: Oxford University Press, 1987, 230-61.

0426 _____. *International Relations of the Asian Muslim States*. New York: The Asia Society, 1986, 41 p.

A. SOUTH ASIA

0427 BANUAZIZI, ALI and MYRON WEINER, eds. *The State, Religion, and Ethnic Politics: Afghanistan, Iran, and Pakistan*. Contemporary Issues in the Middle East Series. Syracuse, NY: Syracuse University Press, 1986, 464 p.
A collection of articles on the impact of religion and ethnic identity on political life in Iran, Afghanistan and Pakistan. The authors underscore the weakness of nationalism as the basis of society and the importance of religion and ethnolinguistic identities.

0428 DIL, SHAHEEN F. "The Myth of Islamic Resurgence in South Asia." *CH*, 78 (April 1980), 165.

0429 EWING, KATHERINE P., ed. *Shari'at and Ambiguity in South Asian Islam*. Berkeley, CA: University of California Press, 1988, 321 p.
A collection of fourteen conference papers, ranging from the sixteenth to the twentieth centuries and including India, Pakistan, Bangladesh, and Malaysia, whose disparate nature is placed under the rubric of the diversity of the Islamic experience. Many of the papers presume a specialist audience.

0430 HARDY, PETER. "Islam and Muslims in South Asia." In *The Crescent in the East, Islam in Asia Minor*. Ed. Raphael Israeli. London: Curzon Press, 1982, 36-61.

0431 _____. "Modern Trends in Islam in India and Pakistan." In *Perspectives on World Religions*. Ed. Robert Jackson. London: University of London, S.O.A.S., 1978, 209-20.

0432 ROBINSON, FRANCIS. "Islam and Muslim Separatism." In *Political Identity in South Asia*. Eds. D. Taylor and M. Yapp. London: Curzon Press, 1979, 78-112.

1. Afghanistan

0433 AZOY, G. WHITNEY. *Buzkashi: Game and Power in Afghanistan.* Symbol and Cultural Series. Philadelphia, PA: University of Pennsylvania Press, 1982, 152p.

0434 CHRISTENSEN, ASGER. "When Muslim Identity Has Different Meanings: Religion and Politics in Contemporary Afghanistan." In *Islam: State and Society.* Eds. Klaus Ferdinand and M. Mozaffari. London: Curzon Press, 1988, 143-54.

0435 EDWARDS, DAVID BUSBY. "Pretexts of Rebellion: The Cultural Origins of Pakhtan Resistance to the Afghan State." Ph.D. diss., University of Michigan, 1986, 575 p.
   Examines the reasons for the development of popular resistance to the Marxist government which took power in Afghanistan in 1978. The principal focus is on the cultural meaning of honor and how the government has tried to appropriate this meaning in order to incorporate Pakhtan tribes within the national framework. Some attention is given to the role of Islamic revival.

0436 GHANI, ASHRAF. "Afghanistan: Islam and Counter-Revolutionary Movement." In *Islam in Asia: Religion, Politics and Society.* Ed. John L. Esposito. New York: Oxford University Press, 1987, 79-96.

0437 HANIFI, M. JAMIL. "Islam in Contemporary Afghanistan." In *The Crescent in the East, Islam in Asia Minor.* Ed. Raphael Israeli. London: Curzon Press, 1982, 23-35.

0438 KARP, CRAIG M. "The War in Afghanistan." *FA*, (Summer 1986), 1027-47.

0439 NABY, EDEN. "The Concept of Jihad in Opposition to Communist Rule: Turkestan and Afghanistan." *SCC*, 19 (Autumn-Winter 1986), 287-300.

0440 _____. "Islam within the Afghan Resistance." *TWQ*, 10 (April 1988), 787-805

0441 ROY, OLIVIER. *Islam and Resistance in Afghanistan.* Trans. from French. Cambridge: Cambridge University Press, 1986, 256 p.
   A major book on the history, ideology and politics of the Afghan *Mujahidin.* Excellent coverage of the nature of Afghan Islamic resistance movements, their organizations, leadership, and attitudes toward the Soviet occupation and its client government in Kabul.

2. India

0442 AHMAD, AKBAR S. "Muslim Society in South India: The Case of Hyderabad." *JIMMA*, 6 (July 1985), 317-31.

0443 BUULTJENS, RALPH. "India: Religion, Political Legitimacy, and the Secular State." *AAAPSS*, 483 (January 1986), 93-109.

0444 HASAN, MUSHIRUL. "Indian Muslims since Independence: In Search of Integration and Identity." *TWQ*, 10 (April 1988), 818-42.

0445 _____. "Pan-Islamism Versus Indian Nationalism: A Reappraisal." *IP*, 2 (July 1986), 16-35.

0446 MARKOVA, DAGMAR. "On the National Consciousness of Indian Muslims." *ArOr*, 54 (1986), 1-18.

0447 MUSHIR-UL-HAQ. "The 'Ulama and the Indian Politics." *IMA*, 10 (November 1979), 69-95.

0448 PILLAI, K. RAMAN. "Muslim Politics in Kerala." *AP*, 7 (1979), 17-24.

0449 REDDY, G. RAM. "Language, Religion and Political Identity--The Case of the Majlis-e-Ittihadul-Muslimeen in Andhra Pradesh." In *Political Identity in South Asia*. Eds. D. Taylor and M. Yapp. London: 1979, 113-37.

0450 SHAHABUDDIN, SYED and THEODORE PAUL WRIGHT, JR. "India: Muslim Minority Politics and Society." In *Islam in Asia: Religion, Politics, and Society*. Ed. John L. Esposito. New York: Oxford University Press, 1987, 152-76.

0451 STEPANIANTS, MARIETTA. "Development of the Concept of Nationalism. The Case of Muslims in the Indian Subcontinent." *MW*, 69 (1979), 28-41.

0452 TROLL, CHRISTIAN W. "Islamic Thought in Modern India". *Islamochristiana*, 13 (1987), 79-98.

0453 _____. "Christian-Muslim Relations in India." In *The Vatican, Islam and the Middle East*. Ed. Kail C. Ellis. Syracuse, NY: Syracuse University Press, 1987, 295-308.

0454 VAHIDUDDIN, SYED. *Islam in India: Studies and Commentaries*. Vol. 3: The Islamic Experience in Contemporary Thought. Ed. Christian W. Troll. Dehli, India: Chanakya Publications, 1986, 293 p.
   Volume three in a series sponsored by the Islamic Section of Vidyajoti, Institute of Religious Studies, Dehli. A selection of writings from the author, a contemporary Indian Muslim thinker, addressing the 'crisis' of religion.

0455 WRIGHT, THEODORE P., Jr. "Inadvertent Modernization of Indian Muslims by Revivalists." *JIMMA*, 1 (Summer 1979), 80-89.

0456 _____. "The Politics of Muslim Sectarian Conflict in India." *JSAMES*, 3 (Spring 1980), 67-73.

0457 YANUK, MARTIN. "The Indian Muslim Self-Image." *IMA*, 4 (November 1973), 78-94.

3. Pakistan

0458 ABBOT, FREEDLAND. "Maulana Maududi on Quranic Interpretation."
MW, 48 (January 1958), 6-19.

0459 ABD, A.R. *Sayyed Maududi Faces the Death Sentence*. Lahore: Islamic
Publications Limited, 1979.

0460 ABDULLA, AHMED. *An Observation: Perspectives of Pakistan: Revival of
Muslim Ummah*. Karachi: Tanzeem Publishers, 1987, 259 p.

0461 ADAMS, CHARLES. "The Ideology of Mawlana Mawdudi." In *South Asia
Politics and Religion*. Ed. D.E. Smith. Princeton, NJ: Princeton University Press,
1966, 371-97.

0462 _____. "Mawdudi and the Islamic State." In *Voices of Resurgent Islam*. Ed.
John L. Esposito. New York: Oxford University Press, 1983, 99-133.

0463 AHMAD, AKBAR S. "Order and Conflict in Muslim Society: A Case Study
from Pakistan." *MEJ*, 36 (Spring 1982), 184-204.

0464 AHMAD, AZIZ. "Activism of the Ulama in Pakistan." In *Scholars, Saints
and Sufis*. Ed. Nikki R. Keddie. Berkeley, CA: University of California Press,
1972, 257-72.

0465 _____. "Mawdudi and Orthodox Fundamentalism in Pakistan." *MEJ*, 21
(Summer 1967), 369-80.

0466 AHMAD, KHURSHID. "The Nature of Islamic Resurgence." In *Voices of
Resurgent Islam*. Ed. John L. Esposito. New York: Oxford University Press,
1983, 218-29.

0467 _____, ed. *Islam: Its Meaning and Message*. London: Islamic Council of
Europe, 1976, 279 p.

0468 AHMAD, K. and Z.I. ANSARI. "Mawlana Sayyid Abul A'la Mawdudi: An
Introduction to His Vision of Islam and Islamic Revival." In *Islamic Perspectives:
Studies in Honour of Sayyid Mawlana Abul A'la Mawdudi*. Eds. K. Ahmad and
Z.I. Ansari. Leicester: The Islamic Foundation, 1979, 359-83.

0469 AHMAD, K. and Z.I. ANSARI, eds. *Islamic Perspectives: Studies In Honour
of Sayyid Abdul A'la Mawdudi*. Leicester: The Islamic Foundation, 1979, 394 p.
Prefacing this collection of essays is a bibliography consisting of 200 entries of
writings by and about Mawdudi.
This *festschrift*, pays tribute to Mawdudi's contributions to Islamic scholarship
and reflects the diversity of interests and viewpoints of the contributing authors,
which include Sayyed Hussein Nasr, Isma'il al Faruqi, Hamid Algar and others.
Discussion covers materialism vs. spiritualism; comparisons between Christianity
and Islam; *tawhid*; intellectual perspectives in the context of contemporary Islam;
twentieth-century scholars and reformers in the Muslim world, with an emphasis
on Mawdudi; Islamic welfare state and economic development; Islamic
jurisprudence; the concept of community; and Muslim minorities.

0470 AHMAD, MUMTAZ. "Islamic Revival in Pakistan." In *Islam in the Contemporary World*. Ed. Cyriac K. Pullapilly. Notre Dame, IN: Cross Roads Books, 1980, 261-73.

0471 _____. "Islamic Revivalism in Asia: Pakistan." In *The Politics of Islamic Revivalism: Diversity and Unity*. Ed. Shireen T. Hunter. Bloomington, IN: Indiana University Press, 1988, 229-46.

0472 _____. "Parliament, Parties, Polls and Islam: Issues in the Current Debate on Religion and Politics in Pakistan." *AJISS*, 2 (1985), 15-28.

0473 _____, ed. *State Politics and Islam*. Indianapolis, IN: American Trust Publications, 1986, 160 p.
A collection of seminar papers by Muslim scholars on Islamic political theory and issues which emerge as Muslims attempt to move from theory to practice. Both Sunni and Shi'i perspectives are represented in these discussions of the nature of an Islamic political and social order.

0474 AHMAD, SAYED R. *Maulana Maududi and the Islamic State*. Lahore: People's Publishing House, 1976.

0475 AHMED, AKBAR S. "The Mulla of Waziristan: Leadership and Islam in a Pakistani District." In *Shariat and Ambiguity in South Asian Islam*. Ed. Katherine P. Ewing. Delhi, India: Adam Publishers and Distributors, 1988, 180-204.

0476 _____. *Pakistan Society: Islam, Ethnicity and Leadership in South Asia*. Karachi: Oxford University Press, 1986, 300 p.
The author has gathered together fifteen of his previously published essays around the three themes: Islam in society, ethnicity and leadership, and contemporary issues. While several of the essays do not fit comfortably within the title of the book, the majority do address important issues about the direction of development in Pakistan and its relationship to Islamic identity and values.

0477 _____. *Religion and Politics in Muslim Society: Order and Conflict in Pakistan*. New York: Cambridge University Press, 1983, 225 p.
A Pakistani anthropologist and government administrator examines the interplay of power, authority and religious status in the tribal society of Waziristan, Pakistan. The author constructs an "Islamic district paradigm" based upon this microcosmic study of religion and politics as witnessed by the challenge to state authority by a local *mullah*, demonstrating the force of Islam in a traditional society undergoing modernization.

0478 AHMED, ISHTIAQ. *The Concept of an Islamic State: An Analysis of the Ideological Controversy in Pakistan*. New York: St. Martin's Press, 1987, 235 p.

0479 AHMED, MUNIR D. "Pakistan: The Dream of an Islamic State." In *Religion and Societies: Asia and the Middle East*. Ed. Carlo Caldarola. Berlin: Mouton de Gruyter, 1982, 261-88.

0480 ALAVI, HAMZA. "Ethnicity, Muslim Society and the Pakistan Ideology". In *Islamic Reassertion in Pakistan*. Ed. Anita M. Weiss. Lahore: Vanguard Books, 1987, 21-48.

0481 AMNESTY INTERNATIONAL. *Islamic Republic of Pakistan An Amnesty International Report*. London: Amnesty International Publications, 1977, 92 p.

0482 BAHADUR, KALIM. *The Jama'at-i-Islami of Pakistan. Political Thought and Political Action*. New Delhi, India: Chetana Publications, 1978.

0483 BAXTER, CRAIG, ed. *Zia's Pakistan: Politics and Stability in a Frontline State*. Boulder, CO: Westview Press, 1986, 122 p.

0484 BROHI, A.K. *Islam in the Modern World*. 2d ed. Ed. Khurshid Ahmad. Lahore: Publishers United, 1975, 323 p.

0485 CLARK, GRACE. "Pakistan's Zakat and Ushr as a Welfare System". In *Islamic Reassertion in Pakistan*. Ed. Anita M. Weiss. Syracuse, NY: Syracuse University Press, 1986, 79-96.

0486 DASKAWIE, M.A.Q. "Legal Aspects of an Islamic Order." *al-Mushir*, 20 (Autumn 1978), 108-14.

0487 EATON, RICHARD M. "The Profile of Popular Islam in the Pakistani Punjab." *JSAMES*, 2 (1978), 74-92.

0488 ESPOSITO, JOHN L. "Pakistan: Quest for Islamic Identity." In *Islam and Development*. Ed. John L. Esposito. Syracuse, NY: Syracuse University Press, 1980, 139-62.

0489 FARUKI, KEMAL A. "Pakistan: Islamic Government and Society." In *Islam in Asia: Religion, Politics and Society*. Ed. John L. Esposito. New York: Oxford University Press, 1987, 53-78.

0490 GILANI, A. *Maududi: Thought and Movements*. Chicago: Kazi Publications, 1978.

0491 HAQ, FARHAT. "Islamic Reformism and the State: The Case of the Jammatt-i-Islami of Pakistan." Ph.D. diss., Cornell University, 1988, 369 p.

0492 HAQUE, ISRARUL. *Towards Islamic Renaissance*. Lahore: Ferozsons, 1987, 256 p.

0493 HUSAIN, MIR ZOHAIR. "The Politics of Islamic Revivalism: A Case Study of Pakistan Under Z.A. Bhutto (1972-77)." Ph.D. diss., University of Pennsylvania, 1985, 607 p.
   Investigates the meaning, characteristics, and causes of contemporary Islamic revival in Pakistan. Features the dynamics between four major types of Muslims: the fundamentalists, the traditionalists, the modernists, and the pragmatists. The latter are conventionally considered to be "secularists", although they engage in varying degrees in the politics of Islam and serve as catalysts in Islamic revival. Prime Minister Bhutto is presented as an example of the "pragmatist" category. The author concludes that as a consequence of global modernization and the resulting spread of Islamic revival, more pragmatist leaders will resort to the politics of Islam in order to legitimize their rule and unite a fragmented citizenry. Such leaders are vulnerable to the politics of Islam, however, because the Islamic revival that they fuel in part may ultimately destroy them.

0494 HUSSAIN, ASAF. *Elite Politics in an Ideological State: The Case of Pakistan.* Folkestone, England: William Dawson & Sons Ltd., 1979, 212 p.
Describes the medieval Muslim state of the Mughal dynasty, the advent of British colonial rule, and the politics of independence in Pakistan. The ideological contributions of Muslim intellectuals to state formation are treated in detail, and the emergence of the power structure of political elites and government is delineated. The role of religious elites is treated in a separate chapter.

0495 _____. "From Nationhood to Umma: The Struggle of Islam in Pakistan." *ATS*, 5 (April 1980), 47-57.

0496 _____. "Islam and Political Integration in Pakistan." In *The Crescent in the East, Islam in Asia Minor.* Ed. R. Israeli. London: Curzon Press, 1982, 62-78.

0497 IQBAL, JAVID. "Islamization in Pakistan." *JSAMES*, 8 (1985), 38-52.

0498 JALIL, YUSUF. "Political Aspects of an Islamic Order." *al-Mushir*, 20 (Autumn 1978), 99-107.

0499 JAMEELAH, MARYAM. "An Appraisal of Some Aspects of Maulana Sayyid Ala Maudoodi's Life and Thought." *IQ*, 31 (1987), 116-30.

0500 KHALID, DETLEV. "The Final Replacement of Parliamentary Democracy by the 'Islamic System' in Pakistan." *Orient*, 20 (1979), 16-38.

0501 KHAN, A.A. *Jamaat-e-islami. Pakistan. Introduction Series No. 2.* Dacca: Maktaba Jamaat-e-Islami, n.d., 18 p.

0502 KHAN, MOHAMMAD ASGHAR, ed. *Islam, Politics and the State: The Pakistan Experience.* London: Zed Books, 1985, 320 p.
Ten Pakistani scholars contribute essays to this volume edited by a former commander-in-chief of the Pakistani Air Force and current leader of a political party (Tehriq-i-Istaqlal. This is a sustained critique of the Islamization program of General Zia ul-Haq (1977-88), former president of Pakistan, and its impact upon national integration, economics, banking, and social change.

0503 KHAN, MOHAMMAD ZAFRULLA. *Ahmadiyyat: The Renaissance of Islam.* London: Tabshir Publications, 1978.

0504 KURIN, RICHARD. "Islamization: A View From the Countryside." In *Islamic Reassertion in Pakistan.* Ed. Anita M. Weiss. Syracuse: Syracuse University Press, 1986, 115-28.

0505 LATIFF, M.R.A. "The Way Ahead for Jamaat-e-Islami." Part I. *Saura al-Islam*, 3 (September-October 1977), 6.

0506 LODHI, MALEEHA. "Pakistan's Shia movement: An interview with Arif Hussaini." *TWQ*, 10 (April 1988), 806-17.

0507 MALIK, HAFEEZ. "Islamic Political Parties and Mass Politicisation." *IMA*, 3 (May 1972), 26-39.

0508 _____. "Martial Law and Islamization in Pakistan." *Orient*, 27 (December 1986), 605-58.

Discusses the various manifestations of Islamic revival in Pakistan since the achievement of independence in 1947, as well as the various interpretations of certain aspects of Islam that have been utilized as a legitimizing source of authority for the power structure of Pakistan.

0509 MAUDUDI, ABUL A'LA. *The Role of Muslim students in the Reconstruction of the Muslim World*. Kuwait: I.I.F.S.O., 1978.

0510 _____. *The Islamic Way of Life*. Ed. and trans. Khurshid Ahmad and Khurram Murad. Chicago: Kazi Publications, 1986, 80 p.

A revised English translation of the views of an important figure in the Islamic revivalist movement, this book offers selections of Mawdudi's writings on a variety of subjects. The book summarizes his views on the Islamic political system, the economic, social and moral principles of Islam, spirituality in Islam and the Islamic concept of life.

0511 MAWDUDI, SAYYID ABUL A'LA. *Jihad in Islam*. Kuwait: International Islamic Federation of Student Organizations, 1977.

0512 _____. *The Moral Foundations of the Islamic Movement*. Lahore: Islamic Publications Ltd., 1976.

0513 _____. *The Process of Islamic Revolution*. Lahore: Islamic Publications, 1970.

An important study by one of the most influential Muslim thinkers/activists of the twentieth century. This relatively brief volume, available in multiple translations, has influenced the thought of contemporary activists from Egypt to Indonesia.

0514 _____. *A Short History of the Revivalist Movement in Islam*. Lahore: Islamic Publications Ltd., 1963.

0515 _____. "Twenty-nine Years of the Jamaat-e-Islami." *The Criterion*, 5 (November-December 1970), 28-623.

0516 _____. *Witness Unto Mankind: The Purpose and Duty of the Muslim Ummah*. Ed. and trans. Khurram Murad. Leicester: The Islamic Foundation, 1986, 80 p.

0517 MAYER, ANN ELIZABETH. "Islamization and Taxation in Pakistan". In *Islamic Reassertion in Pakistan*. Ed. Anita M. Weiss. Syracuse, NY: Syracuse University Press, 1986, 59-78.

0518 McDONOUGH, SHEILA. *Muslim Ethics and Modernity*. Comparative Ethics Series: vol. 1. Waterloo, Ontario: Wilfrid Laurier University Press, 1984, 126 p.

0519 MEHDI, SIBTE. "Jamaat-i-Islami's Policy Towards the Zia Regime." *Saura al-Islam*, 4 (July 1978), 6-17.

0520 _____. "The Way Ahead for Jamaat-i-Islami." *Saura al-Islam*, 5 (January, 1979), 8-16.

0521 METCALF, BARBARA D. "Islamic Arguments in Contemporary Pakistan." In *Islam and the Political Economy of Meaning*. Ed. William R. Roff. Berkeley, CA: University of California Press, 1987, 132-59

0522 MINTJES, H. "Mawlana Mawdudi's Last Years and the Resurgence of Fundamentalist Islam." *al-Mushir*, 22 (Summer 1980), 46-73.

0523 AL-MUJAHID, SHARIF. "The Ideology of Pakistan. *Itt*, 20 (1983), 15-41.

0524 MUSLIM, ABDUL GHAFUR. "Islamization of Laws in Pakistan: Problems and Prospects." *IS*, 26 (Autumn 1987), 265-76.

0525 MUTAHAR, S.H. "Abul Ala Maudoodi: Sublime in Thought and Performance." *Rabitat al-Alam al-Islami*, 6 (October 1979), 5.

0526 _____. "Maudoodi's Views on Islamic Polity." *Rabitat al-Alam al-Islami*, 6 (October 1979), 52-56.

0527 NADVI, S.H.H. *Islamic Resurgent Movement in the Indo-Pak Sub-Continent*. Durban: Academic, 1987, 370 p.

0528 PATEL, RASHIDA. *Islamization of Laws in Pakistan?* Karachi: Faiza Publishers, 1986.
An eminent lawyer and women's leader (Vice-President of the All Pakistan Womens' Association and President of the Pakistan Women Lawyers Association) analyzes the constitutional and legal changes introduced to support the regime of General Zia ul-Haq. The author questions the Islamic as well as legal basis for this process and makes recommendations for a fresh reinterpretation of Islamic law.

0529 QURESHI, SALEEM. "Islam and Development: The Zia Regime in Pakistan." *WD*, 8 (1980), 563-75.

0530 RAHMAN, FAZLUR. "Islam in Pakistan." *JSAMES*, 8 (Summer 1985), 34-61.

0531 RICHTER, WILLIAM L. "Pakistan." In *The Politics of Islamic Reassertion*. Ed. Mohammed Ayoob. London: Croom Helm, 1981, 141-64.

0532 _____. "The Political Dynamics of Islamic Resurgence in Pakistan." *AS*, 19 (June 1979), 547-57.

0533 _____. "The Political Meaning of Islamization in Pakistan: Prognosis, Implications, and Questions." In *Islamic Reassertion in Pakistan*. Ed. Anita M. Weiss. Syracuse, NY: Syracuse University Press, 1986, 129-40.

0534 SAID, HAKIM MOHAMMAD. "Enforcement of Islamic Laws in Pakistan." *HamdIs*, 2 (1979), 61-90.

0535 SAULAT, SARWAR. *Maulana Mawdudi*. Karachi: International Islamic Publishers, 1979.

0536 SAYEED, K.B. "The Jamaat-i-Islami Movement in Pakistan." *PA*, 30 (March 1957), 59-68.

0537 _____. "Mass Urban Protests as Indicators of Political Change in Pakistan." *JCCP*, 17 (July 1979), 111-35.

0538 SHAFQAT, SAEED. "Politics of Islamization: The Ideological Debate on Pakistan's Political System". *AP*, 15 (October 1987), 445-58.

0539 SHAIKH, FARZANA. "Islam and the Quest for Democracy in Pakistan." *JCCP*, 24 (March 1986), 74-92.

0540 SIDDIQI, ASLAM. *Modernization Menaces Muslims*. Lahore: Sh. Muhammad Ashraf, 1974, 296 p.

0541 SIDDIQI, Q.Z., et al. "A Bibliography of Writings by and about Mawlana Sayyid Abul A'la Mawdudi." In *Islamic Perspectives: Studies in Honour of Mawlana Sayyid Abul A'la Mawdudi*. Leicester: The Islamic Foundation, 1979, 3-14.

0542 SIDDIQUI, M. AKHTAR SAEEd. "Enforcement of Shari'ah in the Present Context: An Analysis of the Challenges and the Problems." *JPS*, 34 (1986), 74.

0543 SIDDIQUI, KALIM. *Beyond the Muslim Nation States*. London: The Open Press Ltd., 1980, 16 p.

0544 SIDDIQUI, GHAVAR UDDIN. "An Approach to the Study of Jamaat-i-Islami in Pakistan." Seminar Paper, presented at the Muslim Institute, London, 13 November 1976, 12 p.

0545 WEISS, ANITA M. "The Historical Debate on Islam and the State in South Asia." In *Islamic Reassertion in Pakistan*. Ed. Anita M. Weiss. Syracuse, NY: Syracuse University Press, 1986, 1-20.

0546 _____, ed. *Islamic Reassertion in Pakistan: the Application of Islamic Laws in a Modern State*. Contemporary Issues in Middle East Series. Syracuse, NY: Syracuse University Press, 1986, 176 p.
   This volume is a collection of essays that deal with Islamic resurgence in Pakistan during Zia ul-Haq's rule (1977-88). Essays examine aspects of Zia's Islamization program and cover the historical background of the current resurgence of Islam in Pakistan; legal and economic reforms instituted by Zia's government; the institutionalization of Shari'a-based criminal punishment, courts, and taxation; responses of the rural population to Islamic reform efforts; and the impact of Islamization on Pakistani women. The book is a useful summary of contemporary Islamic revival as it develops in the specific setting of Pakistan.

0547 YUSUF, M. "Iqbal and Maudoodi." *UM*, 1 (January 1980), 8-10.

0548 _____. "Maudoodi: A Formative Phase." *IO*, 1 (1979), 33-43.

0549 ZIA-UL-HAQ, MOHAMMAD. "Enforcement of Nizam-i-Islam." *HamdIs*, 2 (Summer 1979), 3-60.
   Text of the speech announcing the enforcement of the Islamic laws in Pakistan with annexes and constitutional amendments.

0550 ZIRING, LAWRENCE. *Pakistan: The Enigma of Political Development*. Folkestone, Kent; Boulder, CO: Westview, 1980, 294 p.

4. Other

0551 ALI, AMEER. "Politics of Survival: Past Strategies and Present Predicament of the Muslim Community in Sri Lanka." *JIMMA*, 7 (1986), 147-70.

0552 MANIRUZZAMAN, TALUKDER. "Bangladesh Politics: Secular and Islamic Trends." In *Bangladesh*. Vol. I: History and Culture. Eds. S.R. Chakravarty and Narain. New Delhi: South Asian Publishers, 1986, 42-77.

0553 MAUROOF, MOHAMMED. "Muslims in Sri Lanka: Historical, Demographic and Political Aspects." *JIMMA*, 1-2 (1979-80), 183-93.

0554 MOHSIN, K.M. "Trends of Islam in Bangladesh." In *Bangladesh*, Vol I: History and Culture. Eds. S.R. Chkravarty and V. Narian. New Delhi, India: South Asian Publishers, 1986, 28-41.

0555 PHADNIS, URMILA. "Political Profile of the Muslim Minority of Sri Lanka." *InSt*, 18 (1979), 27-48.

0556 SAMARAWEERA, VIVAYA. "Some Sociological Aspects of the Muslim Revivalism in Sri Lanka." *SC*, 25 (1978), 465-75.

B. SOUTHEAST ASIA

0557 ABDULLAH, TAUFIK and SHARON SIDDIQUE. *Islam and Society in Southeast Asia*. Brookfield, VT: Gower Publishing Company, 1986, 360 p.
A collection of studies by Southeast Asian scholars produced under the auspices of the Institute of Southeast Asian Studies in Singapore. Demonstrates the contextualization of Islam in Southeast Asia (Malaysia, Indonesian, Thailand, Singapore, and Philippines) and the diversity of its manifestations politically, socially, and legally.

0558 BRUINESSEN, MARTIN VAN. "New Perspectives on Southeast Asian Islam?" *Anthropologica*, 29 (1987), 519-38.

0559 GUNN, GEOFFREY G. "Radical Islam in Southeast Asia: Rhetoric and Reality in the Middle Eastern Connection." *JCA*, 16 (1986), 30-54.

0560 HAQ, OBAID. "Islamic Resurgence: The Challenge of Change." In *Islam and Society in Southeast Asia*. Eds. Taufik Abdullah and Sharon Siddique. Singapore: Institute of Southeast Asian Studies, 1986, 332-48.

0561 HOOKER, M.B., ed. *Islam in South-East Asia*. Leiden: Brill, 1983, 262 p.

0562 IBRAHIM, AHMAD, SHARON SIDDIQUE, and YASMIN HUSSAIN. *Readings on Islam in Southeast Asia*. Brookfield, VT: Gower Publishing Company, 1986, 424 p.

A volume of forty-eight selected readings on Islam in Southeast Asia which covers the period from the early Islamization of Southeast Asia to the present. Articles are written by Muslim and non-Muslim, indigenous and foreign scholars. Although these selections have appeared elsewhere, their collection in a single volume is most useful for those not having easy access to Southeast Asian materials.

0563 JOHNS, A. "Islam in Southeast Asia: Reflections and New Directions." *Indonesia*, 19 (1975), 33-55.

0564 KESSLER, CLIVE. "The Politics of Islamic Egalitarianism." *Humaniora Islamica*, 2 (1974), 237-52.

0565 MUTALIB, HUSEIN. "Islamic Revivalism in Malaysia: The Middle East and Indonesian Connection." Paper Presented at Third Colloquium of Asian Studies Association of Australia-Malaysian Society, 1981.

0566 PEACOCK, J. *Muslim Puritans: Reformists Psychology in Southeast Asian Islam*. Berkeley, CA: University of California Press, 1978.

0567 TROLL, C.W. "Islam as a Missionary Religion: Some Observations with Special Reference to South and Southeast Asia." *Encounter*, 130 (November-December 1986). [entire issue].

0568 VON DER MEHDEN, FRED R. "The Political and Social Challenge of the Islamic Revival in Malaysia and Indonesia." *MW*, 76 (July-October), 219-33.

0569 _____. *Religion & Modernization in Southeast Asia*. Syracuse, NY: Syracuse University Press, 1986, 232 p.
This volume focuses on the interrelationship of religion (Buddhism, Christianity, and Islam) and modernization in the Southeast Asia (Burma, Thailand, Malaysia, Indonesia, and the Philippines.) The author demonstrates the deficiencies of development theories in the past, often due to biases and limited field research, which led to misconceptions about indigenous cultures and the nature and role of religion in societies.

1. Indonesia

0570 ALFIAN. *Muhammadiyah*. Yogyakarta: Gadja Mada University Press, 1989.

0571 AMIEN, RAIS. "International Islamic Movements and their Influence Upon the Islamic Movement in Indonesia." *Prisma*, 35 (March 1985).

0572 ANWAR, KHAIDIR. "Islam in Indonesia Today." *IQ*, 23 (1979), 99-102.

0573 BOLAND, B. *The Struggle of Islam in Modern Indonesia*. The Hague: Nijhoff, 1982, 283 p.
Slightly revised reprint of the 1971 edition.

0574 DIJK, C. VAN *Rebellion under the Banner of Islam: The Darul Islam in Indonesia.* KITLV Verhandelingen 94. The Hague: Nijhoff Publishers, 1981, 468 p.

0575 FEDERSPIEL, HOWARD. *Persatuan Islam: Islamic Reform in Twentieth Century Indonesia.* Ithaca, NY: Cornell University Press, 1970, 247 p.

0576 HEFNER, ROBERT W. "Islamizing Java? Religion and Politics in Rural East Java." *JAS,* 46 (August 1987), 533-54.

0577 _____. "The Political Economy of Islamic Conversion in Modern East Java." In *Islam and the Political Economy of Meaning.* Ed. William R. Roff. Berkeley, CA: University of California Press, 1987, 53-78.

0578 JACKSON, KARL D. *Traditional Authority, Islam and Rebellion: A Study of Indonesian Political Behavior.* Center for South and Southeast Asia Studies, UC Berkeley: No. 32. Berkeley, CA: University of California Press, 1980, 375 p.

0579 JOHNS, ANTHONY H. "Indonesia: Islam and Cultural Pluralism." In *Islam in Asia: Religion, Politics and Society.* Ed. John L. Esposito. New York: Oxford University Press, 1987, 202-29.

0580 _____. "An Islamic System or Islamic Values? Nucleus of a Debate in Contemporary Indonesia." In *Islam and the Political Economy of Meaning.* Ed. William R. Roff. Berkeley, CA: University of California Press, 1987, 254-80.

0581 KATZ, J.S., and R.S. KATZ. "Legislating Social Change in a Developing Country: The New Indonesian Marriage Law Revisited." *AJCL,* 26 (1978), 309-20.

0582 KIPP, RITA S. and SUSAN ROGERS, eds. *Indonesian Religions in Transition.* Tucson, AZ: University of Arizona Press, 1987, 304 p.

0583 KOENTJARANINGRAT. *Javanese Culture.* Singapore; New York: Oxford University Press, 1985, 350 p.

0584 LIONG, LIEM SOEI. "Indonesian Muslims and the State: Accommodation or Revolt?" *TWQ,* 10 (April 1988), 869-96.

0585 MADJID, NURCHOLISH. "Islam in Indonesia: Challenges and Opportunities." In *Islam in the Contemporary World.* Ed. Cyriac K. Pullapilly. Notre Dame, IN: Cross Roads Books, 1980, 340-57.

0586 _____. "The Issue of Modernization among Muslims in Indonesia: From a Participant's Point of View." In *What Is Modern Indonesian Culture?* Ed. Gloria Davis. Athens, OH: Ohio University Center for International Studies, 1979, 143-55.

0587 McVEY, RUTH. "Faith as the Outsider: Islam in Indonesian Politics." In *Islam in the Political Process.* Ed. James Piscatori. Cambridge: Cambridge University Press, 1983, 199-25.

0588 MUHAMMAD, KAMAL HASSAN. *Muslim Intellectual Responses to "New Order" Modernization in Indonesia.* Kuala Lumpur: Dewan Bahasa dan Pustaka, 1982, 250 p.
An intellectual history by a Malaysian scholar of elite Muslim responses in Indonesia to the socio-political changes of Suharto's "New Order" modernization program from the mid-1960's to the mid-1970's.

0589 NAKAMURA, MITSUO. *The Crescent Arises over the Banyan Tree: A Study of the Muhammadiyah Movement in a Central Javanese Town.* Yogyakarta: Gadja Mada University Press, 1983, 223 p.

0590 NOER, DELIAR. *Administration of Islam in Indonesia.* Monograph Series, No. 58. Ithaca, NY: Cornell Modern Indonesia Project, Southeast Asia Program, Cornell University Press, 1978, 82 p.

0591 _____. *The Modernist Muslim Movement in Indonesia: 1990-1942.* Singapore; New York: Oxford University Press, 1973, 390 p.

0592 PEACOCK, JAMES L. *Purifying the Faith: The Muhammadiyah Movement in Indonesian Islam.* Menlo Park, CA: Benjamin/Cummings, 1978, 118 p.
A fine anthropological study of the Muhammadiyya, an Indonesian reformist movement inspired by the Egyptian Muhammad Abduh's Islamic modernist movement. The author provides an understanding of the inspiration and of the educational and social activities of this modern Islamic reform organization as well as its considerable achievements.

0593 SOEBARDI, S. and C.P. WOODCROFT-LEE. "Islam in Indonesia." In *The Crescent in the East, Islam in Asia Minor.* Ed. Raphael Israeli. London: Curzon Press, 1982, 180-210.

0594 TAPOL. *Indonesia: Muslim on Trial.* London: TAPOL, The Indonesia Human Rights Campaign, 1987, 128 p.
A compelling depiction of the vicissitudes of Muslim activists in Indonesia under the army-dominated Suharto regime.

0595 THOMAS, R. "Islamic Revival and Indonesian Education." *AS*, 28 (September 1988), 897-915.

0596 WAHID, ABDURRAHMAN. "The Nahdlatul Ulama and Islam in Present Day Indonesia." In *Islam and Society in Southeast Asia.* Eds. T. Abdullah and S. Siddique. Singapore: Institute of Southeast Asian Studies, 1986, 175-86.

0597 WOODWARD, MARK R. *Islam in Java: Normative Piety & Mysticism in the Sultanate of Yogyakarta.* Tucson, AZ: University of Arizona Press, 1989, 400 p.

2. Malaysia

0598 ABU BAKAR, MOHAMMAD. "Islam and Nationalism in Contemporary Malay Society." In *Islam and Society in Southeast Asia.* Eds. Taufik Abdullah and Sharon Siddique. Singapore: Institute of Southeast Asian Studies, 1986, 155-74.

0599 _____. "Islamic Revivalism and the Political Process in Malaysia." *AS*, 21 (October 1981).

0600 AL-ATTAS, SYED NAGUIB. *Islam and Secularism*. Kuala Lumpur: Muslim Youth Movement of Malaysia, 1978.
One of Southeast Asia's leading Muslim intellectuals offers an early critique of secularism from a Muslim perspective. This volume is important both for its content and the influence that the author and his ideas have had on a generation of Malaysian youth, in particular those who have become Islamic activists.

0601 _____, ed. *Ethnicity, Class and Development Malaysia*. Kuala Lumpur: Persatuan Sains Social Malaysia, 1984.

0602 ANWAR, ZAINAH. *Islamic Revivalism in Malaysia: Dakwah Among the Students*. Selanger, Malaysia: Pelanduk Publications, 1987, 122 p.
A brief but incisive look at the development of the revivalist activities among Malay students. Documents the turn toward Islam as a vital source of Malay identity, focusing primarily on the role of the student movement in articulating an ideology of dissent and, secondarily, on the rivalry between the two Malay political parties in appealing to Islam as a basis for legitimacy. Decries the polarizing impact of Islamic revivalism on social and political life which exacerbates already deep socio-economic and ethnic tensions.

0603 BARRACLOUGH, S. "Managing the Challenges of the Islamic Revival in Malaysia and Indonesia." *AS*, 23 (August 1983), 958-75.

0604 BUHARUDDIN, SHAMSUL AMRI. "A Revival of the Study of Islam in Malaysia". In *Readings in Malaysian Politics*. Ed. B. Gale. Petaling Jaya: Pelanduk, 1986, 134-44.

0605 CHEEK, AHMAD SHABERY and JOMO KWAME SUNDARAM. "The Politics of Malaysia's Islamic Resurgence." *TWQ*, 10 (April 1988), 843-68.

0606 CROUCH, HAROLD, LEE KAM HING, MICHEAL ONG, eds. *Malaysian Politics and the 1978 Election*. Kuala Lumpur; New York: Oxford University Press, 1980, 330 p.

0607 FUNSTON, N.J. *Malay Politics in Malaysia: A Study of UMNO & Party Islam*. Kuala Lumpur: Heinemann Educational Books (Asia) Ltd, 1980, 326 p.

0608 HAJI ABDULLAH, FIRDAUS. *Radical Malay Politics: Its Origin and Early Development*. Petaling Jaya: Pelanduk Publications, 1985.

0609 HUSIN, ALI S. *The Malays, Their Problems and Future*. Kuala Lumpur: Heinemann Asia, 1982.

0610 HASSAN, MUHAMMAD KAMAL. "Da'wah in Malaysia: Some Personal Observations and Interpretations Regarding Obstacles and Future Strategy". A Paper presented at the International Conference of the 15th Hijra, Kuala Lumpur, Nov. 24-Dec. 4, 1981.

0611 _____ . "The Response of Muslim Youth Organizations to Political Change: HMI in Indonesia and ABIM in Malaysia." In *Islam and the Political Economy of Meaning*. Ed. William R. Roff. Berkeley, CA: University of California Press, 1987, 180-96.

0612 HUSSEIN, S. AHMAD. "Islam and Politics in Malaysia, 1969-1982: The Dynamics of Competing Traditions." Ph.D. diss., Yale, 1988.

0613 KESSLER, CLIVE. "Islam, Society and Political Behavior: Some Comparative Implications of the Malay Case." *BJS*, 23 (March 1972), 33-49.

0614 _____ . "Malaysia: Islamic Revivalism and Political Disaffection in a Divided Society." *SAC*, 75 (October 1980), 3-11.

0615 LEE, RAYMOND L.M. "The Ethnic Implications of Contemporary Religious Movements and Organizations in Malaya." *CSA*, 8 (June 1986), 70-87.

0616 LYON, M.L. "The Dakwah Movement in Malaysia." *RIMA*, 13 (December 1979).

0617 MATHESON V. and A.C. MILNER. *Perceptions of the Haj: Five Malay Texts*. Brookfield, VT: Gower Publishing Company, 1986, 64 p.

0618 MEANS, GORDON P. "Malaysia: Islam in a Pluralistic Society." In *Religions and Societies: Asia and the Middle East*. Ed. Carlo Caldarola. Berlin: Mouton de Gruyer, 1982, 445-96.

0619 _____ . "Malaysia: Islam and Multi-ethnic Politics." In *Islam in Asia: Religion, Politics and Society*. Ed. John L. Esposito. New York: Oxford University Press, 1987, 177-201.

0620 MESS, ZULKARNAINA M., and W. BARNETT PEARCE. "Dakwah Islamiah: Islamic Revivalism in the Politics of Race and Religion in Malaysia." In *Prophetic Religions and Politics: Religion and the Political Order*, vol. 1. Eds. Jeffrey K. Hadden and Anson Shupe. New York: Paragon House Publishers, 1986, 196-220.

0621 MILNE, R.S. and DIANE K. MAUZY. *Malaysia: Tradition, Modernity and Islam*. Boulder, CO: Westview Press, 1986, 125 p.

0622 MILNER, A.C. "Rethinking Islamic Fundamentalism in Malaysia." *RIMA*, 20 (Summer 1986), 48-75.

0623 MUZAFFAR, CHANDRA. *Islamic Resurgence in Malaysia*. Malaysia: Penerbit Fajar Bakti Sdn. Bhd., 1987, 124 p.

0624 NAGATA, JUDITH. "Indices of Religious Resurgence in Malaysia: The Medium and the Message." In *Religious Resurgence, Contemporary Cases in Islam, Christianity, and Judaism*. Eds. Richard T. Antoun and Mary Elaine Hegland. Syracuse, NY: Syracuse University Press, 1987, 35-63.

0625 _____ . "Islamic Revival and the Problem of Legitimacy Among Rural Religious Elites in Malaysia". In *Readings in Malaysian Politics*. Ed. B. Gale. Petaling Jaya: Pelanduk, 1986, 113-33.

0626 _____. *The Reflowering of Malaysian Islam: Modern Religious Radicals and Their Roots*. Vancouver: University of British Columbia Press, 1984, 282 p.
A sociological study of Islamic revivalism in Malaysia which focuses on the major Islamic organizations (ABIM, Darul Arqam, PAS, PERKIM, Tabligh), their history, leadership, ideology, and activities.

0627 _____. "Religious Ideology and Social Change: The Islamic Revival in Malaysia." *MAN*, 53 (Fall 1980).

0628 NOER, DELIAR. "Islam In Indonesia and Malaysia: A Preliminary Study." *RIMA*, (July-December 1975).

0629 PELETZ, M.G. *A Share of the Harvest*. Berkeley, CA: University of California Press, 1988.

0630 SUNDARAM, J.K. and A.H. CHEEK. "The Politics of Malaysia's Islamic Resurgence." *TWQ*, 10 (April 1988), 843-68.

0631 VON DER MEHDEN, FRED R. "Islam, Development and Politics in Malaysia." In *Essays in Islamic and Comparative Studies*. Ed. Isma'il al Faruqi. International Institute of Islamic Thought, 1982.

0632 VON VORYS, KARL. *Democracy Without Consensus: Communalism and Political Stability in Malaysia*. Princeton: Princeton University Press, 1975.

3.   Philippines

0633 ANGELES, VIVIENNE SM. *Islam and Politics: Philippine Government Policies and Muslim Responses, 1946-1976* (Volumes I and II). Ph.D. diss., Temple University, 1987, 444 p.
Examines the Muslim movement in the Philippines, with particular attention given to the MORO National Liberation Front (MNLF), in terms of basic Islamic social and political concepts and theoretical formulations on minority relations. Such concepts as *jihad*, Muslim political obedience, *umma* and the function and place of the Shari'ah help explain how religious identity and the call for an Islamic community affect Muslim political action in the Philippines.

0634 BACHO, PETER. "The Muslim Secessionist Movement in the Philippines." *JIA*, 41 (1987), 153-64.

0635 GOWING, PETER G. "The Moro Rebellion: Why and Wherefore?" *Newsletter*, (Center for the Study of Islam and Christian Muslim Relations.) No. 2 (September 1979).

0636 _____. "The Muslim Filipino Minority." In *The Crescent in the East, Islam in Asia Minor*. Ed. Raphael Israeli. London: Curzon Press, 1982, 211-26.

0637 _____. *Understanding Islam and the Muslims in the Philippines*. Quezon City, Philippines: New Day Publications, 1988, 176 p.

The book contains brief treatment of the Moro Wars and the government programs for Mindanao and secularized Muslims.

0638 GOWING, PETER G. and ROBERT D. MCAMIS, eds. *The Muslims Filipinos*. Manila: Solidaridad Publications, 1974, 311 p.

0639 ISTEIYAQUE, S.M. "Mindano Moro Liberation Movement." *MWLJ*, (Makka) 15 (1988), 50-57.

0640 MADALE, NAGASURA. "The Resurgence of Islam and Nationalism in the Philippines." In *Islam and Society in Southeast Asia*. Eds. Taufik Abdulah and Sharon Siddique. Singapore: Institute of Southeast Asian Studies, 1986, 282-314.

0641 MAJUL, CESAR ADIB. *The Contemporary Muslim Movement in the Philippines*. Berkeley, CA: Mizan Press, 1985, 162 p.
A leading Filipino Muslim intellectual provides an historical interpretation of the stages in the development of the Muslim movement in the Philippines from pre-colonial to contemporary times. Majul traces the evolution of the Muslim community from that of a separate minority struggling to retain its identity within an emerging nation state to the formation of the Moro National Liberation Front in the 1970's with its demand for regional autonomy.

0642 _____. "The Moro struggle in the Philippines." *TWQ*, 10 (April 1988), 897-922.

0643 MASTURA, MICHAEL O. *Muslim Filipino Experience: A Collection of Essays*. Philippine Islam Series, no. 3. Manila: Ministry of Muslim Affairs, 1984, 285 p.
The papers deal with the history of the Muslim community in the Philippines, government policies toward the muslim minority, the constitution,, Islamic laws, and Islamic economics.

0644 MAY, R.J. "The Situation of Philippine Muslims." *JIMMA*, 5 (1984), 427-40

0645 ORTIZ, ALAN TORMIS. "Towards a Theory of Ethnic Separatism: A Case Study of Muslims in the Philippines." Ph.D. diss., University of Pennsylvania, 1986, 375 p.

4. Other

0646 CARROL, LUCY. "Muslim Minorities and Legal Questions in Australia: A Rejoinder." *JIMMA*, 7 (1986), 35-67.

0647 CHE MAN, W.K. "The Malay Muslims of Southern Thailand." *JIMMA*, 6 (1985), 98-112.

0648 IMTIYAZ, ABID ALI. "Forgotten Muslims of Comoro Islands." *IL*, 16 (August 1980), 54-64.

0649 KRAUS, WERNER. "Islam in Thailand." *JIMMA*, 5 (1984), 410-25.

0650 MOON, CHUNG-IN. "Politics and Religion: The Rise of Islam in South Korea." *JSAMES*, 11 (1987), 131-55.

0651 MORIMOTO, ABU BAKR. "Two New Facts Regarding History of Islam in Japan." *ICF*, 2 (April 1979), 19-28.

0652 PROVENCHER, RONALD. "Islam in Malaysia and Thailand." In *The Crescent in the East, Islam in Asia Minor.* Ed. Raphael Israeli. London: Curzon Press, 1982, 140-55.

0653 THOMAS, M. LADD. "The Thai Muslims." In *The Crescent in the East, Islam in Asia Minor.* Ed. Raphael Israeli. London: Curzon Press, 1982, 156-79.

C. SOVIET UNION and CHINA

0654 ABDULLAH, ABDULGHANI. "Islam in Soviet Central Asia." *JIMMA*, 9 (July 1988), 251-54.

0655 ABDURAHMANOV, K. "New Publications by Muslim Religious Board for Central Asia and Kazakhstan." *MSE*, no. 4 (1980), 11-13.

0656 AKINER, SHIRIN. *Islamic Peoples of the Soviet Union.* rev. 2d ed. London: Routledge & Kegan Paul, 1986, 480 p.

0657 AMINI, MUHAMMAD SAFWAT EL-SAQQA. *Muslims in the Soviet Union.* Mecca: Muslim World League, 1980, 58 p.
A tract written by the Assistant Secretary General of the Muslim World League.

0658 ANDERSON, J. "The 'Islamic Factor' in the Soviet Union." *RCL*, 14 (1986), 212-14.

0659 AUGUSTIN, ARCHIMANDRITE. *Islam in Russia.* Research Papers - Muslims in Europe, no. 8. Birmingham, England: Center for the Study of Islam and Christian-Muslim Relations, 1980, 12 p.

0660 BENNIGSEN, ALEXANDRE. "Islam in the Soviet Union." *JSAMES*, 8 (1985), 115-33.

0661 _____. "Official Islam and Sufi Brotherhoods in Soviet Union Today." *Islam and Power.* Eds. Cudsi and Dessouki. Baltimore, MD: Johns Hopkins University Press, 1981, 95-106.

0662 _____. "Unrest in the World of Soviet Islam." *TWQ*, 10 (April 1988), 770-86.

0663 BENNIGSEN, ALEXANDRE and CHANTAL LEMERCIER-QUELQUEJAY. "Muslims Religious Conservatism and Dissent in the USSR." *SCR*, 13 (Winter-Spring 1979), 40-49.

0664 BENNIGSEN, ALEXANDRE and MARIE BROXUP. *The Islamic Threat to the Soviet State.* New York: St. Martin's Press, 1983, 170 p.

Traces the origins of Islam in the USSR, highlighting the friction between Islamic culture in Central Asia and the Caucasus and, the Russian and later the Soviet state. The authors suggest that the USSR's large Muslim population is a likely source of instability. Strongly anti-Soviet and critical of Soviet nationalities policy. Provides information on demographics and life conditions of Soviet Muslims today as well as projections about the future. It also addresses Soviet relations with Muslim countries and the impact of current Islamic revival on religious practices and official Soviet policy.

0665 BENNIGSEN, ALEXANDRE and S. ENDERS WIMBUSH. *Muslim National Communism in the Soviet Union, A Revolutionary Strategy for the Colonial World.* Chicago and London: University of Chicago Press, 1979, 267 p.

0666 _____. *Muslims of the Soviet Empire: A Guide.* Bloomington, IN: Indiana University Press, 1986, 296 p.

0667 _____. *Mystics and Commissars: Sufism in the Soviet Union.* Berkeley and Los Angeles: University of California Press, 1985, 195 p.

Describes the origins, structure, and practices of Sufi orders in Soviet Central Asia and the Caucasus. Focusing on the insurrectionary potential the authors see inherent in the Sufi brotherhoods, described as being the vanguard of dissent in some regions of the USSR. Authors argue that Soviet concerns about the potential effect of revolutionary Islam in Iran has resulted in tighter restrictions on Sufi activities since 1978. Includes a short annotated bibliography of Soviet sources on Sufism in the Soviet Union.

0668 BOBOMUHAMEDOV, P. "Muslims of Daghestan." *MSE*, no. 2 (1978), 7-10.

0669 BROXUP, MARIE. "Islam and Atheism in the North Caucasus." *RCL*, 9 (Spring 1981), 40-48.

Discusses the influence of Tariqas on maintaining a strong Islamic identity among the North Caucasus tribes of Checken and Ingush.

0670 _____. "Islam in Central Asia Since Gorbachev." *AA*, 18 (Old Series Vol. 74) (October 1987), 283-93.

0671 CARRERE D'ENCAUSSE, HELENE. *Islam and The Russian Empire: Reform and Revolution in Central Asia.* Trans. Quintin Hoare. Preface by Maxime Rodinson. Comparative Studies on Muslim Societies, no. 8. Berkeley and Los Angeles: University of California Press, 1988, 267 p.

Originally published in French in 1966, this edition with preface by Maxime Rodinson makes available in English an important source work on traditional Muslim customs and doctrines in Soviet Russia. It traces Islamic heritage in the Khanate of Bukhara from the eve of Russian conquest through the Bolshevik Revolution and political consolidation of Soviet rule. Important features are its presentation of Muslim conventions on property, charity, and political authority and its review of reformist movements in Islam (e.g. Afghani) before discussing the impact of Russian conquest and absorption into the Russian empire. Shows how a reformist ideology developed among Central Asian Muslims in the late nineteenth century.

0672 CHANG, YUSUF HAJJI. "Chinese Islam and the Hui Minority: Past, Present and Future." In *The Legacy of Islam in China: Proceedings of an International Symposium in Memory of Joseph F. Fletcher, April 14-16, 1989*, by the John King Fairbank Center for East Asian Research, 404-33.

0673 DEVLET, NADIR. "Islam in Tataristan." *JIMMA*, 5 (July 1984), 336-44.

0674 DREYER, JUNE T. "The Islamic Community of China." *The Search*, 2 (1980).

0675 GLADNEY, DRU C. "Identifying the Hui in China: Self-Definition, Ethnoreligious Identity, and the State." In *The Legacy of Islam in China: Proceedings of an International Symposium in Memory of Joseph F. Fletcher, April 14-16, 1989*, by the John King Fairbank Center for East Asian Research, 448-98.

0676 _____. "Muslim Tombs and Ethnic Folklore: Charters for Hui Identity." *JAS*, 46 (August 1987), 495-532.
   Discusses the interaction between government policy and religio-ethnic identity in China. Focuses on the importance of Sufi orders and saints' tombs to the continued existence of Islamic practices in China.

0677 HALLIDAY, FRED. "'Islam' and Soviet Foreign Policy." *ASQ*, 9 (Summer 1987), 217-33.

0678 ISRAELI, RAPHAEL. *Muslims in China: A Study in Cultural Confrontation*. London: Curzon Press, 1980, 272 p.
   Uses a sociological approach to study the history of Muslim-state relations and Muslim-Han relations in imperial China. Briefly compares the circumstances of Muslims in China to those of their Jewish and Christian compatriots and of Muslims in India.
   The author dwells on the ramifications of the ideal of *Dar al-Islam* -- the theoretical duty for Muslims to live under Muslim rule -- for Muslims who live as a minority in the non-Muslim world. He characterizes this condition as unstable; however, he fails to account for the absense of rebellion and the long periods of peaceful existence on the part of Muslims in China in spite of their minority status. The book is simplistic in its descriptions of the Muslim community and its struggle to maintain an identity. Assimilation patterns of Muslims in China and the pressures from competing sources of identity are ignored. Simple indications of assimilation such as intermarriage and recruitment into the ranks of the civil and military services, while documented in this study, are not used by the author to temper his superficial argument. Instead the author relies on the facile presumption that an antagonistic relationship persists between the Han Chinese and the dynasty on the one hand and the Muslims, a beleaguered minority, on the other.

0679 _____. "Muslim Plight under Chinese Rule." In *The Crescent in the East, Islam in Asia Minor*. Ed. Raphael Israeli. London: Curzon Press, 1982, 227-45.

0680 KERIMOV, G.M. "Islam in the USSR: Its Nature and Contemporary Forms." In *Utrecht Papers on Central Asia: Proceedings of the First European Seminar on Central Asia in Utrecht, December 16-18, 1985*. Ed. M. Van Damme & H. Boeschoten. Utrecht: University of Utrecht, 1987, 29-42

0681 KHAN, MUHAMMAD M.A. "Popular Islam in Central Asia and Kazakhstan: Comments." *JIMMA*, 9 (July 1988), 258-63.

0682 MACDONALD, PETER K. "The Muslims of Soviet Central Asia: Present Reality and Future Possibilities." *WO*, (Winter 1988), 75-88.
Discusses rising power of Central Asian nationalities and implications for foreign policy.

0683 MOTYL, ALEXANDER J. *Will the Non-Russians Rebel? State, Ethnicity and Stability in the USSR.* Ithaca, NY; London: Cornell University Press, 1987, 188 p.
A study of the Soviet Union's problems with stability which mentions Muslims only briefly in a discussion of the USSR's ethnic groups.

0684 NEWBY, L.J. "The 'Pure and True Religion' in China." *TWQ*, 10 (April 1988), 923-47.

0685 OLCOTT, MARTHA BRILL. *The Kazakhs.* Standford, CA: Hoover Institution Press, 1987, 341 p.

0686 _____. "Soviet Islam and World Revolution." *WP*, 34 (July), 487-504.

0687 PAHTA, GHULAMUDDIN. "Changing Muslim's Status in Eastern Turkestan." *JIMMA*, 7 (1986), 124-33.

0688 PILLSBURY, BARBARA. "Pig and Policy: Maintenance of Boundaries Between Han and Muslim Chinese." In *Minorities: A Text with Readings in Inter-Group Relations.* Ed. B.E. Griessman. Hinsdale, IL: Dryden Press, 1975, 136-45.

0689 _____. "Transformation of Hui Identity in Taiwan and China." In *The Legacy of Islam in China: Proceedings of an International Symposium in Memory of Joseph F. Fletcher, April 14-16, 1989,* by the John King Fairbank Center for East Asian Research, n.p.

0690 PIPES, DANIEL. "Fundamentalist Muslims Between America and Russia." *FA*, 64 (Summer 1986), 939-59.

0691 AL-QADIR, ADB. "Confessions of a Soviet Muslim Rebel." Interview. *Orbis*, 32 (Summer 1988), 432-36.

0692 RAHMATI, RAHMATULLAH AHMAD. "Inside Chinese Turkestan: A Fresh Look." *JIMMA*, 7 (January 1986), 275-82.

0693 RAMET, P., ed. *Religion and Nationalism in Soviet and East European Politics.* Durham, NC: Duke University Press Policy Studies, 1984, 282 p.

0694 RO'I, YAACOV, ed. *The USSR and the Muslim World, Issues in Domestic and Foreign Policy.* London: George Allen & Unwin, 1984, 298 p.
This collection of essays concentrates on the internal dimension as well as foreign policy aspects of Muslim-Soviet relations. Topics covered range from the effects of Soviet language policy in the Turkic republics to the impact of Islamic revival of the late 1970s on the Soviet view of Islam to Soviet policy in Afghanistan, relations with Saudi Arabia, and the problems of Arab communism.

0695 RYWKIN, MICHAEL. "Islam and the New Soviet Man: 70 Years of Evolution". *CAS*, 6 (1987), 22-32.

0696 SHAMS UD DIN. "Demographic Changes and Nationality Problems in Soviet Central Asia, Kazakhstan and Azerbaijan." *IC*, 60 (1986), 27-43.

0697 _____. "Reformist Movements Among the Muslim of Tsarist Russia." *IMA*, 10 (November 1979), 27-50.

0698 _____. "Russian Policy Towards Islam and Muslims: An Overview." *JIMMA*, 5 (July 1984), 321-35.

0699 SOPER, J. "Unofficial Islam: A Muslim Minority in the USSR." *RCL*, 7 (Winter 1979), 226-31.

0700 TING, DAWOOD C.M. "Islamic Culture in China." In *Islam - The Straight Path: Islam Interpreted by Muslims*. Ed. K.W. Morgan. Delhi, India: Motilal Banarsidass, 1987, 344-74.

0701 _____. "Islamic Tradition in Taiwan." *FCR*, 38 (1988), 36-39.

0702 TORU, SAGUCHI. "The Community and Religious Life of Chinese Muslims." In *The Legacy of Islam in China: Proceedings of an International Symposium in Memory of Joseph F. Fletcher, April 14-16, 1989*, by the John King Fairbank Center for East Asian Research, 434-47.

0703 VOLL, JOHN O. "Muslim Minority Alternatives: Implications of Muslim Experiences in China and the Soviet Union." *JIMMA*, 6 (July 1985), 332-53.

0704 _____. "Soviet Central Asia and China: Integration or Isolation of Muslim Societies." In *Islam in Asia: Religion, Politics and Society*. Ed. John L. Esposito. New York: Oxford University Press, 1987, 125-51.

0705 WAARDENBURG, JACQUES. "Western Studies of Islam in Present-Day Central Asia (USSR)" In *Utrecht Papers on Central Asia: Proceedings of the First European Seminar on Central Asia in Utrecht, December 16-18, 1985*. Ed. M. Van Damme & H. Boeschoten. Utrecht: University of Utrecht, 1987, 45-67.

0706 ZHAO-CHUN, IBRAHIM MA. "Islam in China: The Internal Dimension." *JIMMA*, 7 (July 1986), 373-83.

V. EUROPE

0707 ABDULLAH, MUHAMMAD S. "Christian-Muslim Encounter in a German Perspective." In *Islam in a Plural World*. Research Papers - Muslims in Europe, no. 15. Birmingham, England: Centre for the Study of Islam and Christian-Muslim Relations, 1982, 1-11.

0708 _____. *Muslim Religious Education in the Federal Republic of Germany - The Qur'an School Debate*. Research Papers - Muslims in Europe, no. 4. Birmingham, England: Centre for the Study of Islam and Christian-Muslim Relations, 1979, 30 p.

0709 AL-ABOUDI, MUHAMMAD BIN NASR. "Muslim Experience in Eastern Europe: A First Hand Report." *JIMMA*, 7 (1986), 88-116.

0710 ALEXANDER, S. "Yugoslavia: New Legislation on the Legal Status of Religious Communities." *RCL*, 8, (Summer 1980), 119-24.

0711 ALLY, MUHAMMAD MASHUQ. *The Growth and Organization of the Muslim Community in Britain*. Research Papers - Muslims in Europe, no. 1. Birmingham, England: Centre for the Study of Islam and Christian-Muslim Relations, 1979, 10 p.

0712 ANTES, PETER. "Islamic Identity and the Turks in West Germany." In *Muslims in Germany - German Muslims?* Research Papers - Muslims in Europe, no. 28. Birmingham, England: Centre for the Study of Islam and Christian-Muslim Relations, 1985, 1-9.

0713 ANWAR, MUHAMMAD. *The Myth of Return: Pakistanis in Britain*. London: Heinemann, 1979, 278 p.

0714 _____. *Pakistanis in Britain: A Sociological Study*. London: New Century Publishers, 1985, 294 p.

0715 ANWAR, MUHAMMAD and ROGER GARAUDY. *Social and Cultural Perspectives on Muslims in Western Europe*. Research Papers - Muslims in Europe, no. 24. Birmingham, England: Centre for the Study of Islam and Christian-Muslim Relations, 1984, 35 p.

0716 ASSAD, DAWUD. "Mixed Marriages." In *Christian-Muslim Marriages*. Research Papers - Muslims in Europe, no. 20. Birmingham, England: Centre for the Study of Islam and Christian-Muslim Relations, 1983, 3-8.

0717 BADRI, MALIK B. *The Dilemma of Muslim Psychologists*. London: MWH London Publishers, 1979.

0718 BARTON, STEPHEN. "The Bengali Muslims of Bradford." In *What Place for Europe's Muslims?* Research Papers - Muslims in Europe, no. 13. Birmingham, England: Centre for the Study of Islam and Christian-Muslim Relations, 1982, 11-23.

0719 _____. "The Preaching of a Bradford Imam." In *Sermons for Europe.* Research Papers - Muslims in Europe, no. 29. Birmingham, England: Centre for the Study of Islam and Christiam-Muslim Relations, 1986, p. 19.

0720 BHATTI, F.M. "Muslims as Migrants: The Turks in West Germany." *JIMMA,* 1-2 (Winter/Summer 19809), 47-62.
Pays special attention to education of children and adults.

0721 _____. *Turkish Cypriots in London.* Research Papers - Muslims in Europe, no. 11. Birmingham, England: Centre for the Study of Islam and Christian-Muslim Relations, 1981, 20 p.

0722 BOCOCK, R. "Religion in Modern Britain." In *Religion and Ideology.* Eds. R. Bobcock and K. Thompson. London: The Open University, 1985.

0723 COLE, W. OWEN. "Islam in Education in England." In *Islam in English Law and Administration.* Research Papers - Muslims in Europe, no. 9. Birmingham, England: Centre for the Study of Islam and Christian-Muslim Relations, 1981, 2-5.

0724 CRELLIN, CLIFFORD T. *Turkish Education in Cyprus.* C.T Crellin: Statens Trykning Skontor, 1975, 55 p.

0725 CUSTERS, MARTIA. "Muslims in the Netherlands: Newcomers in an Established Society." *JIMMA,* 6 (Jan 1985), 167-80.

0726 DASSETTO, F. and A. BASTERNIF. *The Organization of Islam in Belgium.* Research Papers - Muslims in Europe, no. 26. Birmingham, England: Centre for the Study of Islam and Christian-Muslim Relations, 1985, 20 p.

0727 DE EPALZA, MIKEL. "Muslims in Spain Today." *Newsletter,* (Centre for the Study of Islam and Christian-Muslims Relations) no. 4 (1980), 10-11.

0728 DE JONG, FREDERICK. "Notes on Islamic Mystical Brotherhoods in Northeast Bulgaria." *DI,* 63 (1986) 303-8.

0729 DE WITT, WILLEM. "Mosque Communities in Amsterdam." In *Muslims in the Netherlands.* Ed. J. Slomp, G. Speelman, W. de Witt. Research Papers - Muslims in Europe, no. 37. Birmingham, England: Centre for the Study of Islam and Christian-Muslim Relations, 1988, 24-36.

0730 DOBINSON, M.H.I. "The Lot of the European Muslim." *Minaret Monthly International,* 19 (September 1980), 24-28.
An English convert comments on the manner he was treated by his compatriots.

0731 EMINOV, A. "The Status of Islam and Muslims in Bulgaria." *JIMMA,* 8 (1987), 278-301.

0732 ENGELBREKTSSON, U. *The Force of Tradition: Turkish Migrants at Home and Abroad.* Gothenburg: Acta Universitalis Gothoburgensis, 1978, 309 p.

0733 FATHI, ASGHAR. "The Social and Political Function of the Mosque in the Muslim Community." *IC,* 58 (July 1984), 189-99.

0734　GERHOLM, THOMAS and YNGVE GEORG LITHMAN, eds. *The New Islamic Presence in Western Europe.* London: Mansell Publishing, 1988, 293 p.
　　Contributions focus on the impact of two waves of immigration of Muslims to Western Europe that began in the late 1950s. Articles examine how Muslims have fared in providing education, maintaining religious rituals and ordering family life according to Islamic tradition in the West European context. Four essays focus on the effects of migration on Islamic identity and practice.

0735　HARRISON, S.W. and D. SHEPHARD. *A Muslim Family in Britain.* Exeter: Religious Education Press, 1980, 112 p.

0736　HASNAIN, TAJ. *Female and Muslim: Double Jeopardy?* Research Papers - Muslims in Europe, no. 18. Birmingham, England: Centre for the Study of Islam and Christian-Muslim Relations, 1983, 26 p.

0737　HODGINS, H. "Planning Permission for Mosques - The Birmingham Experience." In *Islam in English Law and Administration.* Research Papers - Muslims in Europe, no. 9. Birmingham, England: Centre for the Study of Islam and Christian-Muslim Relations, 1981, 11-27.

0738　ISLAMIC COUNCIL OF EUROPE. *Muslim Communities in Non-Muslim States.* London: Islamic Council of Europe, 1980, 169 p.

0739　JEFFERY, P. *Migrants and Refugees: Muslim and Christian Pakistani Families in Bristol.* London: Cambridge University Press, 1976.

0740　JOHNSTONE, PENELOPE. *A Decade of European Churches and Islam.* Research Papers - Muslims in Europe, no. 38. Birmingham, England: Centre for the Study of Islam and Christian-Muslim Relations, 1988, 36 p.
　　Analyzes the papers issued by Christian churches regarding the Muslim community in Europe, including the Vatican, Council of European Churches, The Churches' Committee for Migrants in Europe, France, Belgium, The Republic of Germany, Britain, and Switzerland.

0741　JOLY, D. *Making a Place for Islam in British Society: Muslims in Birmingham.* Research Papers, no. 4. Coventry: University of Warwick, 1987, 28 p.
　　The author finds that living in Britain is challenging Muslims to re-evaluate their heritage, especially as pertains to proper male-female relationships.

0742　_____. *The Opinion of Mirpuri Parents in Saltley, Birmingham, About their Children's Schooling.* Research Papers - Muslims in Europe, no. 23. Birmingham, England: Centre for the Study of Islam and Christian-Muslim Relations, 1984, 31 p.

0743　JOLY, D. and J. NIELSON. *Muslims in Britain: An Annotated Bibliography, 1960-1984.* Bibliographies in Ethnic Relations, no. 6. Coventry: Centre for Research in Ethnic Relations, 1985, 35 p.

0744　KEPEL, GILLES. "The Teaching of Sheikh Faisal." In *Sermons for Europe.* Research Papers - Muslims in Europe, no. 29. Birmingham, England: Centre for the Study of Islam and Christian-Muslim Relations, 1986, 20-31.

0745　KERR, DAVID and HASAN ASKARI. "Muslims, Christians and Religious Pluralism: A Case Study of Birmingham, with Special Reference to Religious

Education." *Newsletter*, (Centre for Study of Islam and Christian Muslim Relations) (November 1981), 32-40.

0746 KETTANI, M.A. "Muslims in Southern Europe." *JIMMA*, 1-2 (Winter 1979/Summer 1980), 145-57.
Survey of Muslims in Greece.

0747 KHAN, VERITY SAIFULLAH, ed. *Minority Families in Britain.* London: The Macmillian Press, 1979.

0748 KOOPMAN, D. "Ataturk as seen by Turkish Workers in Europe." *Anatolica*, 8 (1981), 159-77.

0749 KREISER, KLAUS. "Islam in Germany and the German Muslims." In *Muslims in Germany - German Muslims?* Research Papers - Muslims in Europe, no. 28. Birmingham, England: Centre for the Study of Islam and Christian-Muslim Relations, 1985, 9-29.

0750 MAJCHROWSKI, JACEK M. "Islam in Polish Scientific Literature". *JIMMA*, 7 (1986), 84-87.

0751 MILDENBERGER, MICHAEL. "Integration or Segregation - Turks in West Germany." In *What Place for Europe's Muslims?* Research Papers - Muslims in Europe, no. 13. Birmingham, England: Centre for the Study of Islam and Christian-Muslim Relations, 1982, 1-10.

0752 MIRZA, KAWSER. *The Silent Cry: Second Generation Bradford Muslim Women Speak.* Research Papers - Muslims in Europe, no. 43. Birmingham, England: Centre for the Study of Islam and Christian-Muslim Relations, 1989, 32 p.
Based on interviews with Muslim women living in Britain. It discusses such issues as generational conflict, the role of women, the double standard, and the struggle to define what Muslim customs are an essential part of the faith and what can be altered.

0753 MOLLOY, AMINAH. *Attitudes to Medical Ethics Among British Muslim Medical Practitioners.* Research Papers - Muslims in Europe, no. 3. Birmingham, England: Centre for the Study of Islam and Christian-Muslim Relations, 1979, 22 p.

0754 MOURIAUX, RENE and CATHERINE WITHOL DE WENDEN. *French Trade Unionism and Islam.* Research Papers - Muslims in Europe, no. 36. Birmingham, England: Centre for the Study of Islam and Christian-Muslim Relations, 1987, 35 p.
Discusses the rise of Islamic consciousness and the demands for a political role for Islam among second generation Muslim workers in France.

0755 NIELSEN, JORGEN S. "Forms and Problems of Legal Recognition for Muslims in Europe." Research Papers - Muslims in Europe, no. 2. Birmingham, England: Centre for the Study of Islam and Christian-Muslim Relations, 1979, 20 p.

0756 _____. *Islamic Law and Its Significance for the Situation of Muslim Minorities in Europe.* Research Papers - Muslims in Europe, no. 35. Birmingham, England: Centre for the Study of Islam and Christian-Muslim Relations, 1987, 41 p.

0757 _____. "Muslim Children: The Challenge to European Education." In *Muslim Children in Europe's Schools.* Research Papers - Muslims in Europe, no. 17. Birmingham, England: Centre for the Study of Islam and Christian-Muslim Relations, 1983, 24 p.

0758 _____. *Muslim Immigration and Settlement in Britain.* Research Papers - Muslims in Europe, no. 21. Birmingham, England: Centre for the Study of Islam and Christian-Muslim Relations, 1984, 20 p.

0759 _____. *Muslims in Europe: An Overview.* Research Papers - Muslims in Europe, no. 12. Birmingham, England: Centre for the Study of Islam and Christian-Muslim Relations, 1981, 32 p.

0760 _____. *A Survey of British Local Authority Response to Muslim Needs.* Research Papers - Muslims in Europe, no. 30/31. Birmingham, England: Centre for the Study of Islam and Christian-Muslim Relations, 1986, 60 p.

0761 NIELSEN, JORGEN, ed. *The Training of Teachers of the Children of Migrant Workers: Cultural Values and Education in a Multicultural Society.* Strasbourg: Council for Cultural Co-operation, 1982, 45 p.

0762 NORTH, CORNELIUS W. "How Many Ways Forward in Religious Education?" In *Islam and Religious Education in England.* Research Papers - Muslims in Europe, no. 33. Birmingham, England: Centre for the Study of Islam and Christian-Muslim Relations, 1987, 42 p.

0763 PEARL, D. *Family Law and the Immigrant Communities.* London: Jordans, 1986.

0764 _____. "Islam in English Family Law." In *Islam in English Law and Administration.* Research Papers - Muslims in Europe, no. 9. Birmingham, England: Centre for the Study of Islam and Christian-Muslim Relations, 1981, 6-10.
Discusses marriages solemnized in Britain and issues of arranged marriages, dower, divorce, inheritance, polygamy and recognition of Muslim prohibitions of marriage.

0765 _____. "Muslim Marriages in English Law." *CLJ*, 30 (April 1972), 120-43.

0766 POULTER, S.M. *English Law and the Ethnic Minority Customs.* London: Butterworths, 1978, 80 p.

0767 POWER, JONATHAN. *Migrant Workers in Western Europe and the United States.* London: Pergamon Press, 1979, 167 p.

0768 RASMUSSEN, LISSI and JORGEN S. NIELSEN. *A Documentation of Christian Responses to the Muslim Presence in Western Europe.* Research Papers - Muslims in Europe, no. 7. Birmingham, England: Centre for the Study of Islam and Christian-Muslim Relations, 1980, 16 p.

0769 *Resources for Teaching Islam - A Discussion of Problems of Production and Use.* Research Papers - Muslims in Europe, no. 25. Birmingham, England: Centre for the Study of Islam and Christian-Muslim Relations, 1985, 19 p.

0770 ROBINSON, V. *Transients, Settlers and Refugees: Asians in Britain.* London: Virago Press, 1982.

0771 RODINSON, MAXIME. *Europe and the Mystique of Islam.* London: Tauris, 1988, 170 p.

0772 SHADID, W.A. *Moroccan Workers in The Netherlands.* Utrecht: 1977.

0773 SHARIF, R. *Interviews With Young Muslim Women of Pakistani Origin.* Research Papers - Muslims in Europe, no. 27. Birmingham, England: Centre for the Study of Islam and Christian-Muslim Relations, 1985, 1-48.

0774 SHEPHERD, JOHN J. "Religious Education in a Multireligious Society." In *Islam and Religious Education in England.* Research Papers - Muslims in Europe, no. 33. Birmingham, England: Centre for the Study of Islam and Christian-Muslim Relations, 1987, 9-23.

0775 SLOMP, JAN. "Muslim Minorities in the Netherlands." In *Muslims in the Netherlands.* Eds. Jan Slomp, Ge Speelman, and Willem de Witt. Research Papers - Muslims in Europe, no. 37. Birmingham, England: Centre for the Study of Islam and Christian-Muslim Relations, 1988, 2-12.

0776 _____. *Witness to God in a Secular Europe.* Geneva: Conference of European Churches, 1985.

0777 _____, ed. *The Churches and Islam in Europe (II).* Geneva: Conference of European Churches, 1982, 76 p.

0778 SORABJI, CORNELIA. "Islamic Revival and Marriage in Bosnia." *JIMMA*, 9 (July 1988), 331-37.

0779 SPEELMAN, GE. "Muslim Women in the Netherlands: Islam in Transition." In *Muslims in the Netherlands.* Eds. Jan Slomp, Ge Speelman, and Willem de Witt. Research Papers - Muslims in Europe, no. 37. Birmingham, England: Centre for the Study of Islam and Christian-Muslim Relations, 1988, 2-12.

0780 TAMES, RICHARD. "Islam in the Secondary Curriculum." In *Teaching Islam in England.* Research Papers - Muslims in Europe, no. 6. Birmingham, England: Centre for the Study of Islam and Christian-Muslim Relations, 1980, 1-10.

0781 THEUNIS, SJEF. "Migrant Muslims: Moroccans in Utrecht." Research Papers - Muslims in Europe, no. 10. Birmingham, England: Centre for the Study of Islam and Christian-Muslim Relations, 1981, 16 p.

0782 THORNLEY, W. "Some Thoughts of a Mature Convert to the Family of Islam." *YMM*, 7 (September 1980), 3-5.

0783 TIBI, BASSAM. "Islam and Modern European Ideologies." *IJMES*, 18 (February 1986), 15-29.

0784 TWORUSCHKA, UDO. *The Image of Islam in German School Textbooks.* Research Papers - Muslims in Europe, no. 32. Birmingham, England: Centre for the Study of Islam and Christian-Muslim Relations, 1986, 20 p.

0785 WATSON, JAMES. *Between Two Cultures.* Oxford: Basil Blackwell, 1979. The Author argues that analysis of the home society, the migration process and the ongoing interaction between the two societies is crucial to the understanding of the Muslim minority in Britain.

0786 WILKINSON, IAN. *Muslim Beliefs and Practices in a Non-Muslim Country: A Study of Rochdale.* Research Papers - Muslims in Europe, no. 39. Birmingham, England: Centre for the Study of Islam and Christian-Muslim Relations, 1988, 28 p.

0787 WILSON, AMRIT. *Finding a Voice: Asian Women in Britain.* London: Virago Press, 1984.

0788 WOODSMALL, RUTH. *Muslim Women Enter a New World.* Beirut: American University of Beirut Social Science Series 14, 1983.

0789 VILA, JACINTO BOSCH. "The Muslims of Portugal and Spain." *JIMMA,* 7 (1986), 69-83.

VI. MIDDLE EAST

GENERAL

0790 ALI, SHEIKH R. *Oil, Turmoil and Islam in the Middle East.* New York: Praeger, 1986, 238 p.
This book examines how the politics of energy and religion intersect.

0791 ANTOUN, RICHARD T. "Key Variables Affecting Muslim Local-Level Religious Leadership in Iran and Jordan." In *Leadership and Development in Arab Society.* Ed. Fuad I. Khuri. Beirut: American University of Beirut Press, 1981, 92-101.

0792 ATIYEH, GEORGE N. "Middle East Ideologies." In *Middle Eastern Subcultures.* Eds. W.E. Hazen, et al. Lexington, MA: D.C. Heath & Co., 1975, 47-68.

0793 BILL, JAMES A. and CARL LEIDEN. *Politics in the Middle East.* 2d ed. Boston: Little, Brown, 1984, 464 p.

0794 BILL, JAMES A. and JOHN ALDEN WILLIAMS. "Shi'i Islam and Roman Catholicism: An Ecclesial and Political Analysis." In *The Vatican, Islam and the Middle East.* Ed. Kail C. Ellis. Syracuse, NY: Syracuse University Press, 1987, 69-106.

0795 AL FARUQI, ISMA'IL R. *Islam and the Problem of Israel*. London: Islamic Council of Europe, 1980, 114 p.

Provides an Islamist analysis that is increasingly becoming the dominant view, that Israel is an instrument of the age-old Christian hatred of Islam, nurtured to sap the vitality of Muslim nations in order to destroy them.

0796 BORTHWICK, BRUCE M. *Comparative Politics of the Middle East: An Introduction*. Englewood Cliffs, NJ: Prentice-Hall, Inc., 1980, 308 p.

A discussion of Islam illustrates the importance of religion to Middle Eastern political culture, and its contributions to popular resistance to western encroachment.   It deals briefly with traditional Islamic society, Islamic fundamentalism and Islamic socialism. The discussion of Islamic fundamentalism focuses on the *Ikhwan*, its founder Hassan al-Banna, and its rise and fall in Egypt. Allusions are made to parallels between the *Ikhwan* and the Islamic Revolution in Iran. Iran and Shi'ism are discussed in the context of Iranian politics and the Islamic Revolution.   Includes discussion of the Muslim Brotherhood; Egypt; Turkey; Arab World and Iran.

0797 _____. "Religion and Politics in Israel and Egypt." *MEJ*, 33 (Spring 1979), 145-63.

0798 CARROLL, TERRANCE G. "Islam and Political Community in the Arab World." *IJMES*, 18 (May 1986), 185-204.

0799 CURTIS, MICHAEL, ed. *Religion and Politics in the Middle East*. Boulder, CO: Westview Press, 1981, 406 p.

A collection of reprinted essays on the topic written prior to the Islamic revolution in Iran.

0800 DAOUD-AGHA, ADNAN B. "Military Elites, Military-led Social Movements and the Social Structures in Developing Countries: A Comparative Study of Egypt and Syria." Ph.D. diss., University of California at Berkeley, 1970, 463 p.

The rise to power of the Muslim Brotherhood is discussed briefly as a response to adverse economic and political conditions in Egypt. The activities of the Muslim Brotherhood in Syria are also discussed.

0801 DAWISHA, ADEED. *The Arab Radicals*. New York: Council on Foreign Relations, 1986, 192 p.

0802 DEKMEJIAN, R. HRAIR. *Islam in Revolution: Fundamentalism in the Arab World*. Syracuse, NY: Syracuse University Press, 1985, 249 p.

This book was commissioned by the Defense Intelligence Agency of the Department of Defense. It begins with a selective review of the history of Islamist movements, the socio-psychological bases of Islamic revivalism, the constituencies of the revivalists' call, and a taxonomy of Islamist societies and state policies toward Islamic political activism. A great importance is placed on statistical analyses and the classification of regime types as the bases for understanding the official stances taken by the government toward Islamist groups, as well as their likely success in confronting the Islamist challenge.

Part II contains case studies on Egypt, the Muslim Brotherhood and its militant offshoots; Syria and the Syrian Muslim Brotherhood in the milieu of Ba'athist rule; Iraq and Shi'i opposition to Iraqi Ba'athist rule; Saudi Arabia and opposition to the monarchy in the context of rapid modernization; and Islamic fundamentalism in the Arab Gulf states. Both regional and international repercussions are considered in scenarios of possible future developments. The tone is alarmist; the concern is for U.S. global interests.

0803 DESSOUKI, A.E. HILLAL, ed. *Islamic Resurgence in the Arab World*. New York: Praeger, 1982, 286 p.
 A collection of essays which examine the causes of the current Islamic revival as well as the role of Islam in politics and society in the Arab world. Among the topics considered are the effects of modernization and rapid social change, militant anti-west youth groups, politics and religion in Kuwait, the Islamic movement in Syria, Qadhafi's ideology, and an historical account of political thought in Islam.

0804 DONOHUE, JOHN J. "Islam and the Search for Identity in the Arab World." In *Voices of Resurgent Islam*. Ed. John L. Esposito. New York: Oxford University Press, 1983, 48-61.

0805 EICKELMAN, DALE F. *The Middle East: An Anthropological Approach*. 2d ed. Series in Anthropology. Englewood Cliffs, NJ: Prentice-Hall, 1989, 418 p.

0806 ELLIS, KAIL C., ed. *The Vatican, Islam, and the Middle East*. Contemporary Issues in the Middle East Series. Syracuse, NY: Syracuse University Press, 1987, 376 p.

0807 ESPOSITO, JOHN L. *Islam and Politics*. rev. 2d ed. Syracuse, NY: Syracuse University Press, 1987, 302 p.
 A revised edition of a study of Islamic resurgence, analyzing major recent developments in the Muslim world. Includes discussion of the works of Jamal al-Din Afghani, Hassan al-Banna, Sayyid Qutb, Mawlana Mawdudi, Muhammad Iqbal, Ali Shari'ati, and Ruhollah Khomeini. This edition adds the Sudan and Lebanon to the discussion of countries experiencing Islamic revival.

0808 _____. "Islam in the Politics of the Middle East." *CH*, 85 (February 1986), 53.

0809 FADLALLAH, MUHAMMAD HUSAYN. "The Palestinians, The Shi'a, and South Lebanon." Interview. *JPS*, 16 (Winter 1987), 3-10.

0810 HADDAD, YVONNE Y. "The Islamic Alternative." *The Link*, 12, no. 4 (September/October 1979), 1-14.

0811 HEPER, MARTIN, and RAPHAEL ISRAILI, eds. *Islam and Politics in the Modern Middle East*. New York: St. Martin's Press, 1984, 131 p.
 This book endeavors to contribute to the general literature of comparative study of religion and politics. Three country studies are provided: Saudi Arabia, Egypt, and Turkey.

0812 HUNTER, SHIREEN T. "Islamic Iran and the Arab World." *MEI*, 5 (August-September 1987), 17-25.

0813 IZUMISAWA, KUMILO. *Index of Articles on Islam and the Middle East, 1970-1985*. Tokyo: Institute of Developing Economics, 1986, 262 p.

0814 MAYER, ANN ELIZABETH. "Law and Religion in the Muslim Middle East." *AJCL*, 35 (Winter 1987), 127-84.

0815 MUNSON, HENRY. *Islam and Revolution in the Middle East*. New Haven, CT: Yale University Press, 1988, 180 p.
Contains three parts: the first summarizes Islamic history and discusses the distinctions between Shi'ite and Sunni theology and practice and fundamentalist and traditional views; the second discusses Islam and politics in twentieth century Iran, Saudi Arabia, Egypt, and Syria, with some discussion of the social background of fundamentalists; and the third attempts to explain why an Islamic revolution occurred in Iran and is not likely to be repeated elsewhere. Much of the blame is attributed to President Carter's human rights policy.

0816 RAMADAN, SAID. "Three Major Problems Confronting the World of Islam." *IL*, 11 (August 1965), 15-27.
Written by one of the noted leaders of the Muslim Brotherhood, this essay discusses the challenges Muslims faced in the sixties.

0817 SHARABI, HISHAM. "Islam, Democracy and Socialism in the Arab World." In *The Arab Future: Crucial Issues*. Ed. Michael C. Hudson. Washington, DC: Center for Contemporary Arab Studies, Georgetown University, 1979, 95-104.

0818 SIVAN, EMMANUEL. *Radical Islam: Medieval Theology and Modern Politics*. New Haven and London: Yale University Press, 1985, 218 p.

0819 TAYLOR, ALAN R. *The Islamic Question in Middle East Politics*. Boulder, CO: Westview Press, 1988, 150 p.
Addresses the debate concerning the role Islam should play in reconstructing the ideological orientation and institutional framework of politics in the post-Ottoman Middle East. The author describes what he sees as the periodic confrontation between secular nationalism and the Islamic reform movements in Turkey, Iran, and the Arab world, highlighting the deficiencies and eclectic doctrines of each. He distinguishes among the Modernist school associated with the late nineteenth-century Egyptian reformer, Muhammad Abdu, the Wahhabi movement, and contemporary Islamist efforts to repoliticize Islam and create an Islamic state without western ideological vestiges. Among the phenomena considered are Kemalism; the Muslim Brotherhood in Egypt; Revolutionary Iran; the seizure of the Grand Mosque in Mecca in 1979; and Qadhafi's Islamism.

0820 TIBI, BASSAM. "The Iranian Revolution and the Arabs: The Quest for Islamic Identity and the Search for an Islamic System of Government." *ASQ*, 8 (Winter 1986), 29-44.

0821 _____. "Islam and Arab Nationalism." In *The Islamic Impulse*. Ed. Barbara F. Stowesser. London: Croom Helm, 1987, 59-74.

0822 ZUBAIDA, SAMI. "The Quest for the Islamic State: Islamic Fundamentalism in Egypt and Iran." In *Studies in Religious Fundamentalism*. Ed. Lionel Caplan. Albany, NY: State University of New York Press, 1987, 25-50.

A.   ARAB WORLD

0823   DAVIS, ERIC. "Religion against the State, a Political Economy of Religious Radicalism in Egypt and Israel." In *Religious Resurgence, Contemporary Cases in Islam, Christianity, and Judaism*. Eds. Richard T. Antoun and Mary Elaine Hegland. Syracuse, NY: Syracuse University Press, 1987, 145-66.

0824   DAWISHA, ADEED and I. WILLIAM ZARTMAN, eds. *Beyond Coercion: the Durability of the Arab State*. London: Croom Helm, 1988, 310 p.

0825   EDGAR, ADRIENNE L. "The Islamic Opposition in Egypt and Syria: A Comparative Study." *JAA*, 6 (Spring 1987), 82-108.
Compares the contemporary Islamic movements in Egypt and Syria, emphasizing the specific goals, tactics, socioeconomic make-up of the membership, and ideology of each group arguing that they are products of local conditions and cannot be explained by generalized theories of Islamic resurgence. Reviews the history of the Muslim Brotherhood, and finds crucial differences to be more important than similarities between Syrian and Egyptian branches of the organization.

0826   HADDAD, YVONNE Y. "Muslim Revivalist Thought in the Arab World: An Overview." *MW*, 76 (July-October 1986), 143-167.

0827   HALSELL, GRACE. *Prophesy and Politics: Militant Evangelists on the Road to Nuclear War*. Westport, CT: Lawrence Hill & Co., 1986, 210 p.
This book is about Christian Zionism and the activities of its adherents in Israel and the Occupied Territories. It provides an excellent account of Christian and Jewish fervor that has challenged Muslims in the Arab world as well as influenced their perception of a hostile world in which the forces of Christianity and Judaism have combined to destroy Islam.

0828   HUMPHREYS, R. STEPHEN. "Islam and Political Values in Saudi Arabia, Egypt and Syria." *MEJ*, 33 (1979), 1-19.

0829   KECHICHIAN, JOSEPH A. "The Role of the Ulama in the Politics of an Islamic State: The Case of Saudi Arabia." *IJMES*, 18 (1986), 53-71.

0830   IBRAHIM, SAAD EDDIN. *The New Arab Social Order: A Study of the Social Impact of Oil Wealth*. Boulder, CO: Westview Press, 1982, 200 p.

0831   IBRAHIM, SAAD EDDIN, and NICHOLAS S. HOPKINS, eds. *Arab Society: Social Science Perspective*. Cairo: American University in Cairo Press, 1985, 507 p.

0832   LAMB, DAVID. *The Arabs: Journeys Beyond the Mirage*. New York: Random House, 1987, 333 p.
Impressions of a journalist assigned to Cairo in 1980. The author characterizes the actions of today's militant Islamist cells as perversions of 'crazies'. The analysis is superficial, laced with trivial information and riddled with errors. Shows very little comprehension of historical, political, social, economic or cultural contexts. While the author claims to want to strip away American stereotypes and misconceptions about Arabs and Islam, his work is uncritical and

relies heavily on media portrayals of the Middle East in general and public figures such as Qadhafi in particular.

0833 OLSEN, GORM RYE. "Islam: What is Its Political Significance? The Cases of Egypt and Saudi Arabia." In *Islam: State and Society*. Eds. Klaus Ferdinand and Mehdi Mozaffari. London: Curzon Press, 1988, 127-142.

0834 SHARABI, HISHAM. *Neopatriarchy, A Theory of Distorted Change in Arab Society*. New York: Oxford University Press, 1988, 196 p.

0835 SIVAN, EMMANUEL. *Radical Islam: Medieval Theology and Modern Politics*. New Haven, CT: Yale University Press, 1985, 224 p.
Analysis of contemporary Islamic revivalist thought, based primarily on the writings of prominent thinkers from Egypt, Syria and Lebanon. The focus is on the "New Radicals" of Islam, such as Sayyid Qutb, whose ideas are presented as part of a defensive reaction to modernity and the problems facing the Muslim world. Also considered is what Sivan calls the "conservative periphery," a coterie of Islamist preachers (e.g. Sheikh Kishk) who provide support for the radical core, and the secularist (marginalized) Left.

0836 AL-YASSINI, AYMAN. "Islamic Revival and National Development in the Arab World." In *The Arab World: Dynamics of Development*. International Studies in Sociology and Social Anthropology. Eds. B. Abu-Laban and S. McIrvin Abu-Laban. Leiden: E.J. Brill, 1986, 104-121.

1. Egypt

0837 ABUBAKAR, M.A. "Sayyid Kutb: A Study of his Critical Ideas". *M.A. thesis, University of Edinburgh*, 1978.
Includes an extensive biography of Sayyid Qutb, and bibliography of his works. The author argues that Qutb was alienated by the American public's elation at the news of Hassan al-Banna's assassination, and turned to the Muslim Brotherhood as a result.

0838 AGBETOLA, A.S. "Sayyid Qutb on the Social Crime: Stealing." *IS*, 20 (Summer 1981), 87-95.

0839 AJAMI, FOUAD. *The Arab Predicament: Arab Political Thought and Practice Since 1967*. Cambridge: Cambridge University Press, 1981, 220 p.
The "predicament" lies in the incompatible demands arising from the new order offered by the west, and the old order imparted by Islamic civilization. Islamic revivalism is analyzed as an Islamic response to the clash between civilizations. The author discusses the ascendance of religion as a source of solace after the defeat of June 1967. It is precisely because Islam has been able to provide the needed comfort - and serve as a source of authenticity that Islamic revivalism has managed to survive in Egypt. The writings of the Egyptian populist Sheikh Kishk are compared to the works of secular Arab intelligentsia.

0840 _____. "In the Pharaoh's Shadow: Religion and Authority in Egypt." In *Islam in the Political Process*. Ed. James P. Piscatori. Cambridge: Cambridge University Press, 1983, 12-35.

0841 ALTMAN, ISRAEL. "Islamic Movements in Egypt." *JQ*, no. 10 (Winter 1979), 87-105.
Describes the activities of the Muslim Brotherhood and other Islamic groups, the latter being labeled "Mahdist" groups. Because of the Muslim Brotherhood's tolerance of the Sadat regime, the author argues, more militant Islamic groups appeared to challenge Sadat's policies.

0842 ANSARI, HAMIED. *Egypt: The Stalled Society*. Albany, NY: SUNY Press, 1986, 308 p.

0843 AL-ANSARI, HAMIED N. "The Islamic Militants in Egyptian Politics." *IJMES*, 16 (1984), 123-144.

0844 _____. "Sectarian Conflict in Egypt and the Political Expediency of Religion." *MEJ*, 38 (1984), 397-418.

0845 AUDAH, ABDUL QADER. *Islam Between Ignorant Followers and Incapable Scholars*. Kuwait: International Islamic Federation of Student Organizations, 1977, 115 p.

0846 AYUBI, NAZIH N.M. "The Political Revival of Islam: The Case of Egypt." *IJMES*, 12 (1980), 481-499.

0847 AZZAM, MAHA. "The Use of Discourse in Understanding Islamic-Oriented Protest Groups in Egypt, 1971-1981." *BSMESB*, 13 (1987), 150-158.

0848 AL-BANNA, HASSAN. *Five Tracts of Hasan Al-Banna' (1906-1949)*. Trans. and Annotated by Charles Wendell. Berkeley, CA: University of California Press, 1978, 180 p.
A translation of five important texts of Banna's writings: *Between Yesterday and Today; Our Mission; To What Do We Summon Mankind; Toward the Light;* and *On Jihad*. Provides an excellent background of the formative teachings of the Muslim Brotherhood.

0849 _____. *What is our Message?* Lahore: Islamic Publications Ltd., 1974.

0850 BELLO, ILYSA ADE. "The Society of the Muslim Brethren: An Ideological Study." *Itt*, 17 (July-September 1980), 45-56.

0851 BEININ, JOEL. "Islam, Marxism, and the Shubra al-Khayma Textile Workers: Muslim Brothers and Communists in the Egyptian Trade Union Movement." In *Islam, Politics, and Social Movements*. Ed. Edmund Burke, III and Ira M. Lapidus. Berkeley, CA: University of California Press, 1988, 207-227.

0852 BEININ, JOEL and ZACHARY LOCKMAN. *Workers on the Nile, Nationalism, Communism, Islam and the Egyptian Working Class, 1882-1954*. Princeton, NJ: Princeton University Press, 1987, 488 p.
The authors contend that while western attention has focused on Islamic political activism only since the mid-1970s, Islam historically has been an important factor in shaping political consciousness and debate in Egypt. The

book examines in part popular attitudes and practices identified with Islam, the various uses of an Islamic idiom, and the appeal of the Muslim Brotherhood. Describes the relevant parts of Muslim Brotherhood ideology, especially about property, and their role in Egypt's politics in detail. Highlights the Brotherhood's relationship to other political forces in the workers' movement and explains the limited appeal of Islamic politics in the workers' movement in the 1940s and 1950s.

0853 "Call to Revise the Egyptian Civil Code: Recommendations for the Use of Islamic Law." *Cairo Papers in Social Science*, 10 (Spring 1987), 50-64.

0854 FARAH, NADIA RAMSIS. *Religious Strife in Egypt: Crisis and Ideological Conflict in the Seventies*. New York: Gordon and Breach Science Publishers, 1986, 135 p.
    Sectarian conflict in Egypt, including a section on the character of the Islamic revivalist movement: the Muslim Brotherhood and the "neo-Islamic" groups. Both are presented as adopting the same political ideology; the difference is in tactics. Discusses the content of ideology, and Sayyid Qutb's contributions.

0855 GAFFNEY, PATRICK D. "The Local Preacher and Islamic Resurgence in Upper Egypt." In *Religious Resurgence, Contemporary Cases in Islam, Christianity, and Judaism*. Eds. Richard T. Antoun and Mary Elaine Hegland. Syracuse, NY: Syracuse University Press, 1987, 35-63.

0856 _____. "Magic, Miracle and the Politics of Narration in the Contemporary Islamic Sermon." *Rel Lit*, 20 (1988), 111-138.

0857 AL-GHAZZALI, MUHAMMAD. *Our Beginning in Wisdom*. Trans. Isma'il R. el Faruqi. Washington: American Council of Learned Societies, 1953, 145 p.
    An important early response from a member of the Muslim Brotherhood against the secular nationalist trend prevalent in Egypt in the forties. The response deals with the same issues that continue to concern Muslims today: religion and state, role of women, economic justice, Christian-Muslim encounter, nationalism and socialism. Reprinted several times by other publishers.

0858 GILSENAN, MICHAEL. "Trajectories of Contemporary Sufism." In *Islamic Dilemmas: Reformers, Nationalists and Industrialization*. Ed. Ernest Gellner. Berlin; New York: Mouton Publishers, 1985, 187-98.
    This article is based on the author's observations of the Hamidiya Shadhiliya order in Egypt.

0859 GOLDBERG, ELLIS. "Muslim Union Politics in Egypt." In *Islam, Politics, and Social Movements*. Ed. Edmund Burke, III and Ira M. Lapidus. Berkeley, CA: University of California Press, 1988, 228-243.

0860 HADDAD, YVONNE Y. *Contemporary Islam and the Challenge of History*. Albany, NY: SUNY Press, 1982, 257 p.
    An important study of modern Muslim thinking and responses to the challenges of the modern Muslim experience. The author presents a range of Muslim opinions and intellectual orientations, analyzing their sources, outlook, strengths, weaknesses. It includes a discussion and translation of relevent contemporary writings on the idea of history.

0861 _____. "Islamic 'Awakening' in Egypt." *ASQ*, 9 (Summer 1987), 234-259.

0862 _____. "Sayyid Qutb Ideologue of Islamic Revival." In *Voices of Resurgent Islam*. Ed. John L. Esposito. New York: Oxford University Press, 1983, 67-98.

0863 AL-HAKIM, TAWFIQ. *The Return of Consciousness*. Trans. Bayly Winder. Irvington, NY: New York University Press, 1985, 89 p.
  Written in 1974 by one of Egypt's preeminent playwrights, this book is noted as the first published work by someone of the author's stature to repudiate Nasserism. It is disparaging of Egypt's intellectuals for their passivity toward and complicity in the excesses of Nasser's regime. The author, himself a political appointee of Nasser, harshly assesses the policies of the Nasser era. Written from a secular perspective, there are few allusions to the presence of Muslim activists and Nasser's strained relations with the Muslim Brotherhood.

0864 HAMOUD, A. AL-SHARIF ABDU. "Islam and Modern Society: Sources and Dynamics of Contemporary Islamic Revival in Egypt." Ph.D. diss., Vanderbilt, 1988.

0865 HANAFI, HASSAN. *Religious Dialogue and Revolution*. Cairo: The Anglo Egyptian Bookshop, n.d.
  An important reflection by the leader on the Islamic Left.

0866 HASSAN, S. BADRUL. *Syed Qutb Shaheed*. Karachi: International Islamic Publishers, 1980, 56 p.

0867 HANAFI, HASSAN. "The Origin of Modern Conservatism and Islamic Fundamentalism." In *Islamic Dilemmas: Reformers, Nationalists and Industrialization*. Ed. Ernest Gellner. Berlin: Mouton Publishers, 1985, 94-103.
  A personal vintage analysis of Arab predicament by a self proclaimed proponent of the Islamic Left.

0868 HEIKAL, MOHAMMAD. *Autumn of Fury: the Asassination of Sadat*. London: Andre Deutsch, 1983, 290 p.
  In Part III the author discusses the Muslim Brotherhood as an underground political opposition group, whose founder, Hassan al-Banna, created the religious organization as an alternative to the *Wafd*. During Sadat's tenure, part of the Brotherhood was willing to lend its support to the regime; other strains of fundamentalism were uncontrolled by the authorities.

0869 HOMERIN, TH. EMIL. "Ibn 'Arabi in the People's Assembly: Religion, Press and Politics in Sadat's Egypt." *MEJ*, 40 (Summer 1986), 462-78.

0870 HUSAINI, ISHAK MUSA. *The Muslim Brethren: The Greatest of Modern Islamic Movements*. Beirut: Khayat College Book Cooperative, 1956.
  An historical survey of the Muslim Brotherhood in Egypt from its inception in 1928 to 1955.

0871 HUSSEIN, A.   "Islam and Marxism: The Absurd Polarization of Contemporary Egyptian Politics." In *Review of Middle East Studies 2*. London: Ithaca Press, 1976, 71-83.

0872 IBRAHIM, SAAD EDDIN. "Anatomy of Egypt's Militant Islamic Groups: Methodological Notes and Preliminary Findings." *IJMES*, 12 (1980), 423-53.

0873 _____. "Egypt's Islamic activism in the 1980s." *TWQ*, 10 (April 1988), 632-57.

0874 _____. "Islamic Militancy as a Social Movement: The Case of Two Groups in Egypt." In *Islamic Resurgence in the Arab World*. Ed. Ali E. Hillal Dessouki. New York: Praeger, 1982, 117-37.

0875 _____. "A Socio-Cultural Paradigm of Pan Arab Leadership: The Case of Nasser." In *Leadership and Development in Arab Society*. Ed. Faud I. Khuri. Beirut: American University Press, 1981, 30-61.

0876 "Is the Revised Code Islamic? Assessments of Scholars and Critics". *Cairo Papers in Social Science*, 10 (Spring 1987), 71-83.

0877 JANSEN, JOHANNES J.G. "The Early Islamic Movement of the Kharidjites and Modern Moslem Extremism." *Orient*, 27 (March 1986), 127-35.
Examines the conflict within the Islamic world, "in which Moslems accuse each other of not being good Moslems, or even of not being Moslems at all". Analyses the language of *Al-Farida al-Gha'iba, The Neglected Duty*, a document of the contemporary Moslem extremists of Egypt. Compares *al-Farida* with the *Khawarij*.

0878 _____. *The Neglected Duty: The Creed of Sadat's Assassins and Islamic Resurgence in the Middle East*. New York: Macmillan, 1986, 246 p.
An analysis of Egyptian discourse generated by the appearance of a manifesto of *Tafkir wal-hijra*, the Islamist group responsible for the assassination of Sadat. The legal defense of the assassins was based on this tract as an Islamic justification for their actions. Drawing on refutations from al-Azhar, Sufi reactions, and the responses of two popular preachers, the author delineates the positions taken, especially about the issues of political legitimacy and accountability to Islamic law, in response to this tract. He argues that Muslim liberals are growing weaker in the face of the ascendancy of more radical groups, and that the ideas found in this tract circulated and became widespread via oral traditions long before they were written down. A translation of the tract is provided in an appendix.

0879 KEPEL, GILLES. *Muslim Extremism in Egypt: the Prophet and the Pharaoh*. Trans. Jon Rothschild. Preface by Bernard Lewis. Berkeley and Los Angeles: University of California Press, 1985, 281 p.
A study of Islamic movements in Sadat's Egypt. The author argues that "Islamicist thought was reconstructed after 1954 primarily in the concentration camps..." (p. 27), which held many members of the banned Muslim Brotherhood in Egypt. Sayyid Qutb, during his incarceration, "charted the renewal of Islamicist thought of which the contemporary organization are to a large extent the legatees." (p. 23) This book presents the discourse and practice of the Islamicist movement.

0880 KHALID, KHALID M. *From Here We Start*. Trans. Isma'il R. El Faruqi. Washington: American Council of Learned Societies, 1953; reprint, Ithaca, NY: Spoken Language, 165 p.

An important essay on the major issues facing Egypt in the forties by a secularist whose writings were condemned by al-Azhar and by the Muslim Brootherhood. The author retracted his position on Islam and the state in the eighties.

0881 KOTB, SAYYED. *Social Justice in Islam.* Trans. John B. Hardie. Washington: American Council of Learned Societies, 1953; reprint, Los Angeles: Octagon Press, 1969, 298 p.
A translation of what has become a standard text on social justice in Islam written by Sayyid Qutb during his moderate phase.

0882 KUPFERSCHMIDT, URI M. "Reformist and Militant Islam in Urban and Rural Egypt." *JAAS*, 23 (1987), 403-18.

0883 LEISER, GARY. "The Madrasa and the Islamization of the Middle East: The Case of Egypt." *JARCE*, (1985), 29-48.

0884 MAHFOUZ, MUHAMMAD. *The Persecuted: Islamic Organizations in Egypt.* London: Riad El-Rayyes Books, 1988, 256 p.

0885 MARSOT, AFAF LUTFI AL-SAYYID. "Revolutionaries, Fundamentalists, and Housewives: Alternative Groups in the Arab World." *JAA*, 6 (Spring 1987), 178-97.
The author relies heavily on the sociological and political science paradigms of David Apter, Daniel Bell, and Theodore Lowi to discuss the phenomenon of political disaffection in the Arab world asserting that all revolutionary movements arise from a need to instigate change in society that existing institutions fail to accomplish. Similarly, as religion declines in significance in society, anomie is likely to become prevalent unless a comprehensive ideology replaces religion. Paradoxically, if such an ideology does not appear, religion makes a "resurgence" in order to eliminate the growing sense of anomie. Alternative groups such as the *jama'at* arise because of a felt social need. The resort to religious ideology is an effort to address alienation in spiritual, political, and social terms.

0886 MATTHEE, RUDI. "The Egyptian Opposition on the Iranian Revolution." In *Shi'ism and Social Protest.* Eds. R.I. Cole and Nikki R. Keddie. New Haven, CT: Yale University Press, 1986, 247-74

0887 McDERMOTT, ANTHONY. "Mubarak's Egypt: The Challenge of the Militant Tendency." *WT*, 42 (October 1986), 170-74.

0888 MEHDI, SIBTE. "The Way Ahead of the Ikhwan al-Muslimoon." Part 2. *Suara al-Islam*, 3 (February-March 1977).

0889 MITCHELL, RICHARD P. *The Society of the Muslim Brothers.* London: Oxford University Press, 1969, 349 p.
Considered the seminal work on the Muslim Brotherhood in Egypt. Traces the historical development of the Brotherhood through the mid-1950s. In his preface, written in 1968, the author predicts that secularism, including secular nationalism, will continue to overshadow the appeal of the Brotherhood. Includes a short biography of Hasan al-Banna, founder of the Muslim Brotherhood, and a detailed account of the crises of 1948 (the Palestine War) and 1954 (the ban on the Muslim Brotherhood). Also outlines the structure and

ideology of the organization and focuses on the Brotherhood's political role, its orientation toward political power, and the problem of political violence.

0890 MOUSSALLI, AHMED SALAH AL-DIN. "Contemporary Islamic Political Thought: Sayyid Qutb." Ph.D. diss., University of Maryland at College Park, 1985, 192 p.

Focuses on the intellectual and political foundations and principles of revivalism. Author contends that Qutb's writings provide the most important intellectual bases of contemporary Islamic revivalism.

0891 OSLEN, GORM RYE. "Islam: What is Its Political Significance? The Cases of Egypt and Saudi Arabia." In *Islam: State and Society*. Eds. Klaus Ferdinand and Mehdi Mozaffari. London: Curzon Press, 1988, 127-42.

0892 PHILIPP, THOMAS. "Nation State and Religious Community in Egypt: The Continuing Debate." *WI*, 28:n.g. (1988), 379-91.

0893 QUTB, SAYYID. *Islam: The Religion of the Future*. Chicago: Kazi Publications, 1988, n.p.

0894 _____. *Islam and Universal Peace*. Indianapolis, IN: American Trust Publications, 1977, n.p.

0895 _____. *Milestones*. Kuwait: International Islamic Federation of Student Organizations, 1978, 308 p.

Considered to be *the* Islamic revolutionary text of this century, this book was used as a justification for the execution of the author. Its ideas are radically dividing the world into Muslim and un-Islamic, with the latter deserving obliteration. The idealogy was adopted by the radical Egytian movements of *al-Jihad* and *al-Takfir wa'l Hijra* and condemned by the moderates in the Muslim Brotherhood.

0896 _____. *The Religion of Islam*. Kuwait: International Islamic Federation of Student Organizations, 1977.

0897 RUGH, ANDREA B. *Family in Contemporary Egypt*. Syracuse, NY: Syracuse University Press, 1984, 305 p.

A comprehensive anthropological study which seeks to demonstrate the extent the Egyptian family is based upon an indigenous social system whose basic values differ from those of the west. Chapter 11, "Religion," underscores the importance of religion in family life and the impact of the Islamic revival in particular on women's lives.

0898 SID-AHMED, MOHAMMEd. "Egypt: The Islamic Issue." *FP*, 69 (Winter 1987-1988), 22-39.

0899 SIVAN, EMMANUEL. "The Islamic Republic of Egypt." *Orbis*, 31 (1987), 43-53.

0900 VOGT, KARI. "Militant Islam in Egypt: A Survey." In *Egypt Under Pressure: A Contribution to the Understanding of Economic, Social and Cultural Aspects of Egypt Today*. Eds. Marianne Laanatza, et al. Uppsala: Scandinavian Institute of African Studies, 1986, 27-43.

0901 ZAKI, M.A.K. "Modern Muslim Thought in Egypt and Its Impact on Islam in Malaya." Ph.D. diss., University of London, n.d.

2. Iraq

0902 BATATU, HANNA. "Iraq's Underground Shi'a Movements: Characteristics, Causes and Prospects." *MEJ*, 35 (Autumn 1981), 578-94.
Describes the two Shi'a parties that are active in Iraq's underground: *al-Da'wah al-Islamiyah* (the Islamic Call) and *al-Mujahidin* (the Muslim Warriors), and the influence on them of the events in revolutionary Iran.

0903 _____. *The Old Social Classes and the Revolutionary Movements of Iraq, A Study of Iraq's Old Landed and Commercial Classes and of its Communists, Ba'thists, and Free Officers*. Princeton, NJ: Princeton University Press, 1978, 1283 p.
A lengthy work meant to explore the utility of a class analysis of historical social relations in Iraq. Divided into three sections, it covers the economic and social background of landowners, commercial magnates and others of the upper class in pre-republican Iraq (1921-58) in the first section; the history of the Iraqi Communist Party in the second; and the evolution of the Free Officers and the Ba'ath Party, as well as more information about the Iraqi Communist Party, in the third. While heavy emphasis is on the Communist Party, the book also pays some attention to the persistence of sectarian politics; the social roles of the *ulema* class; official use of Islamic symbols as a source of legitimacy and as a means of mobilizing the religiously-oriented against communists; and communist and Ba'athist rhetoric about Islam.

0904 DAWISHA, ADEED I. "Invoking the Spirit of Arabism: Islam in the Foreign Policy of Saddam's Iraq." In *Islam in Foreign Policy*. New York: Cambridge University Press, 1983, 112-28.

0905 "AL-HAKIM, MUHAMMAD BAQIR, head of the Supreme Islamic Revolutionary Council of Iraq." Interview. *MEI*, 5 (1987), 18-24.

0906 MALLAT, CHIBLI. "Religious Militancy in Contemporary Iraq: Muhammad Baqer as-Sadr and the Sunni-Shia Paradigm." *TWQ*, 10 (April 1988), 699-729.

0907 WILEY, JOYCE. "The Islamic Political Movement of Iraq." Ph.D. diss., University of South Carolina, 1988, 287 p.

3. Lebanon

0908 AJAMI, FOUAD. *The Vanished Imam: Musa al Sadr and the Shia of Lebanon*. Ithaca, NY; London: Cornell University Press, 1986, 228 p.
A political biography of the Shi'i cleric Musa al-Sadr, who helped shape the contemporary Shi'ite movement and its institutions in Lebanon. His

disappearance in August 1978 while on a visit to Libya has enveloped him in an aura of mystery and martyrdom.

0909 ALLAH, A. "The Islamic Resistance in Lebanon and the Palestinian Uprising: The Islamic Jihad Perspective." *MEI*, 5 (1988), 4-12.

0910 _____. "The Discovery of the Lebanese Shi'a." *TWQ*, 10 (April 1988), 1047-51.

0911 COBBAN, H. "The Growth of Shi'i Power in Lebanon and its Implications for the Future." In *Shi'ism and Social Protest*. Eds. J.R.I. Cole and N.R. Keddie. New Haven: Yale University Press, 1986, 137-55.

0912 DEEB, MARIUS. *Militant Islamic Movements in Lebanon: Origin, Social Basis and Ideology*. Washington, DC: The Center for Contemporary Arab Studies, Georgetown University, 1986, 22 p.

0913 _____. "Shia Movements in Lebanon: Their Formation, Ideology, Social Basis, and Links with Iran and Syria." *TWQ*, 10 (April 1988), 683-98.

0914 KRAMER, MARTIN. *The Moral Logic of Hizballah*. Occasional Paper, no. 101. Tel Aviv: The Dayan Center for Middle Eastern and African Studies, The Shiloah Institute, Tel Aviv University, 1987, 28 p.

0915 MALLAT, CHIBLI. *Shi'i Thought From the South of Lebanon*. Oxford: Centre for Lebanese Studies, 1988, 42 p.

0916 NORTON, AUGUSTUS RICHARD. *Amal and the Shia: Struggle for the Soul of Lebanon*. Austin, TX: University of Texas Press, 1987, 238 p.
Traces the disintegration of the Lebanese system, attributed largely to sectarianism and external intervention. Identifies the source of current Shi'i activism as predating the Iranian Revolution, emerging from the process of modernization in Lebanon, which included changes in agricultural patterns and began as early as the 1960s. The author gives some attention to Musa al-Sadr and the rivalry for leadership of the Shi'i community after his disappearance. Includes the charter of the Amal movement in an appendix.

0917 _____. "Changing Actors and Leadership Among the Shiites of Lebanon." *AAAPSS*, 482 (November 1985), 109-21.

0918 _____. "The Rise and Decline of Lebanon's Shi'ites." *NL*, 71 (1988), 9-12.

0919 SHAMS AL-DIN, MUHAMMAD MEHDI SHAMS. *The Rising of al-Husayn: Its Impact on the Consciousness of Muslim Society*. Trans. I.K.A. Howard. New York: Methuen, 1986, 218 p.
Translation into English of a work by Sheikh Shams al-Din, one of the leading clerics in Beirut and the vice-president of the Supreme Shi'i Council. A sample of contemporary Lebanese Shi'i socio-religious thought, the book explains significant aspects of Shi'i pilgrimage to Husayn's shrine in Karbala, of poetry mourning Husayn's martyrdom, and of Shi'i rituals commemorating his death.

4.   Saudi Arabia

0920 GOLDBERG, JACOB. "The Shi'i Minority in Saudi Arabia." In *Shi'ism and Social Protest*. Eds. Juan R.I. Cole and Nikki R. Keddie. New Haven, CT: Yale University Press, 1986, 1-29.

0921 AL-MUTAIRI, HEZAM MATER. "An Islamic Perspective on Public Service With Reference to the Hajj Research Center." D.P.A., State University of New York at Albany, 1987, 310 p.
This case study of the Hajj Research Center in Saudi Arabia examines Islamic theory and practice with respect to civil service, its notions and religious importance, with emphasis given to recruiting and selection for civil service jobs. The adoption by the early Islamic state of such administrative concepts as "merit" criterion and accountability - generally considered to be modern "western" concepts - is given significance.

0922 SALAME, GHASSAN. "Islam and Politics in Saudi Arabia." *ASQ*, 9 (Summer 1987), 306-26.

0923 AL-YASSINI, AYMAN. *Religion and State in the Kingdom of Saudi Arabia*. Boulder, CO: Westview Press, 1985, 171 p.
Treats the relationship of Islam to the state in Saudi Arabia. The book begins with a review of classical Islamic political theories and makes a brief comparison between Islamic reform movements in Egypt and Arabia. A chapter is devoted to Wahhabism and its impact on state formation in Saudi Arabia, and another to Wahhabism as state ideology and its utility in maintaining political stability. Religious opposition is given very brief attention in the final chapter and the epilogue.

5.   Syria

0924 ABD-ALLAH, UMAR F. *The Islamic Struggle in Syria*. Berkeley, CA: Mizan Press, 1983, 300 p.
A prescriptive work by a member of the "Islamic Front," a Syrian group founded in 1980 and influenced by the Muslim Brotherhood. This book calls for "jihad" against Asad's Ba'athist government in Syria and its replacement by an Islamic state.

0925 BATATU, HANNA. "Syria's Muslim Brethren." In *State and Ideology in the Middle East and Pakistan*. Eds. Fred Halliday and Hamza Alavi. London: Macmillian, 1988, 112-32.

0926 MAOZ, MOSHE and AVNER YANIV, eds. *Syria Under Assad: Domestic Constraints and Regional Risks*. New York: St. Martin's Press, 1986, 273 p.

0927 RABO, ANNKA. "Nation-State Building in Syria: Ba'th and Islam - Conflict or Accommodation?" In *Islam: State and Society*. Eds. Klaus Ferdinand and Mehdi Mozaffari. London: Curzon Press, 1988, 117-26.

6.   Other

0928 AYOOB, MOHAMMAD. "Oil, Arabism and Islam: The Persian Gulf in World Politics." In *Middle East in World Politics*. Ed. M. Ayoob. Canberra: Australian Institute for International Affairs on the Middle East, 1981, 118-38.

0929 BILL, JAMES A. "Resurgent Islam in the Persian Gulf." *FA*, 63 (Fall 1984), 108-27.

0930 HUREWITZ, J.C. *The Persian Gulf: After Iran's Revolution*. Foreign Policy Association Headline Series, no. 244. New York: The Foreign Policy Association, April 1979, 64 p.

0931 NAKHLEH, EMILE A. "The West Bank and Gaza: Twenty Years Later." *MEJ*, 42 (Spring 1988), 209-26.
      This article discusses the realities of daily life for Palestinians in the Occupied Territories, and the new attitudes of local leaders emerging in the west Bank and Gaza. It reviews the evolution of Israeli policy and of the leadership in the West Bank and Gaza. Islamic fundamentalism is noted as having appeared in the early 1980s; however, no indication is given of its impact or role.

0932 SATLOFF, ROBERT, B. *They Cannot Stop our Tongues: Islamic Activism in Jordan.* Policy Papers, no. 5. Washington, DC: The Washington Institute for Near East Policy, 1986, 33 p.

0933 SHADID, MOHAMMED K. "The Muslim Brotherhood Movement in the West Bank and Gaza." *TWQ*, 10 (April 1988), 658-82.

B. IRAN

0934 ABEDI, MEHDI. "Ali Shariati: The Architect of the 1979 Islamic Revolution in Iran." *IrSt*, 19 (1986), 229-34.

0935 ABEDI, MEHDI and GARY LEGENHAUSEN, eds. *Jihad and Shahadat: Struggle and Martyrdom in Islam*. Essays and addresses by Ayatullah Mahmud Taleqani, Ayatullah Murtada Mutahhari and Dr. Ali Shariati. Houston, Texas: Institute for Research and Islamic Studies, 1986, 300 p.

0936 ABIDI, A.H.H. "The Iranian Revolution: Its Origins and Dimensions." *InSt*, 18 (April-June 1979), 129-61.

0937 _____, ed. *The Tehran Documents*. New Delhi: Patriot Publishers, 1988, 328 p.
      U.S. government documents providing background information about circumstances leading to the Iranian Revolution and the American involvement

in it. Discusses Iran-U.S. relations during the 1960s and 1970s and, specifically, U.S. diplomats' analyses of political events as they unfolded.

0938 ABRAHAMIAN, ERVAND. "'Ali Shari'ati: Ideologue of the Iranian Revolution." *MERIP*, no. 102 (January 1982), 24-28.

0939 _____. *Iran Between Two Revolutions*. Princeton, NJ: Princeton University Press, 1982, 561 p.
   A neo-Marxist analysis of the social bases of Iranian politics principally in the years between the Constitutional Revolution (1905-09) and the Islamic Revolution (1977-79). The book throws some light on the ethnic as well as occupational composition of social classes in Iran. While not the primary focus of this work, the religious establishment is discussed at appropriate points in the book. In the final chapter the author presents a perceptive analysis of the complex variables and events which led to the downfall of the Shah and the consolidation of power under the Islamic Republic.

0940 _____. *The Iranian Mojahedin*. New Haven, CT: Yale University Press, 1989, 307 p.
   Provides a historical analysis of the *Mojahedin-e Khalq* who were instrumental in bringing Khomeini to power, but failed to gain political power. He discusses the ideology of the group, the Marxist influence on their reinterpretation of Islam as well as their socio-economic background.

0941 _____. "The Guerilla Movement in Iran, 1963,-1977." *MERIP*, no. 86 (March/April 1980), 3-21.

0942 _____. "Structural Causes of the Iranian Revolution." *MERIP*, no. 87 (May 1980), 21-26.

0943 AFRACHTEH, KAMBIZ. "Iran." In *The Politics of Islamic Reassertion*. Ed. M. Ayoob. London: Croom Helm, 1981, 90-119.

0944 AFROUZ, ALI. "Dealing with the Counter-Revolutionary Forces." In *The Islamic Revolution: Achievements, Obstacles and Goals*. Ed. K. Siddiqui. London: The Muslim Institute, 1980, 44-48.

0945 AFSHAR, HALEH. "The Iranian Theocracy." In *Iran: A Revolution in Turmoil*. Ed. Haleh Afshar. Albany, NY: State University of New York Press, 1985, 220-43.
   Analyzes the character of the *ulama*, or clerics, their relationship with the state, and their politicization from the 1960s to the present. Discusses "valayeteh faqih", or the rule of the juriconsul as propagated by the ruling elite in the Islamic Republic of Iran, and Khomeini's economic program.

0946 AHMAD, BASHIR. *Iranian Revolution: Its Genesis, Force of Regeneration or Regression?* Rawalpindi: National Defence College, Individual Research Paper, 1979.

0947 AHMAD, EQBAL, ed. *The Iranian Revolution*. London: Institute of Race Relations, 1979. Race and Class Special Issue, Vol. 21, no. 1. Summer 1979.
   This special issue of the British journal Race and Class takes a broad analytical scope and includes essays on Iran's economy and society; the political, economic and social challenges facing the Islamic Republic; the international significance

of the revolution; its treatment in the U.S. media; and its effects on U.S. foreign policy. It also contains an Institute for Policy Studies document on U.S. military involvement in Iran, a bibliography of recent (1980) publications on Iran, and a translation of a lecture by Ali Shari'ati. Useful for information on the initial state of thinking about the revolution and the newly-founded Republic.

0948 _____. "The Iranian Revolution: A Landmark for the Future." *RC*, 21 (1979), 3-11.

0949 AJAMI, FOUAD. "The Impossible Life of Muslim Liberalism: The Doctrines of Ali Shariati and their Defeat". *NR*, no. 3724 (2 June 1986), 26-32.

0950 AKHAVI, SHAHROUGH. "Clerical Politics in Iran Since 1979." In *The Iranian Revolution and the Islamic Republic*. 2d ed. Ed. Nikki Keddie and Eric Hooglund. Syracuse, NY: Syracuse University Press, 1986, 57-73.

0951 _____. "Elite Factionalism in the Islamic Republic of Iran." *MEJ*, 41 (1987), 181-201.

0952 _____. "The Ideology and Praxis of Shi'ism in the Iranian Revolution." *CSSH*, 25 (April 1983), 195-211.

0953 _____. "Ideology and the Iranian Revolution." In *Iran Since the Revolution: Internal Dynamics, Regional Conflicts and the Superpowers*. Ed. Barry Rosen. Boulder, CO: Social Science Monographs, 1985, xi-xx.

0954 _____. "Institutionalizing the New Order in Iran." *CH*, 86 (February 1987), 53.

0955 _____. "Iran: Implementation of an Islamic State." In *Islam in Asia*. Ed. John L. Esposito. Oxford: Oxford University Press, 1987, 27-52.

0956 _____. "Islam, Politics and Society in the Thought of Ayatullah Khumayni, Ayatullah Taliqani, and 'Ali Shari'ati." *MES*, 24 (October 1988), 404-31.

0957 _____. "Islamic Radicalism and Iranian Politics in the Middle East." In *Islamic Fundamentism and Islamic Radicalism: Hearings Before the Subcommittee on Europe and the Middle East of the Committee on Foreign Affairs, House of Representatives, 99th Congress, First Session, June 24, July 15, and September 30, 1985*. Washington, DC: U.S. Government Printing Office, 1985, 125-40.

0958 _____. "The Power Structure of the Islamic Republic of Iran." In *Internal Developments in Iran*. Significant Issues Series, vol. 3. Ed. Shireen Hunter. Washington, DC: Georgetown University Center for Strategic and International Studies, 1985, 1-14.

0959 _____. *Religion and Politics in Contemporary Iran: Clergy - State Relations in the Pahlavi Period*. Albany, NY: SUNY Press, 1980, 255 p.
Reviews the evolution of Shi'a Islam in Iran and its linkage with political action. Traces the history of clergy-state relations in Iran from periods of alignment (1941-58) to periods of estrangement (1959-63).

0960 _____. "Shariati's Social Thought." In *Religion and Politics in Iran, Shi'ism from Quietism to Revolution.* Ed. Nikki R. Keddie. New Haven and London: Yale University Press, 1983, 125-44.

0961 _____. "Soviet Perceptions of the Iranian Revolution." *IrSt*, 19, (Winter 1986), 3-30.

0962 ALBERT, DAVID H., ed. *Tell The American People: Perspectives on the Iranian Revolution.* Philadelphia, PA: Movement for a New Society, 1980, 176 p.

A collection of twelve essays by specialists on Iranian and international politics plus excerpts from prominent Iranians such as Bani-Sadr, Khomeini, Mutahhari and Shari'ati. The book attempts to accomplish two tasks: to portray Iranian grievances against the Pahlavi dynasty and its supporters; and to explore in a preliminary fashion the objectives and ideals of the Islamic Republic of Iran. Since it was published in 1980, the collection is somewhat limited in its analysis and is generally sympathetic to the Islamic Republic. Provides details on U.S.-Iranian relations and the events of the revolution. Some articles are reprints of previously published material.

0963 ALGAR, HAMID. *The Islamic Revolution in Iran: Transcript of a Four Lecture Course at the Muslim Institute, London.* Ed. K. Siddiqui. London: The Open Press, 1980.

0964 _____. "The Oppositional Role of the Ulama in Twentieth Century Iran." In *Scholars, Saints and Sufis: Muslim Religious Institutions Since 1500.* Berkeley, CA: University of California Press, 1972, 231-55.

0965 _____. *The Roots of the Islamic Revolution.* London: The Open Press, 1983, 136 p.

0966 _____, trans and ed. *Islam and Revolution: Writings and Declarations of Imam Khomeini.* Berkeley, CA: Mizan Press, 1981, 460 p.

An English-language translation of some of the most important of Ayatollah Khomeini's essays and speeches, plus selected legal opinions and interviews with the translator/editor, which provide an exposition of Khomeini's ideology through primary materials. Each section is followed by the translator/editor's annotations which help to elucidate Shi'i interpretations and practices.

0967 AMIN, TAHIR. "Iran: Political Economy of an Islamic State." *AJISS*, 2 (1985), 41-62.

0968 AMINI, SOHEYL. "A Critical Assessment of Ali Shariati's Theory of Revolution." In *Iran: Essays on a Revolution in the Making.* Lexington, KY: Mazda Publishers, 1981, 77-104.

0969 AMIRAHMADI, HOOSHANG and MANOUCHER PARVIN, eds. *Post-Revolutionary Iran.* Westview Special Studies on the Middle East. Boulder, CO: Westview Press, 1988, 262 p.

A collection of essays, written by Iranian and non-Iranian specialists, evaluating the nature of and possible future directions for the Islamic Republic of Iran. Topics covered include the impact of the Iran-Iraq war, the role of the military in politics, the labor movement and the left, the political economy of Islamic planning, demographic trends, and U.S.-Iranian trade relations.

0970 AMNESTY INTERNATIONAL. *Law and Human Rights in the Islamic Republic of Iran.* London: Amnesty International, 1980, 216 p.

0971 ANEER, GUDMAR. *Imam Ruhullah Khumaini, Shah Muhammad Riza Pahlavi, and the Religious Traditions of Iran.* Uppsala; Stockholm, Sweden: Almqvist & Wiksell International, 1985, 93 p.

0972 ARJOMAND, SAID AMIR. "Iran's Islamic Revolution in Comparative Perspective". *WP*, 28 (April 1986), 383-414.

0973 _____. "Revolution in Shi'ism." In *Islam and the Political Economy of Meaning.* Berkeley, CA: University of California Press, 1987, 111-31.

0974 _____. "Social Change and Movements of Revitalization in Contemporary Islam." In *New Religious Movements and Rapid Social Change.* Ed. James A. Beckford. London: Sage Publications/UNESCO, 1986, 87-112.

0975 _____. *The Turban for the Crown: The Islamic Revolution in Iran.* New York: Oxford University Press, 1988, 283 p.
The author provides a historical interpretation of the structure of authority in Shi'ism, and the impact of modernization on Iranian society. He analyzes the influence of millenarianism and the clerical structure of Shi'i Islam in the rise of Khomeini as charismatic leader and explains Khomeini's consolidation of power for a constitutional state based on a new interpretation of Islamic principles.

0976 _____, ed. *Authority and Political Culture in Shi'ism.* New York: State University of New York Press, 1988, 393 p.

0977 ASARIA, I. "Iran--A Case Study in Muslim Political Awakening." In *The Islamic Revolution: Achievements, Obstacles and Goals.* Ed. K. Siddiqui. London: The Muslim Institute, 1980, 23-36.

0978 ASKARI, HASAN. "Khomeini and non-Muslims." *Encounter*, No. 71, (January 1981). (Entire Issue)

0979 AYOOB, MAHMOUD MUSTAFA. *Redemptive Suffering in Islam: A Study of the Devotional Aspects of Ashura in Twelver Shiism.* Religions and Society No. 10. The Hague: Mouton, 1978, 299 p.
Presents material on Shi'i devotions much of which was previously inaccessible outside of Iran. Deals specifically with the symbolism of *Ashura* rituals and *ta'ziyah* plays. Summarizes the history of Husayn's martyrdom.

0980 AYOOB, MOHAMMAD. "The Politics of Resurgent Islam." In *Working Paper 21.* Canberra: The Australian National University, The Strategic and Defence Studies Centre, 1980, 1-12.

0981 _____. "Two Faces of Political Islam: Iran and Pakistan Compared." *AS*, 19 (June 1979), 535-66.

0982 BAKHASH, SHAUL. *The Reign of the Ayatollahs: Iran and the Islamic Revolution.* London: Tauris, 1985, 287 p.
A descriptive account of the internal affairs of post-revolutionary Iran. Traces the origins of Iran's Islamic leadership to the events of the 1960s. Focuses

primarily on the personalities of those involved in the overthrow of the Shah and subsequent developments.

0983 BANI-SADR, ABUL HASAN. *Work and the Worker in Islam.* Trans. Hasan Mashadi. Tehran, Iran: The Hamdani Foundation, n.d.

0984 BANI-SADR, ABU AL-HASSAN. *The Fundamental Principles and Precepts of Islamic Government.* Lexington, KY: Mazda Publishers, 1981.

0985 BANI-SADR, ABUL HASAN. "The Twelve Meanings of Martyrdom." *IR*, 2 (July 1980), 8-12.

0986 BANUAZIZI, ALI. "Iran's Revolution Reappraised." *TWQ*, 10 (April 1988), 1041-46.

0987 BASHIRIYEH, HOSSEIN. *The State and Revolution in Iran: 1962- 1982.* New York: St. Martin's Press, 1984, 203 p.

0988 BAYAT-PHILIP, M. "Islam in Pahlavi and Post-Pahlavi Iran: A Cultural Revolution?" In *Islam and Development: Religion and Socio-Political Change.* Ed. J.L. Esposito. New York: Syracuse University Press, 1980, 87-106.

0989 _____. "Shiism in Contemporary Iranian Politics: The Case of Ali Shariati." In *Towards a Modern Iran.* Eds. E. Kedouri and S. Haim. London: Frank Cass, 1980, 155-68.

0990 _____. "Tradition and Change in Iranian Socio- Religious Thought." In *Modern Iran: The Dialectics of Continuity and Change.* Eds. M.E. Bonine & N.R. Keddie. Albany, NY: State University of New York Press, 1980, 37-58.

0991 BAZARGAN, MEHDI. *The Inevitable Victory.* Trans. M. Yusefi. Bedford, OH: Free Islamic Literature, Inc., 1978.

0992 BECK, LOIS. "Revolutionary Iran and Its Tribal Peoples." *MERIP*, no. 87 (May 1980), 14-20.

0993 BEEMAN, WILLIAM O. "Iran's Religious Regime: What Makes it Tick? Will it Ever Run Down?" *AAAPSS*, 483 (January 1986), 73-83.

0994 BEHESHTI, AYATOLLAH. "Autobiography." *EI*, 1 (September 1981), 11-14.

0995 BEHN, W. *The Iranian Opposition in Exile. An Annotated Bibliography.* Weisbaden: Harrassowitz, 1979, 249 p.

0996 _____. *Islamic Revolution or Revolutionary Islam in Iran: a Selected and Annotated Bibliography.* Berlin: Adiyok, 1980, 119 p.

0997 _____. "The Revolution of the Pen: Iranian Underground Publications, 1963-1978." In *Middle East Studies and Libraries.* Ed. B.C. Bloomfield. London: Mansell Publishing, 1980, 13-22.

0998 BENARD, CHERYL and ZALMAY KHALILZAD. *"The Government of God": Iran's Islamic Republic*. New York: Columbia University Press, 1984, 240 p.
Written from a political science perspective. The authors argue that the Iranian Revolution prompts a reevaluation of development theories of the 1950s and more general social science theories, as they apply to Iran, up to the present. In part this book examines the roles of the clerics of various orientations in leading political activism and the clerics' consolidation of power. It also examines mutual images and perceptions as a distorting factor in western-Muslim interaction.

0999 BILL, JAMES. A. *The Eagle and the Lion: The Tragedy of American-Iranian Relations*. New Haven and London: Yale University Press, 1988, 520 p.
An analysis of U.S.-Iranian relations which traces the estrangement between the two nations. In short the author portrays U.S. foreign policy, before and after the Iranian Revolution, as marred by ignorance, a Cold War mentality, narrow economic concerns, and bureaucratic decision-making problems. He also contends that policy of the Islamic Republic is similarly short-sighted and biased, based as it is on fundamental misconceptions about the west and the United States in particular. The primary focus is on American national interests.

1000 _____. "Iran and the Crisis of 1978." *FA*, 57 (Winter 1978-79), 323-42.

1001 _____. "Power and Religion in Revolutionary Iran." *MEJ*, 36 (Winter 1982), 22-47.

1002 _____. *The Shah, the Ayatollah and the United States*. Foreign Policy Association Headline Series no. 285 (Sept/Oct 1987). New York: Foreign Policy Association, 72 p.
As part of the Headline Series of the Foreign Policy Association this pamphlet is meant to stimulate discussion of current events relating to U.S. foreign policy. Reviews the events leading to the downfall of the Pahlavi Shah of Iran, including the role played by the clerics in oppositional politics; the thwarting of U.S. policy in the Gulf; the rise and fall of moderates (e.g. Bakhtiar and Bani-Sadr); the hostage crisis; and the Iran-Iraq War. This is excerpted from the author's book-length work, The Eagle and the Lion: The Tragedy of American-Iranian Relations.

1003 BINDER, L. "Revolution in Iran: Red, White, Blue or Black." *BAS*, 53 (January 1979), 48-54.

1004 BONINE, MICHAEL E. and NIKKI R. KEDDIE, eds. *Continuity and Change in Modern Iran*. Albany, NY: State University of New York Press, 1981, 359 p.

1005 BRASWEL, GEORGE W., JR. "A Mosaic of Mullahs and Mosques: Religion and Politics in Iranian Shi'ah Islam." Ph.D. diss., University of North Carolina at Chapel Hill, 1975, 271 p.

1006 CAMPBELL, W.R. and DJAMCHID DARVICH. "Totalitarian Implications of Komeini's Conception of Islamic Consciousness." *JSAMES*, 8 (1984), 43-72.

1007 CARLSEN, R.W. *Crises in Iran: A Microcosm of the Cosmic Ploy*. Victoria, BC: The Snow Man Press, 1979, 56 p.

1008 CHAMRAN, MUSTAFA. *The Islamic Revolution and the Imposed War.* Tehran: The Ministry of Islamic Guidance, 1982.

1009 CHEHABI, HOUCHANG ESFANDIAN. *Modernist Shi'ism and Politics: The Liberation Movement of Iran.* (Volumes I and II). Ph.D. diss., Yale University, 1986, 598 p.

A case study of the Liberation Movement of Iran, a moderate nationalist party whose ideology is based on Islamic modernism. It places religious modernism in the context of Iranian history and critiques the thought of the Liberation Movement's leading figures: Mehdi Bazargan, Ayatollah S. Mahmud Taleqani, and Ali Shari'ati. It also chronicles the transformation of Iranian political culture from a predominantly secular one to one infused with religious values and symbols.

1010 COLE, JUAN R. "Imami Jurisprudence and the Role of the Ulama: Mortaza Ansari on Emulating the Supreme Exemplar." In *Religion and Politics in Iran, Shi'ism from Quietism to Revolution.* Ed. Nikki R. Keddie. New Haven and London: Yale University Press, 1983, 33-46.

1011 COTTAM, RICHARD W. "The Iranian Revolution." In *Shi'ism and Social Protest.* Eds. Juan R.I. Cole and Nikki R. Keddie. New Haven: Yale University Press, 1986, 55-87.

1012 COTTAM, RICHARD W. *Iran and the United States: A Cold War Case Study.* Pittsburgh, PA: University of Pittsburgh Press, 1988, 298 p.

In part this book analyzes the first ten years of the Islamic Republic of Iran, placing it in historical context. It traces the growth of Iranian political consciousness since World War I and, at appropriate junctures, points out its connection to a religious world view. A political scientist, the author argues that Iran today is in an "era of mass politics" as opposed to the elite politics that characterized the Pahlavi dynasty. Much of the book deals with U.S. policy toward Iran.

1013 DARAVI, REZA. "Islamic Republic of Iran." In *Teaching and Research in Philosophy: Asia and the Pacific.* Paris: UNESCO, 1986, 105-9.

1014 DORMAN, W.A. "Iranian People versus US News Media: A Case of Libel." *RC*, 21 (1979), 57-66.

1015 DREYFUSS, ROBERT. *Hostage to Khomeini.* New York: New Benjamin Franklin House Publishing Co., 1980, 241 p.

Commissioned by Lyndon LaRouche, the thesis of this book is that Khomeini is evil personified, a puppet ("a puffed up, turbaned magician") of the "New Dark Ages" faction that opposes the forces of progress on a global scale. Interestingly, this faction is orchestrated by the British Military Intelligence. It would be an understatement to say that this is an elaborate conspiracy theory which links the Carter Administration, American specialists on Iran, and British intelligence operations with the rise of revolutionary forces in Iran and the spread of "evil" worldwide.

1016 AL-E AHMAD, JALAL. *Gharbzadegi [Weststruckness].* Trans. John Green and Ahmad Alizadeh. Lexington, KY: Mazda, 1982.

Banned from publication in Iran when it was first written in 1963 but distributed widely after the Revolution, the title of this polemical essay has become a phrase to sum up the malaise of modern Iranian society. The author criticizes the advent of western industrialization and influence in Iran and the moral decay and consumerism of Iranian society. He identifies western intentions to destroy Islamic unity and the Shah's complicity in this endeavor.

1017 ELWELL-SUTTON, L.P. "The Iranian Revolution: Triumph or Tragedy?" In *The Security of the Persian Gulf*. Ed. H. Amirsadeghi. London: Croom Helm, 1981, 231-54.

1018 EZZATI, ABUL-FAZL. *The Concept of Leadership in Islam*. London: The Muslim Institute for Research and Planning, 1979.

1019 _____. "Legitimation of the Islamic Revolutionary Movements." *Al-Serat*, 6 (1980), 36-41.

1020 _____. *The Revolutionary Islam and the Islamic Revolution*. Tehran: The Ministry of Islamic Guidance, 1981.

1021 _____. "The Spirit of Islamic Revolution: Government and Constitution." *IDR*, 5 (1980), 26-31.

1022 FARHANG, MANSOUR. "I Witnessed the Most Incredible Celebrations in the Streets of Tehran." *RIPEH*, 3 (Spring 1979), 91-116.

1023 _____. "Resisting the Pharaohs: Ali Shariati on Oppression." *RC*, 21 (1979), 31-40.

1024 AL-FARUQI, I.R. "Islam and the Tehran Hostages." *UM*, 1 (January 1980), 12-13.

1025 FATEMI, K. "The Iranian Revolution: Its Impact on Economic Relations with the United States." *IJMES*, 12 (1980), 303-17.

1026 FERDOWS, ADELE K. "Religion in Iranian Nationalism: The Study of the Fadayan-i Islam." Ph.D. diss., Indiana University, 1967, 235 p.

1027 FISCHER, MICHAEL M.J. "Imam Khomeini: Four Levels of Understanding." In *Voices of Resurgent Islam*. Ed. John L. Esposito. New York: Oxford University Press, 1983, 150-74.

1028 _____. *Iran: From Religious Dispute to Revolution*. Cambridge, MA: Harvard University Press, 1980, 314 p.
    Describes the educational system in Iran and focuses attention on education in Qom. In light of this background information, the author relates the revolutionary events of 1977-79 and the role of the clerics in them. The author argues that the revolution in Iran was shaped by the tradition of religious protest and that the language of the revolution is religious and unique to the Iranian experience.

1029 FISHER, C.B. "The Shah's White Revolution." *MW*, 54 (April 1964), 98-103.

1030 FLOOR, WILLEM M. "The Revolutionary Character of the Iranian Ulama: Wishful Thinking or Reality?" In *Religion and Politics in Iran, Shi'ism from*

Quietism to Revolution. Ed. Nikki R. Keddie. New York and London: Yale University Press, 1983, 73-97.

1031 FORBIS, WILLIAM H. *Fall of the Peacock Throne: The Story of Iran.* New York: Harper and Row Publishers, 1980, 305 p.

Casts recent events in Iran in the light of Cold War hostilities and links them with general global trends toward greater political instability and economic hardship. The style tends to be overly dramatic, highlighting the significance of Persian legends, their heroes and villians, as foreshadows of the cataclysmic events of 1978-79. Discusses the personalities of the Pahlavi imperial court; SAVAK; the impact of oil wealth; the Shah's modernization campaign, including the Literacy Corps; and the doctrine of the Hidden Imam. Understands the appeal of Islam to be reactionary and to counter the headlong rush into modernity initiated by the Shah.

1032 GELLNER, E. "Inside Khomeini's mind." NR, no. 3622, (18 June 1984), 27-33.

1033 GHANI, CYRUS. *Iran and the West: a Critical Bibliography.* London and New York: Kegan Paul International, distributed by Methuen, New York, 1987, 967 p.

This book is a catalog and critical review of mostly English-language books on Iran and, especially, recent Iranian political history. Provides insight into how western influences on Iran are perceived by Iranians, as well as how westerners have regarded Iran. Ghani's comments are especially valuable in chronicling the fall of the Pahlavi dynasty and the rise to power of the clerical regime under Khomeini.

1034 GILANI, AYATOLLAH MOHAMMADI. "Judgement in Islam." *Message of Revolution,* No. 6, n.d., 31-33.

1035 GOODEY, CHRIS. "Workers' Council in Iranian Factories." *MERIP,* no. 88 (June 1980), 5-14.

1036 GRAHAM, ROBERT. *Iran: The Illusion of Power.* New York: St. Martins Press, 1978, 228 p.

Originally published before the Shah's downfall, this book focuses on the inflationary effects of the 1970s' boom in oil prices on the Iranian economy. The author, a news journalist, links Iran's economic problems and the Shah's modernization drive to its political instability. It also discusses SAVAK, the Resurgence Party and the Pahlavi court and mentions in passing the role of the religious establishment in Iranian society. The "illusion of power" refers to Iran's new-found oil wealth and its promise of rapid industrial growth. Revised edition (1980) includes an update following the establishment of the Islamic Republic.

1037 GRIFFITH, WILLIAM E. "The Revival of Islamic Fundamentalism: The Case of Iran." *HamdIs,* 3 (Spring 1980), 47-59.

1038 HAAS, R. "Saudi Arabia and Iran: The Twin Pillars in Revolutionary Times." In *The Security of the Persian Gulf.* Ed. H. Amirsadeghi. London: Croom Helm, 1981, 151-69.

1039 HAERI, SHAYKH FADHLALLA. *Beginnings End.* New York: Methuen, 1987, 210 p.

1040 HAIRI, ABDUL-HADI. *Shiism and Constitutionalism in Iran.* Leiden: E.J. Brill, 1977, 274 p.

Reviews the nineteenth and early twentieth century origins of constitutionalism in Iran, the Shi'i theory of political legitimacy, the role of the clerics in politics, and the functions and writing of a constitution. Focuses on the career of Mirza Muhammad Husayn Na'ini (1860-1936), a constitutional theorist and, as a leading *mujtahid*, one of the highest ranking clerics involved in the Constitutional Revolution of 1906. This book attempts to reconcile democratic constitutional theory with the Shi'i view of legitimate rule, and helps to clarify the Iranian ulema's justification for their political activism in opposing an unjust tyrannical government.

1041 HALLIDAY, FRED. "Iran's Revolution: The First Year." *MERIP*, no. 88 (June 1980), 3-5.

1042 _____. "Iranian Foreign Policy Since 1979: Internationalism and Nationalism in the Islamic Revolution." In *Shi'ism and Social Protest*. Eds. Juan R.I. Cole and Nikki Keddie. New Haven: Yale University Press, 1986, 88-107.

1043 _____. "Theses on the Iranian Revolution." *RC*, 21 (1979), 81-90.

1044 HAMIDI, SHEIKH KHALIL. "Khomeini's Views on the Rule of Shariah." *Rabitat al Alam al Islami*, 6 (June 1979), 54-55.

1045 HANIFFA, M.H. *Iran Under the Islamic Revolution.* Hong Kong: Muslim Heral Publication, n.d.

1046 HARNEY, D. "Some Explanations for the Iranian Revolution." *AA*, 11 (July 1980), 134-43.

1047 HEGLAND, MARY ELAINE. "Imam Khomaini's Village: Recruitment to Revolution." Ph.D. diss., State University of New York at Binghamton, 1986, 909 p.

Focuses on the events leading to the participation of notable residents of the Iranian village of "Aliabad" in the 1979 Iranian Revolution. Traces some of the developments in the village from the early twentieth century until December 1979. Examines the roles of ritual and *taifeh*, or kin-based political factionalism, as they evolved in this period.

1048 _____. "Islamic Revival or Political and Cultural Revolution?" In *Religious Resurgence, Contemporary Cases in Islam, Christianity, and Judaism*. Eds. Richard T. Antoun and Mary Elaine Hegland. Syracuse, NY: Syracuse University Press, 1987, 194-219.

1049 _____. "Two Images of Husain: Accommodation and Revolution in an Iranian Village." In Religion and Politics in Iran, Shi'ism from Quietism to Revolution. Nikki R. Keddie, ed. New Haven and London: Yale University Press, 1983, 218-36.

1050 HEIKAL, MOHAMMED. *Iran: the Untold Story: an Insider's Account of America's Iranian Adventure and its Consequences for the Future.* New York: Pantheon Books, 1982.

Discusses the Iranian revolution as a manifestation of the contradictions created by the forces of western imperialism in Iran. The book focuses on politics and diplomacy to a greater degree than religion; the latter is regarded as a panacea. The reawakening of Islam following the 1967 defeat is addressed in two chapters: "The Resurgence of Islam" and "Khomeini Leads".

1051 HIRSCHFELD, Y.P. "Moscow and Khomeini: Soviet-Iranian Relations in Historical Perspective." *Orbis*, 24 (Summer 1980), 219-40.

1052 HODGKIN, T. "The Revolutionary Tradition in Islam." *RC*, 21 (Winter 1980), 221-38.

1053 HOOGLUND, ERIC J. *Land and Revolution in Iran, 1960-1980.* Modern Middle East Series, No. 7. Center for Middle Eastern Studies. Austin, TX: University of Texas Press, 1982, 191 p.

1054 _____. "Rural Participation in the Revolution." *MERIP*, no. 87 (May 1980), 3-6.

1055 HOOGLUND (HEGLAND), MARY. "One Village in the Revolution." *MERIP*, no. 87 (May 1980), 7-12.

1056 _____. "Religious Ritual and Political Struggle in an Iranian Village." *MERIP*, no. 102 (January 1982), 10.

1057 HUNTER, SHIREEN T. "Iran and the Spread of Revolutionary Islam." *TWQ*, 10 (April 1988), 730-49.

1058 HUSSAIN, ASAF. *Islamic Iran, Revolution and Counter-Revolution.* New York: St. Martin's Press, 1985, 225 p.
Discusses the political culture and Islamic leadership of Iran. In the final chapters the author focuses on the counter-revolutionary threat to the Islamic Republic which he identifies as emanating from three sources: the U.S., the Soviet Union, and other Muslim countries (which uphold a "non-*tawhidi*" Islam).

1059 HUSSAIN, ASAF. "A Select Bibliography of Recent Literature on the Islamic Revolution." *The Muslim World Book Review*, 1 (Winter 1981), 21-24.

1060 HUSSAIN, J.M. "The Role of Tradition in the Occultation of the Twelfth Imam." *Al-Serat*, 6 (1980), 42-52.

1061 IBRAHIM, EZZODIN. *Sunni vs. Shi'ah: A Pitiful Outcry.* Tehran: Islamic Propagation Organization, 1983.

1062 INTERNATIONAL INSTITUTE FOR STRATEGIC STUDIES. "Iran After the Revolution." *SS*, (Spring 1980), 41-47.

1063 _____. "Iran and the Middle East." *SS*, (1978), 50-57.

1064 IOANNIDES, C.P. "The Hostages of Iran: A Discussion with the Militants." *WQ*, 3 (Summer 1980), 12-35.

1065 IRFANI, SUROOSH. *Iran's Islamic Revolution: Popular Liberation or Religious Dictatorship?* London: Zed Books, 1984, 268 p.

1066 IRVING, T.B. "The Looming Crescent: Carter's Canossa." *IR*, 2 (August 1980), 3-8.

1067 _____. "The Stricken Lion." *IO*, 2 (1980), 18-31.

1068 ISMAEL, J.S., et al. "Social Changes in Islamic Society. The Political Thought of Ayatollah Khomeini." *SP*, 27 (June 1980), 601-19.

1069 ISRAELI, R. "The New Wave of Islam." *IJ*, 34 (Summer 1979), 369-90.

1070 JABBARI, AHMAD and R. OLSEN, eds. *Iran: Essays on a Revolution in the Making.* Lexington, KY: Mazda Publishers, 1981, 214 p.

1071 JAMEII, M.M. *The Revolution Which Islam Created.* Tehran: The Hamdani Foundation, n.d.

1072 JANSEN, G.H. "International Islam: Muslims and The Modern World." *The Economist*, 278 (January 1981), 21-26.

1073 JAVADI, ALI ASGHAR HADJ-SYED. *Letters From the Great Prison: An Eyewitness Account of the Human and Social Conditions in Iran.* Trans. by the Committee for Human Rights in Iran. Washington, DC: Committee for Human Rights in Iran, 1978.

1074 JAZANI, BIZHAN. *Capitalism and Revolution in Iran.* Selected Writings of Bizan Jazani. Trans. Iran Committee. London: Zed Publications, 1981, 51 p.

1075 KAZEMI, FARHAD. *Poverty and Revolution in Iran, the Marginal Poor, Urban Marginality, and Politics.* New York and London: New York University Press, 1980, 180 p.
A study of poor rural migrants who, because of dislocation in the agricultural sector, moved into the slums and squatter settlements of Tehran during the 1970s. This study focuses on the impact of the Shah's land reform and industrialization programs and the marginal life of migrants in the city. It also traces the process of political mobilization of the migrant poor in the course of the revolution. Analysis is based on interviews, questionnaires and participant observation. In his conclusion the author summarizes the Khomeini regime's early response to the plight of the urban poor: rhetorical solidarity with the poor, including promises of economic redistribution; and concrete steps to provide food and housing.

1076 KEDDIE, NIKKI R. "Iran: Change in Islam: Islam and Change." *IJMES*, 11 (1980), 527-42.

1077 _____. "Iran: Religious Orthodoxy and Heresy in Political Culture." In *Religion and Societies: Asia and the Middle East.* Ed. Carlo Caldarola. New York: Mouton de Gruyer, 1982, 199-258.

1078 _____. *An Islamic Response to Imperialism, Political and Religious Writings of Sayyid Jamal ad-Din al-Afghani.* Berkeley and Los Angeles: University of California Press, 1983, 212 p.
This revised edition of a 1968 publication has added a treatment of Afghani's legacy and what it has meant for recent trends in Islamic thought and activity of both liberal and revivalist bents. Considered an important work on a major

ideologue of Islamic reformism at the turn of the century whose interpretations of Islam laid the necessary groundwork for the Islamic resurgence of today. Includes translations of some of Afghani's works.

1079 _____. "Oil, Economic Policy and Social Conflict in Iran." *RC*, 21 (1979), 13-29.

1080 _____. "Religion and Irreligion in Early Iranian Nationalism." *CSSH*, 2 (1961-62), 265-95.

1081 _____. "Religion, Society and Revolution in Modern Iran." In *Modern Iran: The Dialectics of Continuity and Change*. Eds. E. Bonine and N.R. Keddie. Albany, NY: State University of New York Press, 1981, 21-36.

1082 _____. *Roots of Revolution: An Interpretive History of Modern Iran (with a section by Yann Richard)*. New Haven and London: Yale University Press, 1981, 321 p.
Discusses the historical linkage of politics and religion in Iran, as well as the intellectual, socio-political, and religious foundations of the 1979 Iranian revolution.

1083 _____. "The Roots of the Ulama Power in Modern Iran." In *Scholars, Saints and Sufis: Muslim Religious Institutions since 1500*. Ed. N.R. Keddie. Berkeley, CA: University of California Press, 1971, 211-29.

1084 _____. "Select Western-Language Bibliography: Shi'ism and Politics, with Special Reference to Iran." In *Religion and Politics in Iran, Shi'ism from Quietism to Revolution*. Ed.Nikki R. Keddie. New Haven and London: Yale University Press, 1983, 237-44.

1085 _____. "Understanding the Iranian Revolution." *CM*, 13 (1980), 38-48.

1086 KEDDIE, NIKKI R. and ERIC HOOGLUND. *The Iranian Revolution and the Islamic Republic: Conference Proceedings*. Washington, DC: Middle East Institute, 1982, 210 p.
A collection of conference papers presented at the Woodrow Wilson International Center for Scholars (May 1982). Includes analyses of the leadership role of the *ulama*, their socio-economic background and political orientations; Iran's relations with the U.S. and Soviet Union; the status of women; rural transformation; and the foreign policy implications of an Islamic ideology. Overall the collection reflects an ongoing attempt at comparative twentieth century history, highlighting at appropriate places the parallels of the Constitutional Movement of 1905-1911 and the Revolution of 1978-79. Contributors have drawn on important primary materials.

1087 KEDDIE, NIKKI R. and MICHAEL E. BONINE, eds. *Modern Iran: the Dialectics of Continuity and Change*. Albany, NY: State University of New York Press, 1981, 464 p.
This collection of essays addresses the complexity of modern Iranian society, demonstrating that politics is not confined to the capital city only. The first paper deals with the role of Islam in Iranian social thought and institutions as well as its impact on the recent revolution.

1088 KEDOURIE, E. "Islamic Revolution." *Salisbury Paper*, 6 (November 1979), 1-5.

1089 KELIDAR, ABBAS. "Ayatollah Khomeini's Concept of Islamic Government." In *Islam and Power*. Ed. Cudsi and Dessouki. Baltimore, MD: Johns Hopkins University Press, 1981, 75-92.

1090 KENNEDY, MOORHEAD. The Ayatollah in the Cathedral: Reflections of a Hostage. New York: Hill & Wang, 1986, 241 p.
Written largely in captivity by a U.S. diplomat held hostage for fifteen months in the U.S. embassy in Tehran. Addresses motivations of Middle Eastern terrorism, and characterizes it as post-colonial religious and national terrorism. In light of the lessons gleaned from British imperial history, the author recounts the parallels with regard to the American role in the Middle East. He points to the signs of waning American influence and also suggests that the use of force to obtain the release of hostages would have been a misguided policy for several reasons. Calls the hostage crisis in Tehran the "Pearl Harbor of the Foreign Service," which highlights the need for fundamental change in the conduct of U.S. foreign policy.

1091 KHAN, M.A. SALEEM. "Religion and the State in Iran. A Unique Muslim Country." *IMA*, 2 (August 1971), 67-88.

1092 KHOMEINI, AYATOLLAH RUHALLAH. *Islamic Government*. Trans. Joint Publications Research Service. New York: Manor Books Ind., 1979.
A series of lectures on Islamic jurisprudence given by Khomeini in Najaf, Iraq, in early 1970. They reflect the Shi'ite doctrinal foundations for social activism on the part of the Shi'ite *ulama* and an Islamic system of government.
For no apparent reason, this edition has appended an "analysis" written by a feature writer for the *New York Post*. The author pulls no punches, beginning by comparing Khomeini to Hitler and *Islamic Government* to *Mein Kampf*. The vitriol escalates from there.

1093 _____. *Sayings of the Ayatollah Khomeini*. Trans. Jean-Marie Xaviere. New York: Bantam Books, 1980.

1094 _____. *Selected Messages and Speeches of Imam Khomeini*. Tehran: Ministry of National Guidence, 1980, 94 p.

1095 KRAMER, MARTIN. *Political Islam*. Washington Papers, no. 73. Foreword by Robert G. Neumann. Beverly Hills, CA and London: Sage Publications, 1980, 88 p.
Examines the relevance of an Islamic world view for contemporary international affairs. Comments on the U.S. government's steps toward instituting "Islampolitik", an agenda or set of policies on the part of a non-Muslim government designed to counter the universal Islamic appeal to *jihad*. Written largely in response to recent events in the Muslim world, especially the Iranian Revolution, this book disparages the idea that Muslim unity exists to the extent that a global Islamic order is imminent.

1096 _____, ed. *Shiism, Resistance, and Revolution*. Dayan Center for Middle East and African Studies series. Boulder, CO: Westview Press, and London: Mansell Publishing Ltd., 1987, 324 p.

A collection of papers originally presented at a conference held in Tel Aviv in 1984 which focuses on Shi'ism in Lebanon, Syria, Saudi Arabia, Kuwait, Bahrain, Afghanistan, Pakistan and India as well as Iran. In general the essays characterize Shi'ism as an ideology of revolutionary violence. The purposes of this volume are to explore the political strategies of Shi'ite movements and to measure the effects of the Iranian Revolution. An alarmist tone is pervasive; the editor identifies Shi'ism as the vehicle of radical change that "will shatter Muslim complacency and discomfit Islam's enemies everywhere."

1097 LAMBTON, ANN K.S. "A Reconsideration of the Position of the Marja Al-Taqlid and the Religious Institution." *StIsl*, 20 (1964), 115-35.

1098 LAQUEUR, WALTER. "Why the Shah Fell." *Commentary*, 67 (March 1978), 47-55.

1099 LEDEEN, MICHAEL and WILLIAM LEWIS. *Debacle, The American Failure in Iran*. New York: Alfred Knopf, 1981, 256 p.
Co-authors Ledeen (who later served as a consultant on Iranian affairs to the National Security Council during the Reagan Administration) and Lewis (a former foreign service officer) provide a shallow, instantaneous analysis of the crises in U.S.-Iran relations, culminating in the Revolution and the hostage-taking. In the preface the authors admit what soon becomes evident, namely, the paucity of footnotes in their account and their partisan motivation in writing this book. Basically the Carter Administration is faulted for its moralistic stance and its abandonment of *realpolitik* in foreign relations. Focuses on the failures of U.S. foreign policy in general. In their conclusion the authors recommend reforming the policy-making bureaucracy with an eye toward shoring up U.S. global hegemony.

1100 LIMBERT, JOHN W. *Iran: At War With History*. Boulder, CO: Westview Press, 1987, 186 p.

1101 LOEFFLER, RHEINHOLD. *Islam in Practice: Religious Beliefs in a Persian Village*. Ithaca: State University of New York Press, 1988, 304 p.

1102 MANOOCHEHRI, ABBAS. "Praxis of a Revolutionary Faith: Ali Shari'ati and Islamic Renaissance." Ph.D. diss., University of Missouri-Columbia, 1988, 223 p.

1103 MANSUR, ABUL KASIM. "The Crisis in Iran: Why the US Ignored a Quarter Century of Warning." *AFJI*, (January 1979), 26-33.

1104 McGEEHAN, R. "Carter's Crises: Iran, Afghanistan and Presidential Politics." *WT*, 36 (May 1980), 163-71.

1105 MENASHRI, DAVID. "Khomeini's Policy Toward Ethnic and Religious Minorities." In *Ethnicity, Pluralism, and the State in the Middle East*. Eds. Milton J. Esman and Itamar Rabinovich. Ithaca, NY: Cornell University Press, 1988, 215-29.

1106 MILANI, MOHSEN M. *The Making of Iran's Islamic Revolution, From Monarchy to Islamic Republic*. Westview Special Studies on the Middle East. Boulder, CO and London: Westview Press, 1988, 361 p.

Reviews twentieth century Iranian political history, including the Constitutional Movement, the Pahlavi dynasty, the June Uprising of 1963, the modernization drive, the 1978-79 Revolution, and the post-revolutionary power struggle. From the vantage point of 1988, the author speculates briefly about who Khomeini's successor might be and whether the Islamic Republic will survive Khomeini's death.

1107 MILLWARD, W.G. "Aspects of Modernism in Shia Islam." *StIsl*, 37 (1973), 111-28.

1108 MINISTRY OF ISLAMIC GUIDANCE. *A Biography of Imam Khomeini.* Tehran: The Ministry, 1982, 24 p.

1109 _____. *A Biography of Martyr Ayatollah Beheshti.* Tehran: The Ministry, 1982, 12 p.

1110 _____. *A Biography of President Martyr Rajai.* Tehran: The Ministry, 1982, 26 p.

1111 _____. *The Imam and the Ommat.* Tehran, The Ministry, n.d.

1112 _____. *Imam Khomeini's Message for Black Friday.* Tehran: The Ministry, 1982, 17 p.

1113 _____. *Imam Khomeini's Message for February 11th.* Tehran: The Ministry, 1982, 27 p.

1114 _____. *Imam Khomeini's Message for April 1st.* Tehran: The Ministry, 1982, 15 p.

1115 _____. *Imam Khomeini's Views on the Superpowers.* Tehran: The Ministry, 1982, 27 p.

1116 _____. *Imam Khomeini's Views and Particularities of Divine Religions.* Tehran: The Ministry, 1982, 31 p.

1117 _____. *The Messages of the Imam of the Ummat.* Tehran: The Ministry, 1981.

1118 MOAZZAM, ANWAR. "Resurgence of Islam: the Role of the State and the Peoples." *BCII*, 2 (October-December 1979), 14-24.

1119 MOMEN, MOOJAN. *An Introduction to Shi'i Islam: The History and Doctrines of Twelver Shi'ism.* New Haven, CT: Yale University Press, 1985, 397 p.
This book begins with a review of Islamic history, concentrating on the formative period, with an eye to explaining the emergence of Twelver Shi'ism. Shi'ite history is then examined in depth. The author sets out the lives and genealogical relationships of the Twelve Imams, Shi'i jurisprudence, eschatology, religious hierarchy, and relationship to popular religion. Twentieth century Iranian political history, and especially the socio-political role of the *ulama*, is treated in a section on contemporary Shi'ism. Also contains very brief descriptions of Shi'ism in such countries as Lebanon, Iraq and Bahrain. Includes a glossary of terms, a chronology of religious and political events in Shi'ite history, and short biographies of prominent Shi'ite *ulama*.

1120 MOTAHARI, AYATOLLAH MORTEZA. "The Nature of Islamic Revolution." In *Iran: a Revolution in Turmoil*. Ed. Haleh Afshar. Albany, NY: State University of New York Press, 1985, 201-19.

1121 MOTTAHEDEH, ROY. *The Mantle of the Prophet: Religion and Politics in Iran*. New York: Pantheon Books, 1985, 416 p.

The author has constructed an account of an Iranian *mullah's* life, beginning with his childhood, continuing through his education and culminating with his achievement of the status of jurisconsultant. While the characters are fictional the description of their lives is very realistic, derived from interviews with Iranians and the author's reading of the curriculum of Iranian religious education. Interwoven into the narrative is a detailed account of Iranian history, including its religious and philosophical traditions, the mystique of Qom (the center of religious education in Iran), and the political struggles of the twentieth century.

1122 MOUSSAVI, AHMED. "The Theory of Vilayat-i Faqih: Its Origin and Appearance in Shi'ite Juristic Literature." In *State Politics in Islam*. Ed. Mumtaz Ahmad. Indianapolis, IN: American Trust Publications, 1986, 97-114.

1123 MUTAHERY, M. *Islamic Movements in Twentieth Century*. Tehran: Great Islamic Library, 1979.

1124 _____. *The Martyr*. Tehran: Great Islamic Library, 1980.

1125 MUTAHHARI, AYATULLAH MURTAZA. *Fundamentals of Islamic Thought: God, Man, and the Universe*. Trans. by R. Campbell with annotations and an introduction by Hamid Algar. Berkeley, CA: Mizan Press, 1985, 235 p.

An exposition of *tawhid*, man and faith, and Islamic methodology and spiritualism by one of the principal architects of revolutionary Iran and a close protege of Imam Ruhollah Khomeini.

1126 _____. *Social and Historical Change: An Islamic Perspective*. Trans. R. Campbell. Berkeley, CA: Mizan Press, 1986, 164 p.

Pre-revolutionary writings of a prominent Iranian religious scholar and ideologue of the 1978-79 Revolution. These essays expound an Islamic justification for political activism, and consider the implications of the arguments over determinism versus free will for historical change. Critiques various social theories of the twentieth century and juxtaposes historical materialism against Islam.

1127 AL-MUZAFFAR, MUHAMMAD RIDA. *The Faith of Shi'a Islam*. Flushing, NY: Tahrike Tarsile Quran, 1986, 80 p.

Written by an Islamic scholar of jurisprudence trained in Najaf, Iraq, this short book reviews the doctrines of Shi'ism, including *tawhid*, prophethood, the Imamate, and eschatology. Briefly explains several basic tenets, such as the necessity of *taqlid*, *ijtihad*, and the position of the *mujtahid*; the attributes of God; predetermination; the justification for *taqiyya*; and the concept of the *mahdi*.

1128 NAJMABADI, AFSANEH. "Iran's Turn to Islam: From Modernism to a Moral Order." *MEJ*, 41 (Spring 1987), 202-17.

1129 NASH, M. "Islam in Iran: Turmoil, Transformation or Transcendence?" *WD*, 8 (1980), 555-61.

1130 NASR, S.H. "Ithna Ashari Shiism and Iranian Islam." In *Religion in the Middle East*. Ed. A.J. Arberry. Cambridge: Cambridge University Press, 1969, 96-118.

1131 _____. *Traditional Islam in the Modern World*. Leiden: E.J. Brill, 1986, 320 p.

1132 NASR, SEYYED HOSSEIN, HAMID DABASHI, and SEYYED VALI REZA NASR, eds. *Shi'ism: Doctrines, Thought, and Spirituality*. Albany, NY: State University of New York Press, 1988, 432 p.
The editors of this volume have selected excerpts from previously published works by scholars of Shi'ism. In their prefatory remarks they have stated that the objective of this book is to dispel the prevailing western view, borne primarily of recent political confrontation, that Shi'ism is a creed of violence. It explores several theological, intellectual, and spiritual aspects of Shi'ism from its origins to contemporary times. Specifically the selections concentrate on Shi'ite doctrines (e.g. revelation and prophesy; *taqiyya*; *ijtihad*; *mut'ah* marriage), religious practices, intellectual and artistic life (Shi'i education, literature, intellectual sciences, art, natural sciences, mathematics), and twentieth century thought.

1133 NEJAD, HASSAN M. "Inequality in an Urban Revolution: The Case of Iran." In *Inequality and Contemporary Revolutions*. Monograph Series in World Affairs, vol 22, bk 2. Denver, CO: Graduate School of International Relations, University of Denver, 1986, 95-109.

1134 NETZER, AMNON. "Islam in Iran: Search for Identity." In *The Crescent in the East, Islam in Asia Minor*. Ed. Raphael Israeli. London: Curzon Press, 1982, 5-22.

1135 NOBARI, ALI REZA, ed. *Iran Erupts*. Stanford, CA: Iran-American Documentation Group, 1978, 237 p.
A collection of reprints on Iran from such newspapers as the *New York Times* and *Le Monde*, this volume (published in late 1978) chronicles the events leading to the 1978-79 Revolution. A valuable source of information on opposition politics, including statements by and interviews with Bani-Sadr and Khomeini. Among the topics discussed are Carter's human rights policy, torture in Iran, and the massacre of Black Friday (8 September 1978).

1136 NOMANI, MOHAMMAD MANZOOR. *Khomeini, Iranian Revolution and the Shi'ite Faith*. London: Al-Furqan Publications, 1988, 197 p.

1137 NOORI, AYATOLLAH YAHYA. "The Islamic Concept of State." *HamdIs*, 3 (Autumn 1980), 71-92.

1138 NOURAIE, F.M. "The Constitutional Ideas of a Shiite Mujtahid: Muhammad Husayn Na'ini." *IrSt*, 8 (Autumn 1975), 234-47.

1139 PAHLAVI, MOHAMMED REZA. *Answer to History*. Chelsea, MI: Scarborough House, 1982, 204 p.

1140 PIPES, DANIEL. "This World is Political: The Islamic Revival of the Seventies." *Orbis*, 24 (Spring 1980), 9-41.

1141 POVEY, T., et al. "From Moguls to Mullahs." *The Middle East*, (March 1979), 25-32.

1142 RAHIMI, A.R. "Hostage Crisis: The Central Islamic Issue." *IR*, 1 (1980), 19-21.

1143 RAJ, C.S. "U.S.-Iran Relations: Post Hostage Phase." *SA*, 4 (February 1981), 537-42.

1144 RAMAZANI, R.K. "'Church' and State in Modernizing Society: The Case of Iran." *ABS*, 7 (January 1964), 26-28.

1145 _____. "Constitution of the Islamic Republic of Iran." *MEJ*, 34 (Spring 1980), 181-204.

1146 RAZA, S.M. "Iran After the Revolution." *UM*, 1 (September 1979), 32-33.

1147 RAZI, G.H. "Development of Political Institutions in Iran and Scenarios for the Future." In *Iran: Essays on a Revolution in the Making*. Eds. A. Jabbari and R. Olsen. Lexington, Kentucky: Mazda Publishers, 1981, 55-76.

1148 RICHARD, YANN. "Ayatollah Kashani: Precursor of the Islamic Republic?" Transl. Nikki R. Keddie. In *Religion and Politics in Iran, Shi'ism from Quietism to Revolution*. Ed. Nickki R. Keddie. New Haven and London: Yale University Press, 1983, 101-24.

1149 RICKS, T. "Background to the Iranian Revolution: Imperialism, Dictatorship and Nationalism, 1872-1979." In *Iran: Essays on a Revolution in the Making*. Eds. A. Jabbari and R. Olsen. Lexington, KY: Mazda Publishers, 1981, 15-54.

1150 RICKS, T.M. "Islamic Republic and Iran Today." *RIPEH*, 3 (Spring 1979), 1-16.

1151 RIZVI, HASAN-ASKARI. *Islamic Reassertion: A Socio-political Study*. Progressive Series No. 46. Lahore: Progressive Publishers, 1981.

1152 RIZVI, S.A.A. *Iran: Royalty, Religion and Revolution*. Canberra, Australia: Marifat Publishing House, 1980.

1153 ROBITALLE, G. "Iran-U.S.: A Conflict of Values." *IR*, 2 (July 1980), 3-7.

1154 RODINSON, M. "Khomeini and 'the Primacy of Spirit'." *MEM*, 22 (May-July 1979), 23-25.

1155 ROSE, GREGORY. "Velayat-e Faqih and the Recovery of Islamic Identity in the Thought of Ayatollah Khomeini." In *Religion and Revolution in Iran, Shi'ism from Quietism to Revolution*. Ed. Nikki R. Keddie. New Haven and London: Yale University Press, 1983, 166-90.

1156 ROSS, LESTER. "Khomeini's Iran and Mao's China: Crises of Charismatic Authority." *ATS*, 5 (September 1980), 150-59.

1157 ROULEAU, E. "Khomeini's Iran." *FA*, 59 (Fall 1980), 1-20.

1158 RUBIN, BARRY. *Paved with Good Intentions: the American Experience and Iran*. New York: Oxford University Press, 1980, 426 p.
A specialist on U.S. policy in the Middle East tells of the impact of mutual misconceptions and ignorance in the deterioration of U.S.-Iranian relations.

1159 RZAI, G.H. "The Background and Emerging Structure of the Islamic Republic in Iran." *RIPEH*, 3, (1979), 1-19.

1160 SACHEDINA, ABDULAZIZ. "Ali Shariati: Ideologue of the Iranian Revolution." In *Voices of Resurgent Islam*. Ed. John L. Esposito. New York: Oxford University Press, 1983, 191-214.

1161 _____. "The Creation of a Just Social Order in Islam." In *State Politics and Islam*. Ed. Mumtaz Ahmed. Indianapolis, IN: American Trust Publications, 1986, 115-32.

1162 SAID, EDWARD W. *Covering Islam: How the Media and the Experts Determine How we See the Rest of the World*. New York: Pantheon Books, 1981, 186 p.
The author, using the analysis he developed in his earlier work, *Orientalism*, critiques American representations of Islam found in media coverage of recent events in Iran. The political and subjective nature of most academic accounts of Islam, as well as the analyses by policymakers and journalists, is linked to the special interests of the experts who produce these accounts. The author argues that media coverage is partial and tends to treat Islam in a reductionist fashion which reinforces superficial, inaccurate and interest-driven conceptions of global politics.

1163 SAIKAL, AMIN. *The Rise and Fall of the Shah*. Princeton, NJ: Princeton University Press, 1980, 279 p.
Analysis is based on interviews with Iranian government officials and leaders of the opposition. The author is critical of the Shah's domestic and foreign policies, which he sees as inherently contradictory. He links these policies and U.S. support for the Shah to the Shah's downfall. Virtually no discussion of the social forces leading the revolution, including the role of the clerics. The main thrust concerns elite politics in pre-1979 Iran, the emergence of Iran as an oil power, and the monarchy's rapid modernization campaign.

1164 SCHAHGALDIAN, NIKOLA B. *The Iranian Military Under the Islamic Republic*. Santa Monica, CA: Rand Corporation, 1987, 164 p.
This study looks at the structural, sociological, and political features of the military of the Islamic Republic of Iran. The impact of the Gulf War as well as internal debates about Islamization of Iranian society and government is examined.

1165 SHANKAR, M. "Iran: Continuing Turmoil." *SA*, 4 (March 1981), 567-75.

1166 _____. "Iran: Internal Struggle Becomes Sharper." *SA*, 4 (February 1981), 525-33.

1167 SHARI'ATI, ALI. "After Shahadat." In *Jihad and Shahadat: Struggle and Martyrdom in Islam*. Ed. and Trans. Farhang Rajaee. Texas: Institute for Research and Islamic Studies, 1986, 244-52.

1168 _____. *Art Awaiting the Saviour*. Trans. H. Fordjadi. Tehran: The Shariati Foundation, 1979.

1169 _____. *Civilization and Modernization*. London: Islamic Students Association, n.d.

1170 _____. *Fatima is Fatima*. Trans. Laleh Bakhtiar. Tehran: The Shariati Foundation, n.d., 226 p.
   Fatima, the daughter of the Prophet Mohammad, is presented as the appropriate role model for contemporary Shi'ite women. Iranian women are exhorted in this book, originally a lecture delivered in 1971, not to deviate from their cultural and religious roots by adopting foreign values and practices.

1171 _____. *Hajj*. Trans. Ali A. Behzadnia and Najla Denny. Houston, TX, Free Islamic Literatures, Inc., 1980, 160 p.

1172 _____. *Islamic View of Man*. Trans. A.A. Rasti. Houston, TX: Free Islamic Literatures, Inc., 1979.

1173 _____. *Martyrdom: Arise and Bear Witness*. Trans. Ali Asghar Ghassemy. Tehran: The Ministry of Islamic Guidance, 1981.

1174 _____. *Marxism and Other Western Fallacies: An Islamic Critique*. Trans. R. Campbell. Berkeley, CA: Mizan Press, 1980, 122 p.

1175 _____. *On the Sociology of Islam*. Trans. Hamid Algar. Berkeley, CA: Mizan Press, 1979, 125 p.

1176 _____. *One Followed by an Eternity of Zeros*. Tehran: The Shariati Foundation, 1979.

1177 _____. *Red Shiism*. Trans. Habib Shirazi. Tehran: The Shariati Foundation, 1979.

1178 _____. *Reflections of a Concerned Muslim on the Plight of Oppressed Peoples*. Houston, Texas: Free Islamic Literatures, Inc., 1979.

1179 _____. *Selection and/or Election*. Trans. Ali Asghar Ghassemy. Tehran: The Shariati Foundation, 1979.

1180 _____. *The Visage of Mohammed*. Trans. A.A. Sachedin. Tehran: Committee for International Propagation of the Islamic Revolution, 1981.

1181 _____. *What Is To Be Done? The Enlightened Thinkers and an Islamic Renaissance*. Ed. and trans. by Farhang Rajaee. Houston, TX: The Institute for Research and Islamic Studies, 1986, 181 p.

1182 _____. *Yea, Brother! That's the Way it Was*. Tehran: The Shariati Foundation, 1979.

1183 SHARIATI, ALI, MAHMUD TALEQANI and MURTADA MUTAHHARI. *Jihad and Shahadat*. Transl. Houston, TX: Institute for Research and Islamic Studies, 1986, 281 p.

1184 SHARIATMADAR, MOHAMMAD KAZIM. *Commandments of Islam According to the Decree of H.H. Ayatullah al-Uzama Agaye al-Haj Sayyed Mohammad Kazim Shariatmadar*. Abr. and Trans. Moulana Syed Shamin-us-Sibtain Rizvi. Qum, Iran: Dar-al-Tabligh-al-Islami, 1976.

1185 SHUJA, SHARIF, M. "Islamic Revolution in Iran and its Impact on Iraq." *IS*, 21 (Autumn 1980), 213-33.

1186 SICHERMAN, H. "Iraq and Iran at War: The Search for Security." *Orbis* 24, 24 (Winter 1981), 711-18.

1187 SIDDIQUI, KALIM. *Islam and Revolution*. Washington, DC: The American Society for Education and Religion, 1981.

1188 _____. "The Islamic Revolution: Achievements, Obstacles and Goals." In *The Islamic Revolution: Achievements, Obstacles and Goals*. Eds. K. Siddiqui, et al. London: The Muslim Institute, 1980, 9-22.

1189 _____. *Khomeini's Iran*. Falls Church, VA: Research and Publications, 1981.

1190 _____. "Revolution and the World's Muslims." *IR*, 1 (August 1979).

1191 _____, ed. *Issues in the Islamic Movement*. London: The Open Press, Ltd., 1982.

1192 _____, ed. *Issues in the Islamic Movement 1981-82*. London: The Open Press, 1983.

1193 _____, ed. *Issues in the Islamic Movement 1982-83 (1402-03)*. London: The Open Press, 1984, 432 p.
This compilation of essays, editorials, and news articles from *Crescent International* and *Muslimedia* presents a 'new paradigm' of Muslim political thought which takes into account the dynamics of history and, specifically, the Muslim experience of European colonialism. The editor presents the case in his introduction where he argues that the Muslim *umma* finds itself divided and debilitated as a result of colonialism and must act to reunite the Muslim world. Topics range from Muslim political culture to capitalism, socialism, education and Zia ul-Haq's policies. Includes a short glossary, a list of articles and an index.

1194 _____, ed. *Issues in the Islamic Movement 1983-84*. London: The Open Press, 1985.

1195 STEMPEL, JOHN D. *Inside the Iranian Revolution*. Bloomington, IN: Indiana University Press, 1981, 336 p.
Written by a U.S. diplomat who was the political officer at the U.S. embassy in Tehran at the time of the Revolution. Analysis is based on interviews with Iranians and Americans both before and after the overthrow of the Shah. Reviews the twentieth century record of American intervention in Iran and

emphasizes U.S. policy failures with regard to Iran. Also discusses the mobilization of anti-Shah forces. In his final chapter the author briefly evaluates the impact of the revolution on Iranian politics and other Muslim countries and predicts continued political turmoil and oppression.

1196 TABARI, AZAR. "Iran's Incomprehensible Revolution." *Khamsin*, no. 12 (Special Issue: Gulf War). London: Ithaca Press, 1986, 87-94.

1197 _____. "The Role of the Clergy in Modern Iranian Politics." In *Religion and Politics in Iran, Shi'ism from Quietism to Revolution*. Ed. Nikki R. Keddie. New Haven and London: Yale University Press, 1983, 47-72.

1198 TABATABAI, ALLAMA SAYYID MUHAMMAD HUSAYN. *Shiite Religion*. Albany, NY: State University of New York Press, 1975.

1199 TABATABAI, S. MUHAMMAD HUSAYN. *Shiite Islam*. Trans. Sayyed Hossein Nasr. Houston, TX: Free Islamic Literatures, 1979, 253 p.

1200 TADEGARI, MUHAMMAD. "Islam: A New School of Thought." *Itt*, 17 (October-December 1980), 9-18.

1201 TAHERI, AMIR. *Holy Terror: The Inside Story of Islamic Terrorism*. London: Hutchinson, 1987, 313 p.

1202 TAHIR KHELI, S. "Proxies and Allies: The Case of Iran and Pakistan." *Orbis*, 24 (Summer 1980), 339-52.

1203 THAISS, GUSTAV. "Religious Symbolism and Social Change: The Drama of Husain." In *Scholars, Saints, and Sufis: Muslim Religious Institutiosn since 1500*. Ed. N.R. Keddie. Berkeley, CA: University of California Press, 1972, 349-66.

1204 TIBI, BASSAM. "The Iranian Revolution and the Arabs: The Quest for Islamic Identity and the Search for an Islamic System of Government." *ASQ*, 8 (Winter 1986), 29-44.

1205 WHETTEN, LAWRENCE L. "The Lessons of Iran." *WT*, 35 (1979), 391-99.

1206 WROBEL, B. *Human Rights in Iran: Testimony on Behalf of Amnesty International*. London: Amnesty International, 1978.

1207 YOSHITSU, M.M. "Iran and Afghanistan in Japanese Perspective." *AS*, 21 (May 1981), 501-14.

1208 ZABIH, SEPEHR. *Iran Since the Revolution*. Baltimore, MD: The Johns Hopkins University Press, 1982, 247 p.
   Characterizes the Islamic Republic as a despotic one-party theocracy. Discusses the institutionalization of power on the part of the post-revolutionary regime in spite of what the author contends was the absense of an ideological consensus. Highlights the political rift in the revolutionary coalition in the months following the overthrow of the Shah, and explains how Khomeini came to dominate the ruling faction. Analyzes in detail the Constitution of the Republic.

1209 _____. *Iran's Revolutionary Upheaval: An Interpretive Essay*. San Francisco, CA: Alchemy Books, 1979, 104 p.

1210 _____. *The Mossadegh Era: Roots of the Iranian Revolution*. Chicago: Lake View Press, 1982, 182 p.
Details the early-1950s nationalist struggle led by Prime Minister Mossadegh. The author emphasizes the role of internal forces, rather than the role of British and American intelligence operations, in creating political instability and the 1952 *coup d'etat* against the Prime Minister. In a postscript he contends that the confrontation between the Shah and nationalist forces in 1951-52 was an important antecedent to the 1978-79 Revolution and that the nationalist struggle continues at present as tensions between clerics and secular nationalists mount.

1211 ZONIS, MARVIN. "The Rule of the Clerics in the Islamic Republic of Iran." *AAAPSS*, 482 (1985), 85-108.

1212 ZUBAIDA, SAMI. "The Ideological Conditions for Khomeini's Doctrine of Government." *Economy and Society*, 11 (1982), 138-72.

1213 _____. "The Quest for the Islamic State: Islamic Foundation in Egypt and Iran." In *Studies in Religious Fundamentalism*. Ed. Lionel Caplan. Albany, NY: State University of New York Press, 1987, 25-50.

C. TURKEY

1214 AHMED, FEROZ. "Islamic Reassertion in Turkey." *TWQ*, 10 (April 1988), 750-69.

1215 ALKAN, TURKER. "The National Salvation Party in Turkey." In *Islam and Politics in the Modern Middle East*. Eds. M. Herper & R. Israeli. New York: St. Martin's Press, 1984, 79-102.

1216 HEPER, METIN. "Islam, Polity and Society in Turkey: A Middle Eastern Perspective." *MEJ*, 35 (Summer 1981), 345-63.
Discusses what is meant by the term "Islamic resurgence", and then suggests that the central concern is whether a "resurgence" of Islam will lead to a popular uprising against the state. The aim of the article is to explore the characteristics of Ottoman-Turkish development that makes Turkey unique, and to explain some aspects of the visibility of Islam in present-day Turkey.

1217 KOPANSKI, A. BOGDAN. "Namik Kemal: A Pioneer of Islamic Revival." *The Muslim World League Journal*, 15 (1988), 38-40.

1218 KUSHNER, DAVID. "Turkish Secularists and Islam." *JQ*, 38 (1986), 89-106.

1219 LUDU, ARNOLD. *Catalyst of Change: Marxist versus Muslims in a Turkish Community*. Austin, TX: University of Texas Press, 1976.
A dense analytical study of local politics and its influence on and relationship to the national political structure.

1220 MAGNARELLA, P.J. "Civil violence in Turkey: its Infrastructural, Social and Cultural Foundations." In *Sex Roles, Family and Community in Turkey*. Ed. C. Kagitcibasi. Bloomington, IN: Indiana University Turkish Studies, 3. 1982.

1221 MARDIN, SHERIF A. "Ideology and Religion in the Turkish Revolution." *IJMES*, 2 (1971), 197-211.

1222 _____. "Turkey, Islam and Westernization." In *Religion and Societies: Asia and the Middle East*. Ed. Carlo Caldarola. Berlin: Mouton, 1982, 171-98.

1223 SARAYI, S. "Politicization of Islamic Re-traditionalism: Some Preliminary Notes." In *Islam and Politics in the Modern Middle East*. Eds. M. Herper and R. Israeli. New York: St. Martin's Press, 1984, 119-28.

1224 TAPPER, RICHARD and NANCY TAPPER. "'Thank God we're Secular!' Aspects of Fundamentalism in a Turkish Town." In *Studies in Religious Fundamentalism*. Ed. Lionel Caplan. Albany, NY: State University of New York Press, 1987, 51-78.

1225 YALMAN, N. "The Center and the Periphery: the Reform of Religious Institutions in Turkey." *CTT*, 38, (1979), 1-23.

Author Index

BENNIGSEN, ALEXANDRE, 0660, 0661, 0662, 0663, 0664, 0665, 0666, 0667
BENOMAR, JAMAL, 0303
BHATTI, F.M., 0720, 0721
BIENEN, HENRY, 0336
BIGGAR, NIGEL, 0023
BILL, JAMES A., 0793, 0794, 0929, 0999, 1000, 1001, 1002
BIN-SAYEED, KHALID, 0379
BINDER, LEONARD, 0024
BINDER, L., 1003
BOBOMUHAMEDOV, P., 0668
BOCOCK, R., 0722
BOLAND, B., 0573
BONE, DAVIS S., 0283
BONINE, MICHAEL E., ed, 1004
BOOTH, MARILYN, 0204
BORTHWICK, BRUCE M., 0796, 0797
BOULBY, MARION, 0304
BOUTALEB, ABDELHADI, 0025
AL-BRAIK, NASSER AHMED M., 0026
BRASWEL, GEORGE W., JR., 1005
BROHI, A.K., 0484
BROWN, GODFREY, 0262
BROWN, RICHARD, 0188
BROXUP, MARIE, 0664, 0669, 0670
BRUINESSEN, MARTIN VAN, 0558
BUHARUDDIN, SHAMSUL AMRI, 0604
BURKI, SHAHID JAVED, 0170
BUULTJENS, RALPH, 0443

CALLAWAY, BARBARA J., 0205, 0206
CAMPBELL, R., trans., 1174
CAMPBELL, W.R., 1006
CARLSEN, R.W., 1007
CARRE, OLIVIER, ed., 0027
CARRERE D'ENCAUSSE, HELENE, 0671
CARROL, LUCY, 0646
CARROLL, TERRANCE G, 0798
CHAMRAN, MUSTAFA, 1008
CHAN, MBYE B., 0337
CHANG, YUSUF HAJJI, 0672
CHAPRA, M. UMER, 0171, 0172
CHATTY, HABIB, 0028
CHE MAN, W.K., 0647
CHEEK, A.H., 0630
CHEEK, AHMAD SHABERY, 0605

CHEHABI, HOUCHANG ESFANDIAN, 1009
CHOUDHURY, MASUDUL, 0173
CHRISTELOW, ALLAN, 0305, 0338, 0339
CHRISTENSEN, ASGER, 0434
CILARDO, AGOSTINO, 0207
CLARK, GRACE, 0485
CLARKE, PETER B., 0340, 0341, 0342
COBBAN, H., 0910, 0911
COLE, JUAN R., 1010; ed., 0029
COLE, W. OWEN, 0723
COLES, CATHERINE H., 0208
COMSTOCK, G.L, 0343
CONN, HARVIE M., 0284
COTTAM, RICHARD W., 1011, 1012
COWARD, HAROLD, 0030
CREEVEY, LUCY E, 0344
CRELLIN, CLIFFORD T., 0724
CROUCH, HAROLD, ed., 0606
CUDSI, ALEXANDER S., 0031
CURTIS, MICHAEL, ed., 0799
CUSTERS, MARTIA, 0725
CUTHELL, DAVID, C., ed., 0139

DABASHI, HAMID, ed, 1132
DADA, EBRAHIM, 0263
DAOUD-AGHA, ADNAN B., 0800
DARAVI, REZA, 1013
DARRAT, ALI F., 0380
DARVICH, DJAMCHID, 1006
DASKAWIE, M.A.Q., 0486
DASSETTO, F., 0726
DAVIS, ERIC, 0032, 0823
DAWISHA, ADEED, 0801, 0904; ed., 0033, 0824
DEEB, MARIUS, 0912, 0913
DE EPALZA, MIKEL, 0727
DE FEYER, KOEN, 0306
DEGENHARDT, HENRY W., ed., 0034
DE JONG, FREDERICK, 0728
DEKMEJIAN, R. HRAIR, 0035, 0036, 0037, 0038, 0802
DENNY, NAJLA, trans., 1171
DESSOUKI, A.E. HILLAL, ed., 0803
DEVLET, NADIR, 0673
DE WENDEN, CATHERINE WITHOL, 0754
DE WITT, WILLEM, 0729
DIJK, C. VAN, 0574
DIL, SHAHEEN F., 0428

Title Index

"Arab Women in the Gulf," 0243
The Arabs: Journeys Beyond the Mirage, 0832
"Are Checking Accounts in American Banks Permissible Under Islamic Laws?"
    0380
Art Awaiting the Saviour, 1168
As the Light Shineth from the East, 0401
"Asian Islam: International Linkages and Their Impact on International
    Relations," 0425
"Aspects of Modernism in Shia Islam," 1107
"Ataturk as seen by Turkish Workers in Europe," 0748
Attitudes to Medical Ethics Among British Muslim Medical Practitioners, 0753
Authority and Political Culture in Shi'ism, 0976
Authority in Islam, from Muhammad to Khomeini, 0096
"Autobiography," 0994
Autumn of Fury: the Asassination of Sadat, 0868
"The Ayatollah in the Cathedral: Reflections of a Hostage," 1090
"Ayatollah Kashani: Precursor of the Islamic Republic?" 1148
"Ayatollah Khomeini's Concept of Islamic Government," 1089

"The Background and Emerging Structure of the Islamic Republic in Iran," 1159
"Background to the Iranian Revolution: Imperialism, Dictatorship and
    Nationalism, 1872-1979," 1149
"Bangladesh Politics: Secular and Islamic Trends," 0552
Beginnings End, 1039
"Behind the Veil: Status of Women in Revolutionary Iran," p. 22; 0244
"Being Muslim and Female," 0235
"The Bengali Muslims of Bradford," 0718
Between Two Cultures, 0785
Beyond Coercion: the Durability of the Arab State, 0824
Beyond the Muslim Nation States, 0543
Beyond the Veil: Male-Female Dynamics in Modern Muslim Society, p. 22; 0228
"A Bibliography of Writings by and about Mawlana Sayyid Abul A'la Mawdudi,"
    0541
A Biography of Imam Khomeini, 1108
A Biography of Martyr Ayatollah Beheshti, 1109
A Biography of President Martyr Rajai, 1110
"Black Africans in the Islamic World: An Understudied Dimension of the Black
    Diaspora," 0351
Both Right and Left Handed, Arab Women Talk About Their Lives, 0249
Buzkashi: Game and Power in Afghanistan, 0433

"Call to Revise the Egyptian Civil Code: Recommendations for the Use of Islamic
    Law," 0853
The Canadian Encyclopedia, 0398
"Canadian Muslims: The Need for a New Survival Strategy," 0375
Capitalism and Revolution in Iran, 1074
"Carter's Crises: Iran, Afghanistan and Presidential Politics," 1104
"A Case of Fundamentalism in West Africa: Wahabism in Bamako," 0335
Catalyst of Change: Marxist versus Muslims in a Turkish Community, 1219
"The Center and the Periphery: the Reform of Religious Institutions in Turkey,"
    1225
"The Centrifugal Forces of Religion in Sudanese Politics," 0307
A Century of Islam in America, 0383
The Challenge of Dawah in Southern Africa, 0263

"Islamic Banking in Pakistan," 0180
"Islamic Banking Operations," 0176
"The Islamic Challenge: Tunisia since Independence," 0304
"The Islamic City-Historic Myth, Islamic Essence, and Contemporary Relevance," 0001
"An Islamic Common Market and Economic Development," 0168
"An Islamic Common Market? Problems and Strategies of Economic Co-operation Among Islamic Countries," 0184
"The Islamic Community of China," 0674
"The Islamic Concept of State," 1137
"Islamic Conversion and Social Change in a Senegalese Village," 0371
"The Islamic Critique of the Status Quo of Muslim Society," 0051
"Islamic Culture in China," 0700
"Islamic Da'wah in North America and the Dynamics of Conversion to Islam in Western Societies," 0411
"Islamic Dynamism in South Africa's Western Cape," 0265
"Islamic Economic: An Approach to Human Welfare," 0193
Islamic Economics: Theory and Practice, 0182
"Islamic Education in the United States: An Overview of Issues, Problems, and Possible Approaches," 0377
"The Islamic Education of an African Child: Stresses and Tensions," 0370
"The Islamic Factor in African Politics," 0260
"The Islamic 'Factor' in the Soviet Union," 0658
Islamic Fundamentalism and Modernity, 0154
"Islamic Fundamentalism and the Women of Kuwait," p. 22
"Islamic Fundamentalism: What it Really is and Why it Frightens the West," 0063
"Islamic Futures: The Shape of Ideas to Come," 0128
Islamic Government, 1092
The Islamic Government's Policy on Womens' Access to Higher Education and its Impact on the Socio-economic Status of Women, 0233
"Islamic Ideals in North America," 0381
"Islamic Identity and the Turks in West Germany," 0712
The Islamic Impact, 0059
The Islamic Impulse, 0140
"Islamic Iran and the Arab World," 0812
Islamic Iran, Revolution and Counter-Revolution, 1058
Islamic Law and Its Significance for the Situation of Muslim Minorities in Europe, 0756
"Islamic Law and Law Reform Discourse in Nigeria: A Comparative Study and Another Viewpoint," 0374
Islamic Law and Society in the Sudan, 0310
Islamic Law in the Contemporary World, 0011
Islamic Law in the Modern World, p. 21
The Islamic Law on Land Tax and Rent, 0178
Islamic Liberalism: A Critique of Development Ideologies, 0024
Islamic Materialism and its Dimensions, 0081
Islamic Messianism: The Idea of the Mahdi in Twelver Shi'ism, 0124
"Islamic Militancy as a Social Movement: The Case of Two Groups in Egypt," 0874
"The Islamic Militants in Egyptian Politics," 0843
"The Islamic Militants in the Politics of Egypt," p. 22
"Islamic Millenarianism in West Africa: A 'Revolutionary' Ideology?" 0340
"Islamic Modernism: Its Scope and Alternatives," 0119
"The Islamic Movement in Tunisia," 0315

Subject Index

This index includes subjects discussed in the essays in Chapters One, Two, and Three and referred to in the Sources documented in Chapter 4. References to the former are by page number; references to the latter are by entry number; the two are separated by a semicolon. Where entries duplicate each other only the annotated entry is noted. Arabic words are in italics.

PAS, pp. 50, 51, 52, 53; 0606, 0607,
  0626
passion play, 0058
patriarchy, 0217
patrimonial society, 0793, 0923
peace, 0002, 0880
  Islamic concept of, 0894
peasants, 0039, 0229, 0903, 1053
penal systems, 0011
People of the Book, 0848
people's committees, 0321
People's Democratic Republic of
  Yemen, 0044, 0217
People's Redemption Party, 0206
People's Republic of Bukhara, 0671
PERKIM, 0626
Persatuan Islam, 0575, 0591
Persia, 0101, 0108, 0203
Persian Gulf, 0029, 0048, 0793, 0928,
  0929, 0930, 1004, 1050, 1163
  U.S. interests in, 0930
Persjarikatan Ulama, 0591
personal relations, 0805
Personal Status Law, 0211, 0228,
  0738
Petit Bourgeoisie, 0056
petroleum, p. 43; 0048, 0106, 0112,
  0146, 0302, 0790, 0793, 0803, 0830,
  0832, 0928, 1012, 1031, 1036, 1079,
  1082, 1163
Philippines, 0064, 0112, 0422, 0557,
  0569, 0634, 0806
philosophy, 0101, 0117, 0561, 1120
piety, 0597
pilgrimage, 0058
PLO. See Palestine Liberation
  Organization
pluralism, 0023, 0108, 0147, 0299,
  0342, 0745
  cultural, 0139, 0422, 0579, 0618
poetry, p. 15; 0211, 0429
policy
  analysis, 0166
  economic, 1079
  makers, 0090, 0930
political action. See activism,
  political
political development, 0048, 0573,
  0578, 0589, 0959, 1164
political economy, 0006, 0052, 0599,
  0632, 0805
political liberation, 1028
political movement, 0591
political parties, 0082, 0321, 0441,

0472, 0591, 0607, 0632
political reconstruction, 0013, 0579,
  0632, 0923, 1195
political struggle, 0116, 0573, 0819,
  0923
political system, 0006, 0084, 0303,
  0607, 0889
political theory, Islamic, 0071, 0123,
  0234, 0473, 0803, 1193
political thought, modern Iranian,
  1082
politics, p. 40; 0002, 0005, 0018, 0023,
  0042, 0045, 0059, 0074, 0080, 0090,
  0106, 0107, 0108, 0109, 0110, 0122,
  0127, 0146, 0147, 0156, 0211, 0305,
  0308, 0477, 0483, 0561, 0578, 0606,
  0632, 0683, 0767, 0793, 0799, 0806,
  0807, 0808, 0811, 0819, 0827, 0879,
  0889, 0924, 0926, 0939, 0959, 1028,
  1086, 1164, 1193
  Egyptian, 0843
  global, 0094
  Malay, 0608
polls, 0472
polygamy, 0045, 0209, 0217, 0241,
  0374, 0764
polytheism, 0514
poor, 1101
popular congresses, 0321
popular Islam, 0277, 0487, 0815, 1119
popular revolt, 0277
populism, 0060, 0356
Portugal, 0788
power, 0031, 0064, 0116, 0203, 0218,
  0790, 0819, 0923, 1036, 1162, 1208
power relationships, 0196, 0923
prayers, p. 41; 0104, 0847. See also
  ritual practices
predestination, 0159
press. See media
price theory, 0182
"Princess" episode, 1162
prisoners of war, 0105
private property, 0048
production, 0182, 0632
prohibitions, 0114
property, 0310, 0629, 0683
  rights, 0094
propogation, 0406, 0411
Protectorate reforms, 0296
protest, 0152, 0537, 1082
  Islamic, 0277, 0338, 0358, 0847
  social, 0029, 0910
psychology, 0053, 0566, 0819

women (*cont'd.*), 0060, 0112, 0122,
0139, 0140, 0203, 0206, 0209, 0218,
0238, 0241, 0251, 0301, 0308, 0325,
0390, 0421, 0423, 0467, 0484, 0528,
0546, 0667, 0752, 0764, 0765, 0788,
0799, 0805, 0815, 0860, 0895, 0897,
1028, 1082, 1086, 1101, 1201
women in Afghanistan, 0257, 0476
women in Africa, 0203, 0257
women in Albania, 0257
women in Algeria, 0211, 0218, 0248,
0249, 0256, 0257
women, Asian in Britain, 0787
women in Bahrain, 0218
women, divorced, 0222
women, dress, 0247. See also zay
shar'i
women, education of, 0211, 0215,
0221, 0229, 0233
women in Egypt, 0195, 0211, 0218,
0219, 0204, 0221, 0247
women in Gulf, 0218, 0243
women, Hausa, 0206
women, health care of, 0221
women in India, 0251
women in Indonesia, 0257
women, influence of, 0223
women in Iran, 0194, 0195, 0198,
0199, 0202, 0211, 0221, 0232, 0238,
0244, 0248, 0251, 0257, 0265
women, Islamic image of, p. 16; 0045,
0059, 0217, 0228, 0238, 0252
women in Jordan, 0218
women in Kuwait, 0218
women in Lebanon, 0218, 0248, 0249
women, legal status of, 0221
women in literature, 0200, 0211, 0221
women in Malaysia, 0221, 0257
women, migrant, 0734
women in Morocco, 0229, 0241, 0251
women in Netherlands, 0779
women in Nigeria, 0205
women in North Africa, 0221
women, orphaned, 0222
women in Pakistan, 0195, 0221, 0225,
0234, 0245, 0258, 0259, 0773, 0793
women in Palestine, 0211, 0239, 0248,
0249, 0257
women, politics and, 0116, 0203,
0206, 0220, 0224
women, poor, 0238
women, religious life of, 0219, 0238
women, revolutionary, 0203
women in Saudi Arabia, 0196

women, seclusion of. See seclusion
women, social networks, 0223
women in South Asia, 0203
women in South Yemen, 0218
women, status and role of, 0116,
0203, 0206, 0220, 0221, 0234, 0252,
0310
women in Sudan, 0214, 0221
women in Syria, 0249
women in Tunisia, 0218, 0221, 0248
women in Turkey, 0195, 0221, 0248,
0255, 0257
women in West Bank, 0239
women, widowed, 0222
women younger-generation, 0196
Women's Action Forum, 0234
women's liberation, 0228
women's magazines, p. 15
women's movement. See movements,
women
women's movement, Egypt, 0221
women's movement, Iran, 0238, 0254
women's movement, Turkey, 0221
women's oppression, 0199
women's organizations, 0234
women's rights, 0202, 0218, 0220,
0234, 0880
women's roles, 0206
women's social position, 0211
women's work, 0196, 0211, 0218,
0220, 0221, 0229, 0230, 0232, 0234
work, 0211, 0308, 1101
workers, 0748, 0924
rights of, 0880
world order, 0026, 0052
world peace, 0894
world view, Islamic, 0160, 1120
World War II, p. 3; 0889, 1012, 1082
worship, 0467, 0847, 1120

Yakan, Fathi, p. 6
Yan Tatsine, 0277
al-Yasar al-Islami, p. 6
Yemen, 0058, 0217, 0218, 0237, 0799
Yezidis, 0666
Yogyakarta, 00597
Yoruba, 0343, 0345
Youth Movement of Malaysia,
Islamic, p. 41
youth, Muslim, 0114, 0334, 0600
Yugoslavia, 0710

zakat, 0006, 0182, 0546. See also
ritual practices

About the Contributors

YVONNE YAZBECK HADDAD is Professor of Islamic History at the University of Massachusetts, Amherst. She has served recently as President of the Middle East Studies Association of North America. She was the editor of *Muslim World* Quarterly (1980-88). Her publications include: *The Islamic Understanding of Death and Resurrection; Contemporary Islam and the Challenge of History; Islamic Impact; Women, Religion and Social Change; Islamic Values in the United States;* and *The Muslims of America.*

JOHN L. ESPOSITO is Professor of Islamic/Middle East Studies and Director of the Center for International Studies at the College of the Holy Cross. He has served as President of the Middle East Studies Association of North America. His publications include: *Islam: The Straight Path; Islam and Politics; The Iranian Revolution: Its Global Impact; Voices of Resurgent Islam; Islam in Transition: Muslim Perspectives; Islam in Asia: Religion, Politics, and Society;* and *Women in Muslim Family Law.*

JOHN OBERT VOLL is a Professor of History at the University of New Hampshire where he has taught Middle East, Islamic and World History for more than 25 years. He is on the Editorial Board of the *International Journal of Middle East Studies* and has served on the board of the Middle East Studies Association and the American Council of Learned Societies. He is the Co-executive Director of the Sudan Studies Association. His publications include: *Islam, Continuity and Change in the Modern World; Historical Dictionary of the Sudan;* and co-author of *The Sudan: Unity and Diversity.*

KATHLEEN MOORE is a Ph.D. candidate in the Political Science Department at the University of Massachusetts, Amherst. Her research has focused on American public law and its implementation by Muslims in the United States.

DAVID SAWAN is a student in the History Department at the University of Massachusetts, Amherst. The focus of his undergraduate studies is the Middle East and he has studied at the American University in Cairo.